IN THE
COMPANY
OF MEN

IN THE COMPANY OF MEN

Male Dominance and Sexual Harassment

Edited by
James E. Gruber
and Phoebe Morgan

Northeastern University Press
BOSTON

Northeastern University Press
Copyright 2005 by James E. Gruber and Phoebe Morgan

Library of Congress Cataloging-in-Publication Data

In the company of men : male dominance and sexual
harassment / edited by James E. Gruber and Phoebe Morgan.
    p.   cm. — (The Northeastern series on gender, crime, and law)
        ISBN 1-55553-638-7 (cl : alk. paper)—
        ISBN 1-55553-637-9 (pa : alk. paper)
    1. Sexual harassment—United States. 2. Sexual
harassment—Europe.   I. Gruber, James. II. Morgan, Phoebe,
1956– III. Series.
HD6060.5.I5   2005
331.4′133′0973—dc22   2004006814

Designed by Amber Frid-Jimenez
Composed in Minion by Coghill Composition Company in
Richmond, Virginia. Printed and bound by Maple Press
in York, Pennsylvania. The paper is Maple Tradebook, an acid-free sheet.

MANUFACTURED IN THE UNITED STATES OF AMERICA
09 08 07 06 05   5 4 3 2 1

CONTENTS

TABLES

PREFACE

Browse any library's holdings or bookstore's inventory and you will find an overwhelming number of publications about sexual harassment. Depending upon the holdings' size, the search term *sexual harassment* can produce a listing of 250 books or more. Within the *Expanded Academic Index* alone, the same search generates more than 2,500 articles, 50 of which have appeared in print in just the last six months. Clearly, sexual harassment is one of the most written about—and therefore discussed—social problems of our time.

The impact of this literature has been significant. Sexual harassment scholarship played a major role in shifting public opinion. A majority of Americans today believe that sexual harassment is wrong and should not be tolerated. Published research has also provided a solid foundation for the development of prohibitive policy. While the frequency and severity of sexual harassment have been reduced in a number of gender-integrated workplaces, the problem appears especially impervious to change within male-dominated workplaces and occupations. In male-dominant settings, unwanted sexual attention is especially problematic: harassment rates are higher than in other settings, and the consequences of it are often more severe. For example, women in the military experience sexual harassment (Bastian, Lancaster, & Reyst 1996, Firestone & Harris 1999) at rates that are 25 to 50 percent higher than those experienced by female federal employees (USMSPB 1995). Also, women in protective services (e.g., fire, police) are exposed to more harassment than civilian employees in the same community (LA Commission on Women 1992, Brown et al. 1995). These women also experience more severe types of harassment—such as pressures for sex and sexual assault—at higher rates (Gruber 2003).

In a variety of ways, each of the thirteen chapters in this collection focuses analytic attention on the relationship between two social problems: male dominance and sexual harassment. Beneath every analysis lie two assumptions: (1) both are complex problems rooted in cultural constructions of gender and institutional roles, identities, and processes, and (2) these processes are inextricably intertwined. Ironically, while sexual harassment's status as a legitimate subject of scholarly study has waxed, attention to the role that male dominance plays in its perpetuation has waned.

The first wave of sexual harassment scholarship placed the problem of patriarchy—specifically, men's dominance of economics, production, and sexuality—at the center of the analysis (see, for example, Farley 1978, MacKinnon 1979, Paludi 1990). But over time, the focus on male dominance has diminished to the point that current research rarely mentions male domination, much less analyzes it. Theory and research, especially in the United States, have drifted from an analysis of sexual harassment as a cultural issue to a narrower focus on it as an organizational problem. As the latter view has gained prominence, a focus on organizational sex ratios, attitudes of leadership, workplace climate, articulation and implementation of effective policies, workshops and training regimes for employees and supervisors, and the like has become stronger. Although these are all important concerns, we see a danger that sexual harassment will become defined primarily as a bureaucratic problem that can be remedied by effective management strategies. By restoring the notion of male dominance as both a normative (i.e., cultural and historical) and a numerical (e.g., workplace sex ratios) phenomenon to sexual harassment theory, this collection attempts a "course correction" in the trajectory of sexual harassment research.

While they employed widely different methods within differing disciplinary traditions, early scholars agreed on three basic propositions: (1) men sexually harass women because they are culturally privileged, (2) social mores and practices sanction their right to do so, and (3) organizations do not adequately protect victims or appropriately punish harassers. Although we owe a great debt to these pioneers, we can now see that these propositions are overly simplistic. They do not, for example, account for the fact that the vast majority of men are not sexual harassers, or that men often sexually harass each other. Recent advances in masculinity studies offer theoretical bases for addressing these issues. This emerging body of literature provides a theoretical frame for appreciating the complexity and fluidity of male dominance (see, for example, Corrigan, Connell, & Lee 1987, Hearn & Parkin 1987, Kimmel 1987, Martin & Jurik 1996). Drawing upon the conceptualization of male dominance within these works, our collection revises and expands the thesis asserted by feminists nearly thirty years ago—that male dominance and sexual harassment are inextricably intertwined. Our collection presents a more complete, albeit more complex, picture of the relationships between these two problems.

The following chapters are products of interdisciplinary links among criminology, psychology, sociology, women's studies, legal studies, and men's studies. The collection cuts a wide swath across a body of innovative theory and research in these areas and presents some of the best work of both emerging and seasoned scholars. We are especially excited about the fact that this is the first edited collection of its kind to integrate research from the United States and Europe. It also presents a range of cultural perspectives. For example, the experiences of both working and professional classes are addressed. The harassment of men as well as women is a concern. Finally, links to intervening social problems like racism and homophobia are explored. We learned a great deal from our contributors—from their previous work as well as from the material they added to this collection. One inference that can be drawn from the following pages is that scholarly definitions of male domination vary considerably across academic paradigms. After much discussion, we all agreed on one basic premise: male domination is multifaceted, consisting of at least two dimensions, numerical and normative (Gruber 1998). These chapters proceed with the assumption that when men outnumber women, those occupations and workplaces can be described as "male dominated." Researchers have typically derived workplace or occupational sex ratios, or determined whether the job was one done traditionally by women or by men, as a means of determining male dominance. But there is also a cultural or ideological dimension of male dominance. When the interests of men are privileged over those of women, where masculinity is prized and femininity disparaged, the workplace culture itself can be labeled "male dominated." This second aspect of male domination has received much less attention than the first over the last two decades. The majority of the chapters in this volume address problems associated with *double dominance*. In other words, they observe experiences and reports from men and women employed in both numerically and normatively male-dominated fields. Normative dominance extends the power of numerical dominance. Normative male dominance is reinforced institutionally through a variety of avenues: through socialization processes (e.g., military boot camp, firefighters, and police academies) that shape masculine hegemonic collective work identities (Chapters 3 and 10), through collective male resistance to organizational policies that promote equal opportunity (Chapters 2 and 12), and through male control of marginalized or nonconforming men through verbal and physical intimidation (Chapters 4 and 7).

Finally, while there is general agreement that sexual harassment has cultural roots, we discovered that definitions, perceptions, and policies regarding it vary widely across nationalities. These differences make cross-national comparisons especially difficult (Chapter 8). We discovered also that experiences and attitudes vary between cultures and among subgroups within society. Blue-collar women's definitions of sexual harassment, for example, do not always correspond with the complaints of professional women. Likewise, when harassment is racialized, the experiences and perceptions of African American women are often quite different from those of their white counterparts (Chapter 13). Because our primary goal is to publish the most innovative work in these areas, the collection is eclectic. We have included material from diverse theoretical perspectives, using different levels of analysis. As a result, the research in this collection ranges from the microlevel (e.g., "girl watching") to the global level (e.g., "corporate violations"). The research methods of our contributors include ethnography, in-depth interviews, surveys, and focus group analysis, as well as cross-national comparisons of survey results. While the full range of male-dominated settings is not represented in our collection, readers will find that the theory and research presented are applicable to a wide variety of male-dominated arenas.

In soliciting manuscripts for this volume, our primary goal was to find innovative theoretical and empirical approaches to the dual issues of male domination and sexual harassment. We hope that the following pages provoke questions as well as provide fresh insights, and we also hope that they will support future scrutiny of the links between sexual harassment and male domination. Striking a balance between the needs of lay and scholarly readers is not easy. Because we wanted to give readers of all levels of expertise access to the innovative ideas these contributors offer, we attempted to keep jargon to a minimum. Throughout the process we shouldered the burdens of editorship equally.

We can only take partial credit for this collection's publication. It is the product of a collaboration of talented and accomplished professionals. We owe our greatest debt to our contributors. Our deadlines were short and our requests for revision many. Our deepest gratitude goes to our NUP editors Sarah Rowley and Emily McKeigue. They were exceptionally available, consistently flexible, and their guidance was always helpful. We are also pleased by the fact that Claire Renzetti believed in the project enough to include it in this prestigious series. Colleagues Nancy Jurik and Michele Paludi read early drafts and provided insightful comments that improved the collection immeasurably. On a more personal note, Phoebe thanks Madeline Adelman for her intellectual and moral support.

Jim thanks the members of the International Coalition Against Sexual Harassment (ICASH) for their continuing efforts to understand the antecedents and consequences of sexual harassment and to develop effective policies and procedures that control the problem.

REFERENCES

Bastian, L., A. Lancaster, and H. Reyst. 1996. *The Department of Defense 1995 Sexual Harassment Survey.* Arlington, Va.: Defense Manpower Data Center.

Brown, J., E. Campbell, and C. Fife-Schaw. 1995. Adverse effects experienced by police officers following exposure to sex discrimination and sexual harassment. *Stress Medicine* 11:221–228.

Corrigan, Tim, Bob Connell, and John Lee. 1987. Hard and heavy: Toward a new sociology of masculinity. In *Beyond patriarchy,* ed. Michael Kaufman, 139–192. Oxford and New York: Oxford University Press.

Farley, Lin. 1978. *Sexual shakedown: The sexual harassment of women on the job.* New York: McGraw-Hill.

Firestone, J., and R. Harris. 1999. Changes in patterns of sexual harassment in the U.S. military: A comparison of the 1988 and 1995 DoD surveys. *Armed Forces and Society* 25 (4): 425–445.

Gruber, James. 1998. The impact of male work environments and organizational policies on women's experiences of sexual harassment. *Gender and Society* 12 (3): 301–320.

———. 2003. Sexual harassment in the public sector. In *Academic and workplace sexual harassment: A handbook of cultural, social science, management, and legal perspectives,* ed. M. Paludi and C. Paludi. Westport, Conn.: Praeger Press.

Hearn, Jeff, and Wendy Parkin. 1985. *Sex at work: The power and paradox of organization sexuality.* New York: St. Martin's Press.

Kimmel, Michael, ed. 1987. *Changing men: New directions in research on men and masculinity.* Newbury Park, Calif.: Sage.

Los Angeles Commission of the Status of Women. 1992. Report on the city of Los Angeles 1992 sexual harassment survey. Los Angeles: Commission on the Status of Women.

MacKinnon, Catharine. 1979. *Sexual harassment of working women: A case of sex discrimination.* New Haven, Conn.: Yale University Press.

Martin, Susan, and Nancy Jurik. 1996. *Doing justice, doing gender.* Thousand Oaks, Calif.: Sage.

Paludi, Michele. 1990. *Ivory power: Sexual harassment on campus.* New York: State University of New York Press.

United States Merit Systems Protection Board. 1995. Sexual harassment in the federal workplace: Trends, progress, and continuing challenges. Washington, D.C.: U.S. Government Printing Office.

EDITORS AND AUTHORS

Dave Baigent wrote the first U.K. degree in Uniformed Public Service and currently directs the Fire Service Research and Training Unit for the service. He holds a Ph.D. in sociology and publishes research about the social construction of masculinity and the fire service. He joined the London Fire Service at the age of eighteen and retired after thirty-one years as an operational firefighter.

Carrie N. Baker, J.D., Ph.D., is Assistant Professor of Sociology and Anthropology at Berry College (Rome, Georgia) and directs the Women's Studies Program. Her research interests include women's legal status in the United States, women's political activism, and feminist legal and political theory. Her dissertation, "Sex, Power, and Politics: The Origins of Sexual Harassment Policy in the United States," traces the emergence and development of the issue of sexual harassment from the second wave of the women's movement.

NiCole T. Buchanan, Ph.D., is an Assistant Professor in the Department of Psychology at Michigan State University. Her research examines the intersection of race and gender in workplace harassment, gendered and racial components of interpersonal violence, and coping and resilience among women of color. Her work appears in *Psychology Policy and the Law* (1999), *Women and Therapy* (2001, 2002), *Journal of Vocational Behavior* (2001), C. M. West, ed., *Violence in the Lives of Black Women: Battered, Black, and Blue* (2003), and A. R. Gillem & C. A. Thompson, eds., *Biracial Women in Therapy: Between the Rock of Gender and the Hard Place of Race* (2004).

Carla Corroto holds a Ph.D. in sociology from Ohio State University and a master's of architecture from the University of Illinois. She has practiced architectural design and now teaches courses on design and professionalism. Her research interests include the intersection of race and gender in architecture practices and in design. Her latest publication, "The Politics of Masculinity and Sacred Space," appears in *Journal of Architectural Education*.

Robert S. Done teaches organization behavior and human resource management courses. His research interests include gender issues in organizations and technology in society. His publications include a chapter ("Sexual Harassment") in R. K. Unger, ed., *Handbook of the Psychology of Women and Gender* (with Barbara Gutek), and two recent journal articles: "Resolving Conflict Within the Organization: Creating Win-Win Solutions with Mediation," *Industrial-Organizational Psychologist* 36:28–33; and "The Utility of the Reasonable Woman Standard in Hostile Environment Sexual Harassment Cases: A Multimethod, Multistudy Examination," *Psychology, Public Policy, and Law* 5:569–629 (with Gutek, O'Connor, Melancon, Stockdale, and Geer).

Melissa Sheridan Embser-Herbert holds a Ph.D. and is Associate Professor of Sociology at Hamline University in Saint Paul, Minnesota. She authored *Camouflage Isn't Only for Combat: Gender, Sexuality, and Women in the Military* and with Aaron Belkin published "A Modest Proposal: Privacy as a Flawed Rationale for the Exclusion of Gays and Lesbians from the U.S. Military" in *International Security* (2002).

James Gruber is Professor of Sociology at the University of Michigan, Dearborn. He has researched sexual harassment for over twenty years, and his work has appeared in *Sex Roles, Social Science Quarterly, Work and Occupations, Psychology of Women Quarterly,* and *Gender and Society*. His most recent publications include "Sexual Harassment in the Public Sector," in Paludi and Paludi, eds., *Academic and Workplace Sexual Harassment: A Handbook of Social Science, Legal, Cultural, and Management Perspectives* (2003); "Not Taking It Anymore: Women Who Report or File Complaints of Sexual Harassment," *Canadian Review of Sociology and Anthropology* (with Sandy Welsh, 1999); and "The Impact of Male Work Environments and Organizational Policies on Women's Experiences of Sexual Harassment," *Gender and Society* (1998).

Jeff Hearn is Research Professor in Sociology at the University of Huddersfield, United Kingdom, and Academy Fellow and Professor at the Swedish School of Economics, Helsinki, Finland. He has published widely on gender, sexuality, violence, organizations, and management. His most recent books include *Gender, Sexuality and Violence in Organizations* (with Wendy Parkin), *Gender Divisions and Gender Policies in Top Finnish Corporations* (with Anne Kovalainen and Teemu Tallberg), and *Information Society and the Workplace* (coedited with Tuula Heiskanen). His current research topic is "Men, Gender Relations, and Transnational Organizing, Organizations, and Management."

Kaisa Kauppinen holds a Ph.D. from Helsinki University, where she teaches as a docent. She is Research Manager at the Finnish Institute of Occupational Health, and her interest areas include comparative research on gendered economic and occupational inequality and the impact on women's well-being. She has a number of publications on sexual harassment and mobbing, as well as on women in leadership positions.

Michael S. Kimmel is Professor of Sociology at State University of New York, Stony Brook. His most recent publications include *Men's Lives* (6th ed., 2003), *The Politics of Manhood* (1996), *Manhood: A Cultural History* (1996), and *The Gendered Society* (2000). He edits *Men and Masculinities*, an interdisciplinary scholarly journal, and two book series: Men and Masculinity at the University of California Press, and the Sage Series on Men and Masculinities. A spokesperson for the National Organization for Men Against Sexism (NOMAS), he lectures extensively on campuses in the United States and abroad.

Phoebe Morgan is Associate Professor of Criminal Justice at Northern Arizona University. She teaches courses about women, law, and research methods. She has published on the topics of sexual harassment complaints, women's litigation, victim claiming, and multicultural education. In 1992 she cofounded Sociologists Against Sexual Harassment (which later became the International Coalition Against Sexual Harassment). Her most recent publications include "Sexual Harassment: Violence Against Women at Work," in Renzetti, Edleson, and Bergen, eds., *The Violence Against Women Source Book* (2001); "Risking Relationships: Understanding the Litigation Choices of Sexually Harassed Women," *Law and Society Review* (1999); "Tuna Fish and Pissing Contests: Gender and Domination on the Internet," in Ronai, Zsemblik, and Feagin, eds., *Everyday Sexism in the Third Millennium* (with Kimberly J. Cook, 1997); and "The Power of Law and the Sexual Harassment Complaints of Women," *National Women's Studies Association Journal* (Special Issue on Sexual Harassment, 1996).

Saara Patoluoto graduated from the University of Sheffield in 2000 and has been working as a researcher at the Finnish Institute of Occupational Health since 2002. Before 2002 she worked as a research assistant in the Helsinki School of Economics, Center for Markets in Transition. Her research interests include women in leadership, equality in Finnish working life, and women in male-dominated occupations. She speaks fluent Russian and is interested in researching women leaders in Russia.

Wendy Parkin is now retired from her post as Principal Lecturer in Sociology and Social Work at the University of Huddersfield, United Kingdom. Her key works, in collaboration with Jeff Hearn, include the early introduction of the concept of gender into the field of organization studies, to be followed by the development of the concept of "organization sexuality," in *"Sex" at "Work": The Power and Paradox of Organisation Sexuality* (1987, 1995). A particular interest has been issues of sexuality in residential organizations, which has led to recent work on organization violations in *Gender, Sexuality and Violence in Organizations* (2001).

Beth A. Quinn is Associate Professor of Sociology at Montana State University, Bozeman. She received her Ph.D. in criminology, law, and society from the University of California, Irvine. Drawing primarily on feminist and masculinity theories and on neo-institutional organizational theory, her research focuses on legal complaint-making and discrimination law and has been published in journals such as *Law and Social Inquiry* and *Gender and Society*. She is currently exploring how human resources personnel understand and deal with employment discrimination law.

Tyson Smith is a Ph.D. candidate at State University of New York, Stony Brook. He is currently doing ethnographic research on professional wrestlers performing in Long Island, New York.

Margaret S. Stockdale is Professor of Psychology at Southern Illinois University, Carbondale, and Program Director for the Applied Psychology doctoral program. Her research interests concern gender and diversity issues in the workplace as well as the surveillance and evaluation of public health interventions. Her recent publications are found in *Psychology, Public Policy and the Law; Journal of Vocational Behavior;* and *Psychology of Women Quarterly*. She recently coedited *The Psychology and Management of Workplace Diversity* (with Faye Crosby). She teaches both undergraduate and graduate courses in workplace diversity, organizational psychology, and applied social science research methods.

Greetje Timmerman is Associate Professor of Gender Studies at the University of Groningen and in the Education and Gender Studies Department, the University Centre for Gender Studies. In 1997 and 1998 she led a study project commissioned by the European Commission to evaluate sexual harassment in European Union member states. In 1999 she coordinated the first large-scale survey of unwanted sexual behavior in secondary schools in the Netherlands, commissioned by the Ministry of Education, Culture and Science. Her recent research areas include sex education of adolescents, feminization of the teaching and medical professions, and gender and educational careers. Her latest research can be found in *Sex Roles* and in the *Journal of Youth and Adolescence* (with Bajema, Cristien, Bonink, and Marjan). She has a chapter in *Seksuele Intimidatie op School: Omvang, Aard en Aanpak* (*Sexual Harassment at School: Incidence, Types, and Policies*).

Kristen Yount received her Ph.D. in sociology from the University of Colorado. Currently, she is a Professor at Northern Kentucky University and directs the Sociology Program. She teaches courses on the environment, gender, race, and social movements. Previous research concerned gender relations and harassment among coal miners. At present, she evaluates programs and policies regarding redevelopment and contaminated properties for the U.S. Environmental Protection Agency. Her most recent publications include *What Are Brownfields? Finding a Conceptual Definition* (2003); "Financing Redevelopment of Brownfields," in White, Bingham, and Hill, eds., *Economic Development in the 21st Century* (2003); and *Insuring Redevelopment at Contaminated Urban Properties*, forthcoming, in *Public Works, Public Policy*.

Part I

Men, Domination, and Sexual Harassment

The first wave of sexual harassment research placed women's experiences of sexual harassment at the center of analysis. Subsequent waves turned attention toward women's response strategies and then to organizational responses and their impact. Similarly, earlier scholarship on patriarchy focused on how women experienced male dominance. In both cases, studies from the standpoint of female victims pushed the experiences of men to the margins. Only recently have scholars begun to investigate the place of men in sexual harassment and their experiences of male dominance. While the approaches vary widely, the seven chapters in this section have one thing in common: they all place the attitudes and behaviors of men at the center of analysis.

In the first two chapters, Done and Quinn shift attention from female victims and their experiences toward the experiences of the men who harass them. Although Done's analysis is quantitative and Quinn's qualitative, in each case they break new theoretical ground by framing their analyses with criminological theory. The result is a greater understanding of what motivates some men to harass women. In addition to setting new horizons for the research of male dominance and sexual harassment, their findings suggest new approaches to policy and organizational practice. For example, Done's work suggests that the Propensity to Sexually Harass and the Self Control Scales are reliable instruments for identifying employees at high risk of committing sexual harassment. Evaluating such risk could be useful for both deterrent and rehabilitative purposes. Quinn's study highlights the critical role that fun plays in sexual harassment, suggesting that those with the responsibility to transform organizational culture need to take more seriously the pleasures of sexual harassment.

Chapters 3 and 4 are ethnographic studies of men's experience of male dominance. From an insider's standpoint, Baigent reveals the hierarchy of firefighting men and exposes how the informal culture and the authorities within it normalize harassment. Similarly, Yount's chapter digs deeper into the gendered and occupational practices that support a harassing culture. By employing the term *harazzment*, she dissects the overlap between friendly and hostile forms of harassment. Both authors point to new directions in the management of sexual harassment. Baigent argues that formal policies prohibiting sexual harassment will have little impact until informal practices are called into question and reformed. In a similar vein, Yount links the quality of working conditions to both sexual harassment and male dominance. As a coping mechanism, harazzment is likely to continue as long as the working conditions for miners remain dangerous and demoralizing.

Chapters 6 and 7 are some of the first to focus specifically on the problem of men's victimization. In Chapter 6, Stockdale proposes a new theoretical model that can accommodate the seemingly contradictory reality of the sexual harassment of men. She identifies four dimensions that have been either understudied or ignored: approach versus rejection harassment and opposite-sex versus same-sex harassment. These four dimensions allow a place for male victims within sexual harassment theory. Through an analysis of U.S. court opinions regarding cases filed by men, Chapter 7 considers the conundrum of same-sex harassment and the harassment of men by men. Drawing upon legal scholarship, it shows how sexual harassment against men is not only a valid violation but should also be actionable under current laws.

Chapter 5 is not about men per se but rather about the links between harassment and the bullying physical violence that occurs at work. Building on their earlier work linking male dominance to work violence, Hearn and Parkin question the partitioning of various types of work-related violence. They argue that sexual harassment, bullying, and physical violence occur across interconnected continua. These types of problems are on the rise, in part because policies that treat them as discrete problems fail to meaningfully address them.

1 JUST MEN OUT OF CONTROL?
Criminology and the Likelihood to Sexually Harass

Robert S. Done

Across various disciplines, research has consistently connected male dominance and sexual harassment. Sociologist Lin Farley (1978), for example, was one of the first to link sexual harassment with patriarchy. Organizational studies have discovered a correlation between sexual harassment prevalence and gender skew (i.e., settings in which a disproportionate number of workers are of one gender) (Gutek & Morasch 1982). Legal scholars argue that sexual harassment is both a cause and consequence of an androcentric justice system (MacKinnon 1979). And psychologists note a relationship between the acceptability of sexual harassment and the privileging of men's sexual desires (Fitzgerald & Weitzman 1990).

By highlighting the fact that sexual harassment is most often committed by men against women, feminist criminologists have compared sexual harassment to violent crimes against women like rape and battering (Morgan 2001), and critical criminologist James Messerschmidt (1986, 1993) has classified sexual harassment as a form of white-collar crime. With these exceptions, mainstream criminology has neglected its study. Even though the motivation to commit illegal behavior is a mainstay of criminological inquiry, criminologists have not used this research to understand why some men sexually harass while others do not. This chapter conceptualizes sexual harassment as crime and then draws upon the mainstream criminological understanding of internal factors affecting crime perpetration to analyze men's responses to a survey that measured their self-control and likelihood to sexually harass. The analysis reveals the extent to which self-control predicts the likelihood to sexually harass, as it does the likelihood to commit other crimes.

CONCEPTUALIZING SEXUAL HARASSMENT AS CRIME

Legally speaking, sexual harassment is a civil rights violation. The U.S. Equal Employment Opportunity Commission (EEOC) officially recognizes sexual harassment as an actionable form of employment discrimination. As such, formal complaints become civil actions and are litigated accordingly. Initially, U.S. feminists and women's activists applauded the move to cast sexual harassment as a civil rights violation, because doing so recognizes institutional liability and affords victims substantial compensation for their losses (MacKinnon 1979). But more recently, feminists have noted the inability of civil action to hold accountable the individuals who commit sexual harassment (MacKinnon 1987). In fact, while the complaints themselves are civil in nature, the behaviors named in them are often violations of specific crime statutes (Morgan 1996). Most sexual harassment research relies upon the EEOC's definition of what constitutes sexual harassment. While such reliance has given us clear estimates of the problem as defined by civil law, it ignores the criminality of sexual harassment.

A review of official crime statistics makes clear that crime is a male-dominated institution. Even though men are disproportionately victims of crime, with few exceptions (e.g., shoplifting and prostitution), the perpetrators of crime are overwhelmingly male (Newburn & Stanko 1994). In fact, the gender skew is greatest in violent crime—the vast majority of scenarios involve men assaulting, harassing, or stalking women to whom they are intimately related or sexually attracted (Bachman 1998). The statistical profile of sexual harassment mirrors that of other forms of violence against women. Nearly 86 percent of its victims are women, while only 7 percent of the perpetrators are women (U.S. Merit Systems Protection Board 1995). For these reasons, this analysis places sexual harassment on the continuum of violent crime against women, and therefore considers it an appropriate subject of criminological analysis.

Until recently, criminological investigations of violence against women have focused disproportionately on the victims. The criminological literature is dominated by studies of how women experience violence such as rape, battering, and abuse. Much less has been published on the perpetrators of these crimes. Sexual harassment scholarship is similarly skewed; it focuses on the prevalence of victimization and the effects it has on women (for exceptions, see Pryor 1987 and Pryor & Stoller 1994). Although criminology has much research on crime motivation, this literature has been underutilized in the study of violence against women and has hardly been applied to analyses of the motivation to sexually harass.

Early feminist criminology identified the primary motivation to commit any form of violence against women as the need to assert power and maintain control over them (Websdale & Chesney-Lind 1998). In a patriarchal society such as ours, men use violence against women because they can—in other words, they have the physical, social, and economic power to do so. In a patriarchal society, violence, or even the mere possibility of it, is an effective means to control unruly women and keep them in their place (Messerschmidt 1986). From this viewpoint, sexual harassment is a spillover of male dominance from the home to the workplace, from the private to the public sphere. Gutek and Morasch's (1982) study of sex-role spillover and sexual harassment draws striking parallels. As greater numbers of women have moved into the public world of work, violence against them has followed them there. At work, men sexually harass women to assert and maintain their dominance of specific workplaces, entire occupations, and simply wage labor in general (Farley 1978, MacKinnon 1979, Morgan 2001).

More recently, critical criminologists have built on feminist conceptualizations to argue that a primary motivator for the commission of most crimes—and especially violent crimes against women—is the need to construct a masculine identity (Messerschmidt 1986, 1993, Stanko 1994). This "doing gender" perspective asserts that in the absence of other more viable options, males commit crime to demonstrate their manliness (Hobbs 1994, Levi 1994), and a common strategy is the denigration of all things feminine—especially women (Connell 2000). Defining and preserving masculinity through sexual harassment are not only the provinces of criminals. Indeed, by observing criminal justice workers through this "doing gender" lens, Martin and Jurik (1996) show how sexual harassment works to preserve the male dominance of these occupations. In short, the "doing gender" lens sharpens our view of how the need to be masculine affects the likelihood to commit crime. It furthers our understanding of the motivation to dominate women and how crimes against women gratify the need to "be a man."

CRIMINOLOGY AND THE RISK OF CRIMINALITY

While most perpetrators of violence against women are men, the vast majority of men never commit such crime. This is true across all categories of violence against women, including sexual harassment. Clearly, there is variation in perpetration. Some men are more likely than others to sexually harass women. What increases this likelihood? Empirical research to date sheds considerable light on the social and structural conditions that produce violence against women in general and sexual harassment in particular. Such external factors as gender ratio (Gutek & Morasch 1982), social acceptability (Essed 1992), and power differential (Pryor 1987) have been found to be significant predictors of sexual harassment. But far less is known about the internal factors affecting the likelihood to commit sexual harassment. Fortunately, mainstream criminology offers the tools to explore this missing link.

Within this literature lies an extensive study of the internal drives and inhibitions influencing the motivation to commit crime. A particularly robust factor is self-control. Gottfredson and Hirschi (1990) find a variety of deviant behaviors—criminal and noncriminal—that provide immediate gratification. These behaviors are also exciting or risky, provide primarily short-term benefits, require little preparation, and often cause pain for the victim. Accordingly, criminals are those who seek immediate gratification, such as "sex without courtship" (p. 89), and they are insensitive to others. Those who engage in deviant behavior lack the self-control to delay the immediate gratification that deviance provides, without regard to the age, ethnicity, education, income, or employment history of the perpetrator.

Gottfredson and Hirschi's (1990) studies of self-control explain why some people commit crime while others do not. They observe that although a criminal act provides short-term gratification to the perpetrator, it can inflict long-term harm on the victim. Thus to achieve immediate gratification and to avoid hurting others would be the ideal goal. The factor differentiating the two is individual self-control. Self-control checks the temptation to trade on the welfare of others, and instead motivates one to be considerate of others. Those with less self-control are more likely than those with more of it to immediately gratify their desires at the expense of others. Self-control, then, checks the impulsive gratification of desire and delays gratification until it can be achieved through sanctioned channels.

A significant body of empirical research supports the significance of self-control as a factor affecting the likelihood to commit crime. The criminal behaviors studied in this empirical scrutiny have included crimes against property (e.g., theft) and people (e.g., assault) (Burton et al. 1998, Evans et al. 1997, Grasmick et al. 1993, Longshore 1998, Longshore & Turner 1998, Longshore, Turner, & Stein 1996, Wood, Pfefferbaum, & Arneklev 1993). The relationship between self-control and criminal behavior has been studied among high school students (Wood et al. 1993), college students (Gibbs & Giever 1995, Gibbs, Giever, & Martin 1998), and adults (Burton et al. 1998, Evans et al. 1997, Grasmick et al. 1993, Keane, Maxim, & Teevan 1993).

On the continuum of criminological orientation with mainstream theory at one end and critical theory at the other, the self-control theory of violent crime occupies the opposite pole of the structural emphasis of feminism. The most fundamental difference between the two is locus of action. Gottfredson and Hirschi (1990) consider crime to be a coincidental by-product of an individual's search for pleasure, whereas feminist criminologists consider crime to be an artifact of the dominant (i.e., patriarchal) social structure. Gottfredson and Hirschi focus their attention on internal factors, while feminist and critical criminologists study external ones.

Some would argue that the differences between them are irreconcilable. Despite these differences, there is convergence on one important point: regardless of whether the pressure comes from within or without, violence against women is the outcome of desire. Both self-control and social control impact men's motivations to dominate.

Currently, our knowledge about the types of men likely to commit sexual harassment is more descriptive than proscriptive. Knowing what kinds of men are most likely to sexually harass is important, but identifying the internal motivations of those individuals is equally essential to understanding this type of behavior. Thus, in this chapter I conceptualize self-control as a significant but underappreciated link connecting male domination and sexual harassment. To test this link, statistical data are examined to reveal the significance of self-control as a predictor of the likelihood to sexually harass. The primary hypothesis examined here is that men who have low self-control are more likely to sexually harass women than men with high self-control. Second, my analysis will explore the extent to which this relationship is affected by structural or external factors such as age, ethnicity, education, committed relationship status, income, or work status.

The data used to conduct these tests are the responses of 164 men to a survey questionnaire. The questionnaire contained items that measured the respondents' self-control (independent variable) and the likelihood that they would sexually harass a woman (dependent variable). In addition, responses to a set of questions provided the demographic data needed to examine how social structure affects the relationship between self-control and the likelihood to sexually harass.

MEASURING THE LIKELIHOOD TO SEXUALLY HARASS

Within mainstream criminology, the likelihood to commit crime is a common focus of empirical study. In contrast, relatively little effort has been made to measure the likelihood to commit sexual harassment. Pryor's (1987) Likelihood to Sexually Harass Scale (LSHS) is the most widely used scale today. The LSHS is a questionnaire consisting of ten different vignettes, each describing men in positions of control over employment benefits for a woman. Following each vignette, the respondent answers the same set of questions. The first asks if the respondent would provide the thing or opportunity to the woman, the second asks if the respondent would provide the thing or opportunity to the woman in exchange for sexual favors, and the third asks if the respondent would ask the woman to meet later for dinner to discuss the thing or opportunity.[1]

Consistently, applications of the LSHS find it to be a reliable and valid measure. The LSHS has been used to test relationships between the likelihood to sexually harass and the likelihood to rape (Malamuth 1981), sexual attitudes (Burt 1980, White et al. 1977), authoritarianism (Berkowitz & Wolkon 1964), machiavellianism (Christie & Geiss 1970), and measures of dominance (Berkowitz & Wolkon 1964). Pryor and Stoller (1994) report that scores on the LSHS significantly predict confidence in recognizing dominance and sexuality. Bargh et al. (1995) find that the LSHS significantly predicts the cognitive association between power and sex. Rudman and Borgida (1995) report that those who score high on the LSHS are more likely to ask sexist questions in a staged employment interview than those who score low on the scale. Finally, in a behavioral study of under-graduate men (Pryor 1987), scores on the LSHS significantly pre-dicted a female research confederate's interpretation of respondent behavior as being sexual or not. Thus, the LSHS is a consistent and valid measure of the likelihood to sexually harass.[2]

MEASURING SELF-CONTROL

Because self-control has been a focus of mainstream criminology for some time, a variety of reliable and valid self-control measures exist. Those most visible to the general public are the subsets of questions within psychometric inventories such as the Minnesota Multiphasic Personality Inventory and the California Psychological Inventory. Because of the large number of items and the time constraints of the study, these instruments were removed from consideration. Two shorter measures of self-control, the Ego Control VI Scale and the Self-Control Schedule (Rosenbaum 1980), were also considered. Both of these scales were eliminated because neither reflects the mul-tidimensional construct defined by Gottfredson and Hirschi (1990), and neither has experienced wide use.

Grasmick et al.'s (1993) Measure of Self-Control (MSC) contains the structure[3] defined by Gottfredson and Hirschi (1990) and has been widely used. The MSC contains twenty-four items, such as "I often do whatever brings me pleasure in the here and now, even at the cost of some distant goal."[4] Following the successful use of the MSC initially reported by Grasmick et al. (1993), Wood et al (1993), Longshore et al. (1996), and others have used it to test the relation-ship between self-control and criminal behavior.

The Measure of Self-Control (Grasmick et al. 1993) is the scale most suited to explore the proposed relationship between self-con-trol and the likelihood to sexually harass. Its relevant structure, acceptable reliability,[5] and direct application make it the most appropriate scale to test the usefulness of Gottfredson and Hirschi's criminological theory in predicting the likelihood of sexual harassment, a behavior that is not criminal per se but that is predicated on domination and self-gratification.

METHOD

Data on self-control and the likelihood to sexually harass were collected from men with extensive employment and supervisory experience. The sample consisted of 164 men summoned for jury duty in the southwestern United States who volunteered to participate in the study (see Table 1.1). Most respondents were white and 46 to 55 years of age. More than three-quarters had at least some college education, and the majority were in a committed relationship. Many reported working at least forty hours per week and had at least fifteen years of work experience. Finally, a majority of respondents had supervisory experience. These demographic characteristics suggest that the sample was composed of men in a position to sexually harass women, that is, employed men in a position to condition employment benefits on sexual favors. This form of sexual harassment, quid pro quo, is the form reflected in each of the vignettes of Pryor's (1987) LSHS.

The questionnaire administered included demographic items and slightly modified versions of the MSC (Grasmick et al. 1993) and the LSHS (Pryor 1987). Both scales were modified to include six-point response scales. The response scale of the MSC was anchored by (1) does not describe me and (6) does describe me. The response scale of the LSHS was anchored by (1) not very likely and (6) very likely. The questionnaire was administered to men in a jury pool as they waited to be summoned to a courtroom. Participants were given as much time as they needed to complete the questionnaire, and researchers assured the participants of the anonymity of their responses to all questions.

Table 1.1

Characteristics of the Likelihood to Sexually Harass Sample

Characteristic ($N = 164$)	% of Sample
Age	
18–25	11.0
26–35	19.5
36–45	24.5
46–55	28.0
56–65	7.9
Over 65	9.1
Ethnicity	
Asian	1.9
Black	1.2
Hispanic	12.4
Native American	1.9
White	82.6
Education	
High school or less	16.0
Vocational school	8.6
Some college	36.2
Bachelor's degree	12.9
Graduate work	26.4
Committed Relationship	
No	14.6
Yes	85.4
Income	
None	2.5
<$30,000	28.6
$30,001–$60,000	43.5
$60,001–$90,000	14.3
>$90,000	11.1
Hours Employed	
None	14.1
<20	0.6
20–39	8.0
40 +	77.3
Years Employed	
<15	27.8
15–24	21.6

Table 1.1 *(continued)*

Characteristics of the Likelihood to Sexually Harass Sample

Characteristic (*N* = 164)	% of Sample
Years Employed	
25–34	26.5
35 +	24.1
Supervisory Experience	
No	9.1
Yes	90.9

RESULTS

Because a single question fails to capture the complexity of concepts like self-control and the likelihood to sexually harass, scaled indexes of multiple questions were employed. A reliable and valid measure of concepts like these is one in which the items within an index are related but exclusive. In other words, they measure the same concept, but in different ways. Before testing the relationship between these two concepts, the analysis began with a test of the reliability and validity of the scales themselves. Thus, the data were collected with the MSC (Grasmick et al. 1993) and the LSHS (Pryor 1987).

The items in the MSC and the LSHS produced reliability coefficients of .83 and .95, respectively. These findings compare favorably with those reported by others (e.g., Grasmick et al. 1993, Pryor 1987) and suggest that both measures have high levels of internal consistency. As a result, the average response for each question was adopted for subsequent hypothesis testing.

Next, before testing the statistical significance of self-control as a predictor of the likelihood to harass, correlations were generated to confirm the relationship between these two variables. The resulting coefficient, .26, was statistically significant ($p < .001$). Furthermore, it indicates that about 7 percent of the variation in responses can be explained by the degree of self-control. While this percentage may seem modest, the ability to account for this 7 percent moves us even closer to understanding why some men harass and others do not.

Finally, regressions tested the statistical significance of self-control as a predictor of the likelihood to sexually harass. The tests controlled for the effects of such external factors as age, ethnicity, education, relationship, income, employment, and supervisory experience.

Initially, some of the demographic variables were ordinally measured, but for (1) statistical power, (2) empirical validity, and (3) theoretical purposes, these demographic characteristics were then recoded into two categories (see Table 1.2). With respect to the first, statistical power is the ability to determine the probability that a relationship between variables exists. Too little power may result in the conclusion that a relationship exists when it does not or that a relationship does not exist when it does. With regard to the second, although ordinal data are often subjected to statistical analyses that require interval (or better) data, this technique is commonly accepted in the social sciences. The difference between being Asian and black is not likely to be the same as the difference between being black and Hispanic. Thus, it is more persuasive to consider the responses of ethnic minorities to their white counterparts, since the latter share a common characteristic.

Similar logic was applied to the other demographic variables. Of course, two of the demographic variables were already dichotomous and required no manipulation. The third reason for dichotomizing the demographic variables is theoretical. The purpose of this study was to test the hypothesis that if we controlled for the effects of external factors, the internal factor of self-control would predict the likelihood to sexually harass. To discover that self-control predicts the likelihood to sexually harass only for white men over 65 years of age who have attended vocational school is of little theoretical (or practical) use. More significant would be the finding that self-control is a consistent and significant predictor of the likelihood to sexually harass for all men. This approach is also consistent with Gott-

Table 1.2

Demographic Groupings of the Likelihood to Sexually Harass Sample

Grouping ($N = 64$)	% of Sample
Age	
18–45	55.0
46 +	45.0
Ethnicity	
Nonwhite	17.4
White	82.6
Education	
Less than bachelor's degree	60.7
Bachelor's degree or more	39.3
Committed Relationship	
No	14.6
Yes	85.4
Income	
<$60,001	74.6
$60,001 +	25.4
Hours Employed	
<40	22.7
40 +	77.3
Years Employed	
<25	49.4
25 +	50.6
Supervisory Experience	
No	9.1
Yes	90.9

fredson and Hirschi's (1990) position that self-control is a general predictor of criminal behavior.

A series of regression equations tested the statistical significance of self-control as a valid predictor of the likelihood to sexually harass (see Table 1.3). In the first analysis, the average scores on the MSC and all of the demographic variables were simultaneously regressed on the average scores on the LSHS. Self-control was the only statisti-

Table 1.3

Predictors of the Likelihood to Sexually Harass

Characteristic	b
Self-control	.24[a]
Age	−.01
Ethnicity	.02
Education	−.01
Committed relationship	−.03
Income	.07
Hours employed	.04
Years employed	−.03
Supervisory experience	.07

R-square: .070.
[a]$p < .001$.

cally significant predictor of the likelihood to sexually harass. Together, all the independent variables in this regression model explained 7 percent ($p < .001$) of the variation in the likelihood to sexually harass.

To allow the strongest variables to prove themselves while eliminating the truly insignificant variables, a stepwise regression was conducted. This procedure, which retains and analyzes only those variables with statistical merit, recognized only self-control as a significant predictor of the likelihood to sexually harass ($b = .24, p < .001$).

Based on these findings, a final regression analysis was conducted for only self-control. All the other insignificant variables in the equation (all the demographics) were excluded. In this analysis, self-control ($b = .24, p < .001$) explained 6 percent ($p < .001$) of the variance in the likelihood to sexually harass. Thus, the external factors tested (ethnicity, age, relationship, employment, supervisory experience, etc.) account for less than 1 percent of the variation in the responses to the index of questions measuring the likelihood to sexually harass.

DISCUSSION

These findings support the proposition that when one controls for external factors like age, ethnicity, relationship status, employment, and supervisory experience, the internal factor of self-control significantly affects the likelihood of harassment. As mentioned before, all men are not sexual harassers. In fact, most are not. Self-control is a significant element of a constellation of factors determining the types of men who are at higher risk of committing sexual harassment than others. When one controls for the effects of external factors like those tested in this study, men with low self-control are significantly more likely to sexually harass than men with high self-control. In light of previous research emphasizing structural factors, the fact that self-control exhibited more explanatory power than the demographics measured is a significant finding.

It is theoretically plausible that age would affect likelihood. For example, in patriarchal Western society older men tend to have more authority than younger ones. The opportunity to dominate others increases with age. As men get older, they are more likely to have subordinates at work and therefore have greater opportunity to harass those with less power. Conversely, with age comes the opportunity to learn from past mistakes and to choose not to misbehave. In fact, criminality peaks in the late teenage years and declines steadily throughout life. In either case, however, controlling for the other demographics, age failed to predict the likelihood to sexually harass.

Similarly, Messerschmidt's (1986, 1993) structured action theory suggests that ethnicity would structure self-control and therefore the likelihood to sexually harass. White men experience numerical and hierarchical superiority in most organizations. Accordingly, it would be expected that this superiority would be used to dominate women, who are typically fewer in number and occupy the lower rungs of the organizational ladder. Alternatively, men of an ethnic minority may be challenged to define their masculinity in organizations controlled by white men. By dominating and sexually harassing women, men of color distance themselves from women and identify their common ground with white men, namely, gender. Although both of these perspectives are plausible, ethnicity did not reveal itself as a significant predictor of the likelihood to sexually harass.

It is also easy to believe that education could influence the likelihood to sexually harass. Historically men have possessed more higher education than women. This privilege has granted them both institutional and social power. Intellectual domination could easily segue into physical domination through sexual harassment. On the other hand, as men become more educated they may not need to prove their superiority; rather, they may develop more respect for humanity and treat women with respect and support. As likely as either of these positions may seem, education was not a predictor of the likelihood to sexually harass.

Those who believe that the likelihood to sexually harass is driven by the need for sex may also believe that whether or not a man is in a committed relationship would predict his likelihood to sexually harass. The commitment of a man to a relationship would seem to be a strong indicator that his needs are being fulfilled by that relationship. As such, he would have no reason to exploit vulnerable women at the workplace to gratify his needs. It is also possible that a committed relationship is the product of traditional patriarchal values and a reflection of a man's status as the head of a household. Drawing upon the spillover theory (Gutek & Morasch 1982) in those cases, a spillover of patriarchal values from the home to the office would increase the entitlement of those men to sexual gratification. But in this case whether or not a man was in a committed relationship had no influence on his likelihood to sexually harass.

The employment variables could also be used to construct a logical explanation for the likelihood to sexually harass. Men who work full-time and earn high incomes where they have worked for many years have much more to lose if they are caught sexually harassing others. Part-time or minimum wage employees who earn little more than their unemployment benefits provide might see sexual harassment as a way to get a "leg up" over their female competitors. Alternatively, men who work full-time in prestigious positions may sense that women in the organization, like the company jet, exist for their utilization, while the proletariat may sense that women are their equal and not subject to their domination. However logical they may be, neither of these perspectives nor any of the employment variables were statistically significant predictors of the likelihood to sexually harass.

The list of external variables included in these analyses is by no means definitive. Research and theory implicate the significance of a number of other factors. Recent work on masculinity (Connell 2000, Martin & Jurik 1996, Messerschmidt 1993), for example, suggests that sexual harassment is a means of both accomplishing hegemonic masculinity and of resisting it. Given this proposition, future replications should consider including measures of masculinity. Specifically, one hypothesis is that as a sense of masculinity decreases the likelihood to sexually harass increases. The demographic variables examined here are likely to be included in definitions of masculinity (employment status, income, etc.), and none of these variables proved significant. Thus, it is unlikely that masculinity (or any other variable that could be defined by the demographic variables studied here) will be useful in predicting the likelihood to sexually harass.

CONCLUSION

Men sexually harassed women long before it became illegal to do so. From the earliest scholarship, feminists (e.g., Farley 1978, MacKinnon 1979) have conceptualized sexual harassment as a form of violent crime against women. Today, sexual harassment is recognized as a vehicle for dominating women in the same ways that other violent crimes like rape and battering are (Morgan 2001). Male domination through crime serves both instrumental and expressive purposes. Men who exchange employment benefits for sexual favors are using sexual harassment as a tool to achieve personal gratification. Men who assault and rape women perpetrate crime to express social and physical superiority over them. The economic and physical dominance of women is clear in both instances.

Mainstream criminologists Gottfredson and Hirschi (1990) would consider sexual harassment and shoplifting to be similar because both provide immediate gratification of an internal or personal desire. Critical criminologist Messerschmidt (1993) would consider sexual harassment and sexual assault to be similar in that both accomplish masculinity in a patriarchal capitalistic society. Psychologist Pryor's (1987) work on measuring the likelihood to sexually harass was based in part on the likelihood to commit the crime of rape. Sigler and Johnson's (1986) work also supports the criminalization of sexual harassment. Ironically, the conceptualization of sexual harassment has emerged from psychology and not from criminology.

In this chapter I have argued that sexual harassment can be conceptualized as a crime against women. Framed within a mainstream criminological perspective, my analysis highlights an overlooked link—self-control—to be a significant factor connecting male dominance with sexual harassment. In the study of violent crimes against women, feminist criminologists have foregone analyses of internal factors, focusing on external or structural factors affecting the likelihood of perpetration. My analysis shows that the effects of internal factors like self-control should not be dismissed. They also matter. Given its extensive history in the study of internal motivations, I have drawn upon mainstream criminology to test the contribution that self-control might make.

This research has important implications for theories of sexual harassment and criminal behavior. Self-control appears to be a personality trait that can predict the likelihood of sexual harassment. This study identified similarities between crime and sexual harassment, including empirical evidence on the prevalence of male perpetrators and the dominant effect that crime and sexual harassment have on their victims. Because of the similarities between sexual harassment and crime, these findings provide strong support for the conceptualization of sexual harassment as a behavior analogous to crime and one that can be predicted with self-control. Further theoretical developments on the cause(s) of sexual harassment must account for the empirical findings reported here. I propose that mainstream and critical criminological understandings of the likelihood to sexually harass need not be mutually exclusive. Perhaps external *and* internal factors conspire to affect a man's willingness to sexually harass.

These findings have a number of implications for research as well. The results support the use of the Measure of Self-Control in studies of self-control and noncriminal but otherwise deviant behavior such as sexual harassment. Fortunately, quid pro quo sexual harassment is less common than hostile work environment sexual harassment. Although less severe, hostile work environment sexual harassment is more pervasive and requires attention. However, the Likelihood to Sexually Harass Scale captures only quid pro quo sexual harassment. To more completely understand sexual harassment, it is incumbent on researchers to develop a single measure that captures the likelihood to engage in both quid pro quo and hostile work environment sexual harassment.

Finally, these findings have a number of implications for those whose job it is to reduce sexual harassment and other deviant behaviors in their organizations. Although this research does not demonstrate that self-control can be perfectly measured or that it is a perfect predictor of the likelihood to sexually harass, it does suggest that self-control may be a useful criterion in the development and use of employment screening instruments. Since organizations are increasingly being held liable for hiring individuals who later harm others, it is imperative that human resource managers avail themselves of research such as this to improve the employee selection process.

The link between male domination and crime against women is clear. The link between male domination and sexual harassment is just as strong. This chapter weaves these two forms of domination together to create a unique contribution to our understanding of the link between male domination and sexual harassment. Beyond the logical and theoretical arguments that have connected crime and sexual harassment as forms of male domination, the findings reported here represent the first empirical evidence that there exists a single factor that predicts not only the likelihood to commit crime but also the likelihood to sexually harass.

NOTES

My thanks to Michael Gottfredson, Barbara Gutek, and Ken Koput for their assistance and to Phoebe Morgan and James Gruber for their helpful comments.

1. The LSHS items are on a five-point scale anchored by (1) not at all likely and (5) very likely.
2. Pryor (1987) reported reliability coefficients of .90, .93, and .95 in three different samples. Pryor and Stoller (1994) reported a reliability coefficient of .93. Bargh et al. (1995) reported reliability coefficients of .85 and .91 in two samples.
3. Gottfredson and Hirschi (1990) define lack of self-control as impulsivity; a preference for simple tasks, risk-seeking behavior, and physical activity; self-centeredness; and a quick temper.
4. Response options are (1) strongly disagree; (2) disagree somewhat; (3) agree somewhat; or (4) strongly agree.
5. Grasmick et al. (1993) use of the Measure of Self-Control produced a reliability coefficient of .81 in a sample of adults in the midwestern United States. Based on a sample of undergraduate students, Wood et al. (1993) reported a reliability coefficient of .88.

REFERENCES

Bachman, R. 1998. The factors related to rape reporting behavior and arrest: New evidence from the National Crime Victimization Survey. *Criminal Justice and Behavior* 25:8–29.

Bargh, J. A., P. Raymond, J. B. Pryor, and F. Strack. 1995. Attractiveness of the underling: An automatic power-sex association and its consequences for sexual harassment and aggression. *Journal of Personality and Social Psychology* 68:768–781.

Berkowitz, N. H., and G. H. Wolkon. 1964. A formal choice form of the F scale free of acquiescent response set. *Sociometry* 27:54–65.

Burt, M. 1980. Cultural myths and supports for rape. *Journal of Personality and Social Psychology* 38:217–230.

Burton, V. S., Jr., F. T. Cullen, T. D. Evans, L. F. Alarid, and R. G. Dunaway. 1998. Gender, self-control, and crime. *Journal of Research in Crime and Delinquency* 35:123–147.

Christie, R., and F. Geiss. 1970. *Studies in machiavellianism.* New York: Academic Press.

Connell, R. W. 2000. *The men and the boys.* Cambridge: Polity.

Essed, P. 1992. Alternative knowledge sources in explanations of racist events. In *Explaining one's self to others: Reason-giving in a social context,* ed. M. L. McLaughlin and M. J. Cody, 199–224. Mahwah, N.J.: Erlbaum.

Evans, T. D., F. T. Cullen, V. S. Burton, Jr., R. G. Dunaway, and M. L. Benson. 1997. The social consequences of self-control: Testing the general theory of crime. *Criminology* 35:475–504.

Farley, L. 1978. *Sexual shakedown: The sexual harassment of women on the job.* New York: McGraw-Hill.

Fitzgerald, L. F., and L. M. Weitzman. 1990. Men who harass: Speculation and data. In *Ivory power: Sexual harassment on campus,* ed. M. A. Paludi, 125–140. Albany: State University of New York Press.

Gibbs, J. J., and D. Giever. 1995. Self-control and its manifestations among university students: An empirical test of Gottfredson and Hirschi's general theory. *Justice Quarterly* 12:231–255.

Gibbs, J. J., D. Giever, and J. S. Martin. 1998. Parental management and self-control: An empirical test of Gottfredson and Hirschi's general theory. *Journal of Research in Crime and Delinquency* 35:40–70.

Gottfredson, M. R., and T. Hirschi. 1990. *A general theory of crime.* Stanford, Calif.: Stanford University Press.

Grasmick, H. G., C. R. Tittle, R. J. Bursik, Jr., and B. J. Arneklev. 1993. Testing the core empirical implications of Gottfredson and Hirschi's general theory of crime. *Journal of Research in Crime and Delinquency* 30:5–29.

Gutek, B. A., and B. Morasch. 1982. Sex-ratios, sex-role spillover, and sexual harassment of women at work. *Journal of Social Issues* 38:55–74.

Hobbs, D. 1994. Mannish boys: Danny, Chris, crime, masculinity and business. In *Just boys doing business? Men, masculinities and crime,* ed. T. Newburn and E. A. Stanko, 118–134. New York: Routledge.

Keane, C., P. S. Maxim, and J. J. Teevan. 1993. Drinking and driving, self-control, and gender: Testing a general theory of crime. *Journal of Research in Crime and Delinquency* 30:30–46.

Levi, L. 1994. Masculinities and white-collar crime. In *Just boys doing business? Men, masculinities and crime*, ed. T. Newburn and E. A. Stanko, 234–252. New York: Routledge.

Longshore, D. 1998. Self-control and criminal opportunity: A prospective test of the general theory of crime. *Social Problems* 45:102–113.

Longshore, D., and S. Turner. 1998. Self-control and criminal opportunity: Cross-sectional test of the general theory of crime. *Criminal Justice and Behavior* 25:81–98.

Longshore, D., S. Turner, and J. A. Stein. 1996. Self-control in a criminal sample: An examination of construct validity. *Criminology* 34:209–228.

MacKinnon, C. A. 1979. *Sexual harassment of working women: A case of sexual discrimination.* New Haven, Conn.: Yale University Press.

———. 1987. *Feminism unmodified: Discourses on life and law.* Cambridge: Harvard University Press.

Malamuth, N. 1981. Rape proclivity among males. *Journal of Social Issues* 37:138–157.

Martin, S. E., and N. C. Jurik. 1996. *Doing justice, doing gender.* Thousand Oaks, Calif.: Sage.

Messerschmidt, J. W. 1986. *Capitalism, patriarchy, and crime: Toward a socialist feminist criminology.* Totowa, N.J.: Rowman and Littlefield.

———. 1993. *Masculinities and crime.* Lanham, Md.: Rowman and Littlefield.

Morgan, P. 1996. The power of law and the sexual harassment complaints of women. *National Women's Studies Association Journal* 9:23–42.

———. 2001. Sexual harassment: Violence against women at work. In *Sourcebook on violence against women*, ed. C. M. Renzetti, J. L. Edleson, and R. K. Bergen, 209–222. Thousand Oaks, Calif.: Sage.

Newburn, T., and E. A. Stanko. 1994. When men are victims: The failure of criminology. In *Just boys doing business? Men, masculinities and crime*, ed. T. Newburn and E. A. Stanko, 153–165. New York: Routledge.

Pryor, J. B. 1987. Sexual harassment proclivities in men. *Sex Roles* 17:269–290.

Pryor, J. B., and L. M. Stoller. 1994. Sexual cognition processes in men high in the likelihood to sexually harass. *Personality and Social Psychology Bulletin* 20:163–169.

Rosenbaum, M. 1980. A schedule for assessing self-control behaviors: Preliminary findings. *Behavior Therapy* 11:109–121.

Rudman, L. A., and E. Borgida. 1995. The afterglow of construct accessibility: The behavioral consequences of priming men to view women as sexual objects. *Journal of Experimental Social Psychology* 31:493–517.

Sigler, R. T., and I. M. Johnson. 1986. Public perceptions of the need for criminalization of sexual harassment. *Journal of Criminal Justice* 14:229–237.

Stanko, E. A. 1994. Challenging the problem of men's individual violence. In *Just boys doing business? Men, masculinities and crime*, ed. T. Newburn and E. A. Stanko, 32–45. New York: Routledge.

U.S. Merit Systems Protection Board. 1995. *Sexual harassment in the federal workplace: Trends, progress, continuing challenges.* Washington, D.C.: U.S. Government Printing Office.

Websdale, N., and M. Chesney-Lind. 1998. Doing violence to women: Research synthesis on the victimization of women. In *Masculinities and violence*, ed. L. H. Bowker, 55–81. Thousand Oaks, Calif.: Sage.

White, L. A., W. A. Fisher, D. Byrne, and R. Kingma. 1977. *Development and validation of affective orientation to erotic stimuli: The Sexual Opinion Survey.* Paper presented at the meeting of the Midwestern Psychological Association. Chicago, Illinois.

Wood, P. B., B. Pfefferbaum, and B. J. Arneklev. 1993. Risk-taking and self-control: social psychological correlates of delinquency. *Journal of Crime and Justice* 16:111–130.

2 / TOWARD A CRIMINOLOGY OF SEXUAL HARASSMENT

Beth A. Quinn

I fear that the title of this chapter risks promising too much; criminology is a wide-ranging field and sexual harassment is a multilayered, complex phenomenon. To avoid the offense, I begin by clarifying what I do *not* intend by invoking the term *criminology*. I follow with a discussion of the logic and usefulness of constructing criminologies of sexual harassment. The paper then turns to two analyses. The first documents the predominance of a *victimological* perspective in sexual harassment research and assesses its limitations and dangers. The second proposes a *criminological* approach and explores how this different tack can expand our understanding of the phenomenon of sexual harassment.

By invoking criminology, I am not arguing for the criminalization of sexual harassment. While I agree with legal scholar Steven Schulhofer (1998) that quid pro quo harassment is a violation of sexual autonomy—and thus appropriately within the scope of criminal law—I do not address that issue here. The purpose of this paper is not to call for statutory regulation. Instead, the goal is to adopt a criminological stance as a means of theorizing about the *etiology* of sexual harassment.

The first reason I employ the term *criminology* is to highlight a tendency within sexual harassment research to focus on victims rather than on perpetrators. In other words, most sexual harassment research is *victimological* rather than criminological. Victimological investigations center on the victim and ask questions about victim behavior, consider the demographic distribution of the victimized, and measure the effects of victimization. These are important questions, to be sure. However, this tendency toward victimology has resulted in an incomplete, and potentially distorted, understanding of sexual harassment perpetration.

It is this need to make more explicit the role and perspective of the perpetrators of sexual harassment—who are largely men (Quinn 2000b)—that points to the importance of a criminological approach. In the field of criminology, even when victims figure prominently (as in murder, for example), criminologists logically focus on the perpetrator in their inquiries. Research questions like "Why do they do it?" not "How do the victims experience it?" are most common. A reasonable question, then, is why such questions have not figured more predominantly in sexual harassment research.

Second, in advocating a criminological approach, I do not make much use of "traditional" criminological theory. Historically, the theoretical perspectives occupying mainstream criminology—e.g., social learning, strain theory, and control theories—have tended to ignore gender as a social category, an identity, and a field on which power is played (Messerschmidt 1993, Chesney-Lind 1997). Fixing this omission is not as easy as simply adding gender as another demographic category; the limitations of these theories go beyond their silence on gender. What is required are theoretical tools that make explicit the operation of gendered social structures (Messerschmidt 2000) and the processes of "doing gender" (West & Zimmerman 1987) in everyday contexts.

But traditional criminology, as Katz (1988) has aptly observed, tends to concentrate on background characteristics to the exclusion of the "foreground"—the experiential, the phenomenological. This has resulted, among other things, in the dual problems of over- and underprediction: many individuals with the requisite background characteristics do not perpetrate, while many who do not share these backgrounds do. This is evident in sexual harassment research as well. Demographic analyses have established the fact that most men are not sexual harassers. And while researchers readily point out that fact, they do not, and perhaps cannot, *explain it*. To adequately do so requires a shift in focus from the experiences of the sexually harassed to the motivations of those who harass.

This is not, however, a call for more psychological explanations. Instead, it is a call for an exploration of how differences among socially embedded men shape their sexual harassment experiences and behaviors. As Messerschmidt (1993:62) argues, "articulating the gendered content of men's behavior and of crime . . . requires a different theoretical lens—one that focuses on a sociology of masculinity." And this logic of performance is thoroughly socially constructed. The propensity to sexually harass is not merely a psychological trait; it makes sense in some contexts to some men because of the social and experiential context in which they are operating. As with Messerschmidt's (2000) delinquent boys and Katz's (1988) "bad asses," sexual harassment is a form of gender-situated action. Our research questions and methods need to reflect this.

We need theories that "can make comprehensible the minutiae of experiential details in the phenomenal foreground, as well as explain the general conditions that are most commonly found in the social backgrounds of these forms of criminality" (Katz 1988:10). To understand the production of sexually harassing behavior—as with many deviant behaviors—we need to explore the subjective, phenomenological logic of its production as well as the contextual, social background. This leads to a shift in focus to questions such as "What animates harassers?" "What do they 'get out of' the acts?" and "Why?" Much sexual harassment research and theory have simply *assumed* these motivations instead of empirically examining them.

Third, I offer no hope for, or direction toward, *a* criminology of sexual harassment. The literature clearly characterizes sexual harassment as a constellation of behaviors, with various causes, effects, and outcomes. The phenomenon of sexual harassment is multifaceted, and it is unlikely that different forms share etiologies (Gruber 1992). Likewise, among criminologists there is a growing acknowledgment of the multiple causes of criminal behavior and a corresponding call to produce "crime-specific" theories. Thus, we also need a "crime-specific" criminology of sexual harassment. For this analysis I will construct a criminology for only one type of sexual harassment—a rather common, pervasive, and less serious form that I have labeled "girl watching" (Quinn 2002). My analysis by no means suggests that the motivations animating this form of sexual harassment can be generalized to other forms, such as quid pro quo harassment. Indeed, the present analysis may fail even to explain all forms of *girl watching*. The goal is simply to draw upon a finite set of field observations of girl watching to explore the viability of new criminological frames that can inform future empirical analyses of sexual harassment.

In sum, I am proposing that a shift in focus from a victimological approach to a criminological one brings into view salient links between male dominance and sexual harassment that have to date been underexplored if not ignored altogether in the empirical literature. The following pages describe the steps taken to arrive at this proposition. The first part documents my critique of the existing literature. The results establish the preponderance of victim-oriented research and note gaps in the few efforts to study perpetration. The second part utilizes data from an organizationally bounded ethnography to illustrate how a criminological approach may enrich our understandings of the social phenomenon of sexual harassment.

THE VICTIMOLOGY OF SEXUAL HARASSMENT

To confirm my suspicions that a victimological approach dominates empirical research on sexual harassment, using the keyword *sexual harassment*, I searched multidisciplinary databases for recently published empirical studies.[1] Based on the abstract, each article was coded as having a (1) victimological, (2) criminological ("etiological"), or (3) mixed approach. In addition, the types of methods used, the research questions pursued, and the discipline of the journal were coded.

While the analysis is limited, the results are suggestive. Of the seventy-four empirical studies published and indexed by these databases in those two and a half years, 71 percent took an exclusively victim-focused approach. Of those, 79 percent reported survey findings and 14 percent were experiments. Less than 10 percent reported findings from qualitative studies (e.g., interviews, ethnographic or archival analyses). Research questions about victim demographics, their organizational and social locations, and victims' subjective experiences of harassment and the harms they sustain are more common than questions about the etiology of sexual harassment, that is, *why* harassment happens. More than half (57 percent) of these studies were concerned primarily with the question of prevalence and/or victim outcomes.

The predominance of the victimological approach is especially problematic because it perpetuates an overly dualistic understanding of sexual harassment: it either *normalizes* or *pathologizes* men's harassing behavior. When sexual harassment is normalized, the fact that many men do not engage in it is obscured. When it is pathologized, the everyday means by which male dominance is mundanely and regularly reproduced is neglected. When we assume the causation of perpetration rather than study it, sexual harassment is too easily reduced to a simple problem of perception and differing opinions or, in contrast, of individual pathologies.

Still, some work on sexual harassment has employed a criminological frame. About 11 percent of recently published articles focused, at least in part, on the etiology of sexually harassing behavior. Extensions of Pryor's "Propensity to Harass" measure (e.g., Pryor 1987) predominate this literature, and these studies mark a crucial first step toward developing a type of criminology of sexual harassment. However, a review of Pryor's work and that of his colleagues illustrates the need for more criminological studies. While these studies rely on direct observation of potential and actual perpetrator behavior, the measures of sexual harassment focus on the more obvious and less controversial forms of harassment—quid pro quo harassment—and the factors analyzed are primarily psychological. They establish a clear link between the motivation to harass and sexist ideology and rape myth acceptance, but they reveal little about the social factors producing the link and the meaning of sexually harassing behavior, especially for the more common *hostile work environment* harassment.

Ironically, in some of these studies, the validity of suggested motivational factors is questionable, since they were measured by either victim perception or the self-reports of men. For example, Begany and Milburn (2002) base their analysis on scores on self-report instruments of the likelihood to harass. Their results tell us more about what men think or believe they would do than what they actually do—their actual social practices.

In another vein, researchers have attempted to match victimization rates with victims' organizational position and organizational climate, a line of questions that can be traced to Kanter's (1977) *Men and Women of the Corporation*, one of the first analyses to consider the ways in which organizations are explicitly gendered. Researchers such as Collinson and Collinson (1989) and Hearn (1985) expand on this idea, and I draw on their theoretical insights in my subsequent analysis. In terms of sexual harassment, Gruber (1998), for example, has found evidence for organizational effects on the prevalence of harassment and varied structural vulnerabilities for individual women (see also Mueller, De Coster, and Estes 2001, Rogers & Henson 1997, and Williams, Giuffre, & Dellinger 1999). By taking a more macrolevel approach, this research fills in the gaps left by psychological studies of perpetration. Yet it tells us little of the social processes through which organizational structures encourage and sustain *everyday practices* of sexual harassment.

In sum, the pattern of research is clear: the preponderance of current research continues to pursue questions of prevalence, victim perception, and response strategies. A modest proportion of the current literature does address perpetrator's motivations and links them to ideological and organizational factors. Yet, how the perpetration of harassment is normalized and how those who commit it experience harassment remain understudied.

In the next section I illustrate a criminological, phenomenological analysis. Rather than discuss the phenomenon of sexual harassment in all its varieties, I focus on the production and meaning of a particular set of verbal remarks and sexualized behaviors displayed by men: shared sexual bantering and "girl watching"[2]—the act of men sexually evaluating women, often in the company of other men. It may be a shared message of "check it out," boasts to other men of their sexual prowess, or explicit comments about a woman's body or imagined sexual acts with her. The target may be an individual woman or a group of women, or simply a photograph or other representation. The status of these behaviors as sexual harassment may often be contested, but it is this very ambiguity—this slip between deviant and normal behavior—that makes it a fruitful site to explore the (re)production of male dominance in the everyday work world.

LA PERRUQUE MASCULINE AND SNEAK THRILL

In previous work (Quinn 2002) I argue that some forms of hostile work environment sexual harassment should be understood not only as acts directed against particular women but also as the means by which men bond with one another *as men*. While the targeted women may certainly experience it as harassing and disempowering, the men may not always be engaged in the behavior for this explicit effect. In this form of harassment, women are the objects around which men build masculine identities and relationships, rather than

subjects—at least to the men—to be harassed. When women complain about their behavior, the men may be truly baffled, since they
"understand her primarily as an object, and objects do not object"
(Quinn 2002:398).

In the present analysis, I extend this argument to suggest that girl
watching may also serve as a gendered form of worker resistance. In
the language of French social theorist Michel de Certeau, girl watching may also function as a kind of "*la perruque*," a practice whereby
"the worker's own work is disguised as work for his employer"
(1984:25). It is a tactic—a small, limited act of resistance—played on
the grounds of the opposition (in this instance, the employer) with
the goal of "getting away with something." While de Certeau describes this in the context of men using their employer's tools to
make objects for their own use, it may also include a secretary writing her version of the great American novel between company
memos. The crucial point is that in *une perruque*, nothing is stolen
but *time*.

This form of tactical resistance may also include (at least from
the employer's perspective) the wasting of time or "goofing off."
Rather than time used for personal material production, as in de
Certeau's example, workers may also use their employer's time for
personal social (re)production. The formalized workplace attempts
to (en)force a separation between the personal and the professional,
controlling the worker's time purchased through the labor contract.
Workers, however, may insert the personal to resist the hierarchy
and structure imposed by the rationalized organization. But it is
resistance with a smile, or borrowing from Katz (1988), it is a
"sneaky thrill." It is *fun*, and does not undermine the system per se.
Paraphrasing James Scott's (1990) pithy image of resistance strategies, the sneaky thrill has more in common with "the peasant silently
farting as the king rides by" than the sabotage of the Luddites.

Connell (1995:179) argues that "pure economic rationality is in-
compatible with men's categorical authority over women. . . . In
however limited a way, the instrumental rationality of the market-

place has a power to disrupt gender." Gender, however, may be employed to disrupt the rationality and discipline of an alienating workplace (Cockburn 1983). This is similar to Hearn's observation that men's mutual displays of sexuality ("cocking a snoot") may be a form of resistance to management, a way to "humaniz[e] an alienating workplace" (1985:115). This resistance can take many forms, and I suggest that the "girl watching" may be one of them. As resistance, girl watching is most likely employed by men who are disempowered in their organization or profession in some way. Men may experience disempowerment—or more accurately, challenges to their masculine privilege—in a number of ways, for example, through class and race oppression, through differential access to technological and cultural capital, and because of differing talents and personal charisma. In these instances, the discourses of masculinity may be poached for sources of power and tactical maneuvers (Messerschmidt 2000). To girl watch is to draw on and display one's supposed dominant status as a man through the assertion and insertion of a (masculine) sexuality into the purportedly formal rational workplace (Collinson & Collinson 1989). It asserts: "If nothing else, at least I am a man."

GIRL WATCHING

Diego enjoys girl watching. A Filipino man in his late thirties, he works in the shipping and receiving department of Acme, a multinational technology firm. Diego is aware that Acme has policies against displaying pornographic pictures in the workplace ("they made a rule that we ain't suppose to have that") However, he admits with a satisfied grin that the men in his area have a pornographic photograph hidden on the inside of a cabinet door. "When you open [the cabinet], it's there." It is obvious from Diego's description that the men get great satisfaction from their shared furtive viewing as they go about their work.

It seems somewhat absurd that these men would go to such trouble to hide a small pornographic picture. Why then is such pleasure taken in their resistance to its prohibition? Sexual harassment policies that require the removal of such displays, especially in a geographically secluded and primarily male department such as Diego's, prevent men from using girl watching as a game to assert masculine identities. The prohibition itself, however, simultaneously provides fodder for the use of girl watching as *la perruque*. It is a fairly easy rule to break and offers a small means by which the men may collectively assert their power against Acme's management. The pleasure of the act, then, lies not so much in the viewing of the picture as in the shared knowledge that they are "getting away with something" and that they are doing it as *men*.

Sid, a white man in his early forties, works in facilities management at the same company. In the course of his interview, he acknowledges that his job is traditionally male dominated and might even be characterized as "macho." However, Sid experienced a great deal of frustration in his job, the primary source being his boss, a man whom Sid described as "overbearing." He told a story of girl watching that also implies the *perruque masculine* function of girl watching. Sid evoked an image of a particularly beautiful and sexily dressed secretary whom the men used as a distraction from their everyday activities. It is a familiar story, one that several men told.

[Consider a] secretary who, let's say, wears short dresses [or] skirts, a low cut collar, just, she's [pause] just pretty. [. . .] [If she] asks for [paper to be delivered upstairs], it's taken care of right away because they want to go up and see what she's wearing today, what she's looking like, that kind of thing. O.K.? And there might be a fight over who is going to deliver it.

While this foray to the second floor is conducted in the context of the men's regular duties (e.g., making deliveries), it is clear that its main purpose is as a girl-watching expedition. We may also safely assume that the winner of the fight ("there might be a fight") is charged with the added duty of reporting back to the other men ("see what she's wearing today"). This is clearly a form of "homosexual" play (Butler 1990). I would argue, however, that it also works as *la perruque masculine*, a way to waste time and to disrupt the rational, formalized structure of their workplace by asserting a shared masculine (hetero)sexuality.

That girl watching can be disruptive to the workings of the company was most clearly revealed in interviews with the Human Resources (HR) officers at Acme. Christy, a senior HR representative, admitted that "guys will come sniffing around, and they will impede productivity. [pause] You know, guys will give up productivity for girl sniffing." While she employs somewhat more colorful terminology, it is clear that she is referring to girl watching.

In an ironic (and probably not all that uncommon) use of sexual harassment law to effect a sort of gender discrimination, Jenny and Christy implied several times that both a woman's attractiveness and her putative tolerance of sexual harassment sometimes influenced hiring and assignment decisions. For example, only one woman, Peggy, was assigned to Diego's department at the time of the interview, and this woman was given the job because Christy deemed her "street smart."[3] The men in this department were known to engage in rude talk, sexual pranks, and girl watching, and Christy was sure that some women would "not last" in that environment. Rather than challenge the men's behavior, the HR representatives simply kept "prissy women" out of the department.

The function of girl watching as *la perruque* was best illustrated through Christy's account of a manager who supposedly did not want attractive women assigned to her division.

> [This] particular manager is very, very sensitive to hiring young attractive women. Because to her, she's a workhorse. She's a nose-to-the-grind-stone [pounds on desk], a task master [five quick pounds on desk]. . . . [She believes that if] you get an attractive girl . . . the boys [will] come sniffing around. And it drives her absolutely crazy. Just crazy, because she thinks that she's losing all this productivity from her employee because the boys are sniffing.

The lost productivity, at least from the perspective of this manager, is that of the attractive woman. However, it is also apparent that this game is a way for the men to waste time, since they "give up productivity for girl sniffing."

To engage in girl watching at work, then, can function as a way for men to effect *une perruque masculine*, and its power is produced both through its form and its content. The content—the comments, the acts, the attitudes—are similar to those of the other forms of girl watching that draw their power from discourses of asymmetrical heterosexuality and hegemonic masculinity (Quinn 2002). It is the form, however, that gives this type of girl watching its power as *une perruque masculine*. As resistance, girl watching draws its power from its status as a form of rule breaking. In "being bad"—in boldly breaking the rules or even asserting that one is beyond the rules—a form of masculinity with much resonance in North American culture is evoked (Kimmel 1996, Messerschmidt 2000). The media are filled with depictions of the man who steps easily over sacred boundaries and breaks rules that others dare not touch. We are to admire him; he is a "real man." He is the cowboy of the old west and the rogue cop in the latest summer movie. It is their untoward character that makes his actions thrilling and that constitutes their power. That it is prohibited, unseemly, and illegitimate makes it a particularly powerful avenue for enacting an oppositional or rogue masculinity and contesting the disciplining of the workplace (Messerschmidt 2000).

Is the workplace, however, really a setting of desexualization and rationalization? Should we consider men using gender to bolster their power in an organization a form of resistance? Organizational researchers such as Collinson and Collinson (1989), for example, have argued convincingly that it is more accurate to say that (hetero) sexuality is built into organizations rather than an alien presence to be excluded (see also Rogers & Henson 1997). For most men, their workplaces require a successful expression of masculinity, and heterosexuality is invariably mandatory (Connell 1995, Hearn 1985). In addition, human relations theory points to the importance of informal relationships in producing and maintaining employee morale and in smoothing the operations of even the most formalized organization (e.g., Pringle 1989). Thus, what I have argued to be a form of resistance to organizational discipline may actually be necessary to its maintenance.

The crux of the matter lies here: girl watching and other forms of masculine sexual displays are recognized by neither the men nor their employers as legitimate parts of work or central to its functioning. This is true even in the absence of sexual harassment laws, and even if these practices are, in fact, implicitly *built into* the organization. Practices such as girl watching are understood to be distractions from work, a playful imposition or reassertion of the personal into the public, and a form of male bonding (Lyman 1987, Willis 1981). Even if managers condone or even contribute to these acts, they remain outside the formal role and mission of most organizations. Indeed, it is the fact that they are unacceptable that makes them a powerful resource for constructing a particular form of masculinity.

That girl watching does not threaten the organization—and may even help reproduce particular social forms and organizational goals—is not fatal to its function as *une perruque masculine* or as sneaky thrill. Especially in a climate of increased attention to sexual harassment policies, the act of girl watching is understood by many men to be something that, as one of my interview subjects explained, "you have to be more careful about now." It is also, however, still very common in their workplaces. In this aspect, similarities to the performances of masculinity chronicled by Willis (1981) in his study of working-class "lads" are suggested. Willis found that through their radical and anti-establishment behavior rooted in a particular form of masculinity, the lads were effectively tracked into unstable, low-paying, and highly disciplined jobs, the same jobs, in fact, that their fathers held. Thus, in their seeming resistance, they aligned themselves with the masculinity of their fathers, and like their fathers, reproduced their class location (see also MacLeod 1992).

The introduction of sexual harassment law may also have an unintended and ironic effect on the play of masculine "games" such as girl watching. It becomes more costly to get caught when well-developed sexual harassment policies are in place and enforced, yet this increased price may ironically increase the thrill. When acts are premised on a masculinity that seeks to show it is above or beyond the law, part of the fun comes from "getting away with something." Sexual harassment policies raise the bar on how careful one must be, but they also increase the thrill when one is successful. In being more dangerous, especially for men in the lower echelons of workplace hierarchies, the act presents a more powerful opportunity to show one is "still a man."

Thus, when men "girl watch," the *target* may not be women (although they are certainly its objects), but rather the *disciplining structures of the workplace*. As *une perruque masculine*, some sexually harassing behavior, such as girl watching, may be attempts by men to playfully elide (whether they are conscious of it or not) the contradiction of their structural position: they are both workers who are required to obey, and men who are expected to display strength, dominance, and independence (Pateman 1988). Like Katz's (1988) adolescent shoplifters and street elites, "crime" is ironically used to (re)assert a powerful *moral* self.

This analysis has several implications for our understanding of the dynamics of sexual harassment and the processes by which it helps reproduce male dominance. First, because the direct target of the behavior may not be a particular woman, men may misunderstand and resist women's attempts to terminate the behavior (through the filing of sexual harassment claims, for example). Second, women's effective resistance may be thwarted by their recognition of the complexity of motivations (Quinn 2000a). Women's affiliation with their male coworkers' resistance may result in their unwittingly supporting the reproduction of male dominance. Third, attempts to control this behavior through sexual harassment policies may be rendered ineffective by the very content of this form of masculinity: in "rogue" masculinity, to break the rules is to show one is a man (Willis 1981, Messerschmidt 2000). The imposition of additional rules simply raises the bar and increases the power of a successful act of resistance.

CONCLUSION

This paper outlines a possible etiology for one form of sexual harassment. Drawing on de Certeau's (1984) analysis of worker resistance and Katz's (1988) analysis of the seduction of the sneaky deviant thrill, I suggest that the cause of one form of sexually harassing behavior may be located in its function as a masculinized tactic of worker resistance. Viewed from a criminological or etiological perspective, rather than solely a victimological one, the complex, ongoing social production of sexually harassing behavior is revealed. As such, common interventions for sexual harassment—legal claims, workplace training—are called into question, as are questions about women's interpretations of and responses to it. We must refocus our attention on the complex social production of sexual harassment, and the only reasonable way to do that is to study the perpetrators directly. As criminologists know, this is a difficult but essential goal.

We can begin this process by revisiting the astute observations of the original feminist theorists of sexual harassment, such as Catharine MacKinnon (1979, 1987) and Lin Farley (1978). They recognized sexual harassment as both an instance of male domination and a mechanism by which that domination is perpetuated. But they also failed to examine the phenomenological positioning of the men who are its actors. The present work draws on more recent studies of masculinity to suggest that the social construction and performance of various forms of masculinity are often at the root of sexually harassing behavior. Most interestingly, the etiology of some harassing behavior may lie not in individualized attempts to assert dominance over individual women, but in the co-construction of masculine identities by men. One impetus for such behavior may be men's experiences of their workplaces as sites of emasculation effected through discipline and hierarchy. As men attempt to reassert masculine privilege against these organizations, women are both their victims and possibly—in their identification with the men as workers—their co-conspirators. Thus the examination of sexual harassment as an embedded social process gives us another view of the complex nature of the intersectionality of multiple forms of domination, a perspective that, unfortunately, as been seriously lacking in the sexual harassment literature.

To acknowledge the "fun," "thrill," or "resistance" in some forms of sexually harassing behavior implies a diminishment neither of the culpability of the harasser nor of the harm caused to women. It is clear that the impetus for the resistance and the logic of the thrill are born from masculinities that presume male dominance and privilege. This analysis no more implies acceptance of the behavior than Katz's analysis of "righteous slaughter" promotes murder. On the contrary, refocusing our work on the development of criminologies of sexual harassment provides new frames for examining the complex phenomenon of sexual harassment as a form and practice of male domination.

NOTES

1. The databases were Social Science Citations, Academic Universe Expanded, PsychInfo, and Criminal Justice Abstracts. Searches were limited to academic articles published between January 2000 and July 2002. While nonempirical articles were excluded (e.g., legal analyses), the full range of social science methodologies was included, such as surveys, experiments, interviews, cases studies, and ethnographies.

2. The term *girl watching* emerged from my interviews of eighteen men and twenty-five women in 1994–95. A complete explanation of the methods used in this study may be found in Quinn (2002).

3. In her interview, Peggy refused to define acts of girl watching and other sexualized acts by her coworkers as sexual harassment, but she was

clearly upset by them. Diego, in fact, commented in his interview that he did not know how Peggy was able to put up with it. For more discussion of Peggy and the logic of her refusal to claim these harms as sexual harassment, see Quinn (2000a).

REFERENCES

Begany, J. J., and M. A. Milburn. 2002. Psychological predictors of sexual harassment: Authoritarianism, hostile sexism, and rape myths. *Psychology of Men and Masculinity* 3 (2): 119–126.

Butler, J. 1990. *Gender trouble: Feminism and the subversion of identity.* New York: Routledge.

Chesney-Lind, Meda. 1997. *The female offender: Girls, women, and crime.* Thousand Oaks, Calif.: Sage.

Cockburn, C. 1983. *Brothers: Male dominance and technological change.* London: Pluto.

Collinson, D. L., and M. Collinson. 1989. Sexuality in the workplace: The domination of men's sexuality. In *The sexuality of organization,* ed. J. Hearn and D. L. Sheppard. Newbury Park, Calif.: Sage.

Connell, R. W. 1995. *Masculinities.* Berkeley: University of California Press.

de Certeau, M. 1984. *The practice of everyday life.* Berkeley: University of California Press.

Farley, L. 1978. *Sexual shakedown: The sexual harassment of women on the job.* New York: McGraw-Hill.

Gruber, J. E. 1992. A typology of personal and environmental sexual harassment research and policy implications for the 90s. *Sex Roles* 26 (11/12): 447–464.

———. 1998. The impact of male work environments and organizational policies on women's experiences of sexual harassment. *Gender and Society* 12 (3): 301–320.

Hearn, J. 1985. Men's sexuality at work. In *The sexuality of men,* ed. A. Metcalf and M. Humphries. London: Pluto.

Kanter, R. M. 1977. *Men and women of the corporation.* New York: Basic Books.

Katz, Jack. 1988. *Seductions of crime.* New York: Basic Books.

Kimmel, M. S. 1996. *Manhood in America: A cultural history.* New York: Free Press.

Lyman, P. 1987. The fraternal bond as a joking relationship: A case study of the role of sexist jokes in male group bonding. In *Changing men: New directions in research on men and masculinity*, ed. M. S. Kimmel, 148–163. Newbury Park, Calif.: Sage.

MacKinnon, C. A. 1979. *The sexual harassment of working women*. New Haven: Yale University Press.

———. 1987. *Feminism unmodified*. Cambridge: Harvard University Press.

MacLeod, A. E. 1992. Hegemonic relations and gender resistance: The new veiling as accommodating protest in Cairo. *Signs: Journal of Women in Culture and Society* 17 (3): 533–557.

Messerschmidt, J. W. 1993. *Masculinities and crime: Critique and reconceptualization of theory*. Lanham, Md.: Rowman and Littlefield.

———. 2000. *Nine lives: Adolescent masculinities, the body, and violence*. Boulder, Colo.: Westview Press.

Mueller, C. W., S. De Coster, and S. B. Estes. 2001. Sexual harassment in the workplace: Unanticipated consequences of modern social control in organizations. *Work and Occupations* 28 (4): 411–446.

Pateman, C. 1988. *The sexual contract*. Stanford, Calif.: Stanford University Press.

Pringle, R. 1989. Bureaucracy, rationality and sexuality: The case of secretaries. In *The sexuality of organization*, ed. J. Hearn and D. L. Sheppard, 158–177. Newbury Park, Calif.: Sage.

Pryor, J. B. 1987. Sexual harassment proclivities in men. *Sex Roles* 17 (5/6): 269–290.

Quinn, B. A. 2000a. The paradox of complaining: Law, humor, and harassment in the everyday work world. *Law and Social Inquiry* 25 (4): 1151–1183.

———. 2000b. Sexual harassment-adult/workplace. *Encyclopedia of criminology and deviance* (vol. 3), 363–368. London: Taylor and Francis, Ltd.

———. 2002. Sexual harassment and masculinity: The power and meaning of "girl watching." *Gender and Society* 16 (3): 386–402.

Rogers, J. K., and K. D. Henson. 1997. "Hey, why don't you wear a shorter skirt?" Structural vulnerability and the organization of sexual harassment in temporary clerical employment. *Gender and Society* 11 (2): 215–238.

Schulhofer, S. J. 1998. *Unwanted sex: The culture of intimidation and the failure of law*. Cambridge, Mass.: Harvard University Press.

Scott, J. 1990. *Domination and the arts of resistance: Hidden transcripts.* New Haven, Conn.: Yale University Press.

West, C., and D. H. Zimmerman. 1987. "Doing gender." *Gender and Society* 1:125–51.

Williams, C. L., P. A. Giuffre, and K. Dellinger. 1999. Sexuality in the workplace: Organizational control, sexual harassment, and the pursuit of pleasure. *Annual Review of Sociology* 25:73–93.

Willis, Paul. 1981. *Learning to labor: How working class kids get working class jobs.* New York: Columbia University Press.

3 FITTING IN
The Conflation of Firefighting, Male Domination, and Harassment

Dave Baigent

By any measure, firefighting is a male-dominated occupation. Numerically speaking, the fire service is overwhelmingly white and male. In the United Kingdom, for example, 99 percent of firefighters are men and 98.7 percent of them are white (HMCIFS 2002). Similarly, in the United States 97 percent of firefighters are male. Of those, only 9 percent are black and less than 6 percent are Hispanic (NFPA 2001). Culturally speaking, the work of firefighting is extremely masculinized. The assumption persists that simply because they are females, women lack the basic necessities to effectively fight fires. Thus, like other doubly dominated occupations, such as law enforcement and corrections, manliness and heterosexuality are implied occupational requirements (Martin & Jurik 2000). Harassment in various forms has been one of several strategies employed to exclude those deemed not man enough to do the job, and this would likely include anyone who openly challenged rules on compulsory heterosexuality.

Since the 1970s feminists and women's liberation activists around the world have challenged the myth that women cannot or should not fight fires. Within the United States and the United Kingdom, the passage of antidiscrimination laws promised to expedite the integration of a diverse workforce at fire stations and to protect members of gender and ethnic minorities from hostile resistance. In fact, it was through the filing of discrimination complaints that nearly 16 percent of U.S. black females currently working as firefighters obtained purchase in this doubly dominated career (Yoder & Aniakudo 1997). Despite the institution of strict prohibitions against discrimination and harassment, both are endemic to the firefighting service. The lack of progress suggests a certain naiveté about how the double bind of sexism and racism operates within occupations like firefighting. Perhaps there are processes at play that are more subtle and less salient than those that current public policy recognizes. Through the analysis of ethnographic data, this chapter identifies one such process—the informal socialization (initiation) of new firefighters by their supervisors and coworkers to their role at work.

Rarely has the fire station been the setting for academic inquiry. The public image of firefighting is clear (Cooper 1986), but the firefighting lifestyle has managed to escape the scholarly eye. What little we know about station house relations comes from the firsthand experiences of the few women (mostly black) working in the U.S. fire service (see, for example, Yoder & Aniakudo 1997) and from those white women in the United Kingdom who have spoken out, often needing the law to do so (IT 1995). While research from the "outsider within" standpoint exposes the diversity of ways that women firefighters are harassed, this vantage point is not the best location from which to observe the subtle ways in which men firefighters construct and maintain their masculine image and hierarchy. The observations that support the analysis in this chapter were recorded from an "insider without" standpoint. In other words, I conducted the observations as an academic, a man, and a former firefighter with thirty years of firefighting experience. This unique combination of identities afforded me access to a world not readily apparent to those uninitiated into it.

The following pages describe in greater detail the methods used to observe the initiation of probationers into firefighting work, the socialization process itself, the various ways it impacts on those who participate in it, and how this informal socialization subverts formal efforts to integrate firefighting and eliminate harassment. I conclude with two propositions. First, I argue that while the suitability of *all* firefighters—men and women—is rigorously tested, it is easier for men than women to find their place in the social order. Second, I note that men are able to fit in more easily than women because the accomplishment of effective firefighting is conflated with the achievement of masculinity (Connell 2000, Martin & Jurik 2000).

METHODS

This chapter's analysis comes from qualitative data collected between 1996 and 2003 in a variety of fire service locations. The data set is primarily narratives gleaned from conversations with firefighters solicited as part of a larger ethnographic study of gender, masculinities, and social relations in the U.K. firefighting service (Baigent 1996, 2001a, 2001b, Baigent & Hill 2003). Included are 84 longitudinal interviews with seven firefighters during their initial training (two women and five men) and over 300 interviews with firefighters in their first year of service (probies) through to chief officers and union officials. Ages of those observed range between 18 and 55.

This chapter focuses specifically on firefighters' comments regarding a particularly important aspect of fire service culture—the socialization of probationers by more experienced members to the watch. Analysis relies primarily on firefighters' comments but also includes my own reflections regarding this rite of passage.

Because firefighters not only work together but also live together for extended periods of time, they work hard to keep their relations at the station private, including the way they protect their masculine image as the white knight that protects the public from the red devil—fire (for the patriarchal dividend that goes with this, see Connell 1995). As a result, outsiders are rarely given a glimpse of everyday life among firefighters. Access to this information was only gained because I was both a man and a former firefighter with more than thirty years of experience. These credentials established my status as an "insider" and therefore allowed access as "one of them." As a consequence, I was able to talk with firefighters about the probationary process. My pro-feminist stance (Hearn 1994) and my training in critical research afforded enough social and professional distance to question assumptions about the naturalness or the necessity of that process.

THE IMPORTANCE OF FITTING IN

Once aspiring firefighters successfully complete their training programs, they are assigned to a watch (a shift or unit at a station) for a probationary period of time. Advancement to probationary status (proby) means that the firefighter has demonstrated the initial skills needed to be able to operate firefighting equipment. But being capable is not enough. All firefighters must learn about the particular skills of firefighting, and to learn these they must first demonstrate their ability to "fit in" with the informal hierarchy operating on their watch. During the probationary period, the ability of all "probies" to line up with the existing hierarchy is therefore put to the test. Those who do not fit in are either persuaded to change or are winnowed out.

The term *fitting in* is common currency in the fire service. Every proby knows that the ability to fit in is critical to his acceptance. Nowhere in the formal job description is there any mandate for it. Yet, every firefighter knows that the ability to fit in with one's watch is an essential requirement. Older members of the watch assume the responsibility of fitting probies in. This means teaching probies the importance of finding their place, testing their ability to fit in, and disciplining or correcting those who are not fitting in. When asked to explain what "fitting in" means, Ted responded, "Like when we were new, until they think they can trust you, you are not going to be accepted. You are, but it takes time to get in, and then they know they can trust you and you fit in." Ted is arguing that the watch need to know they can trust any newcomer before they accept him. So, probationers are treated with caution until they prove their ability to fit in. Given the dangers of firefighting and the necessity of teamwork, it is not surprising that the ability to fit in is important. While on the surface Ted appears to be referring to the necessity of trustworthiness in emergencies, he is also referring to the expectation that probies find a way to fit in with informal hierarchies operating at the station.

Alf, a seasoned member of another fire service, described in greater detail how the hierarchy of his particular watch is organized and the place of probies within it:

> I work on a watch strength of sixteen; if you take out the four officers, they have to administer, you are talking about twelve firefighters; we have female, ethnic minorities, two of . . . I am the longest serving firefighter . . . there is another guy who has got 4 years less than me and the rest go down from 15 years to 10 to 5 to six months. . . . I find that the 15 to 20 year intake resent the attitude that he has got far more than I do. But, I am not so sure that is because I am 45 and they are 35 and they are still fiery and up for an argument. I suppose that when I was 35 I was the same . . . let them argue it out, it's not that important . . . the five year blokes are well tuned in with the blokes who have only done two years . . . so they gradually step into line with each other. So there is always somebody on the watch that you have got a rapport with; you know there is somebody behind you; somebody in front of you. Somebody you can relate to or with, whether he has done a few years more or a few years less. And there are outspoken personalities who dig their heels in and not accept any change, they are becoming more rare, more often than not people gradually come to accept change and reform. You know there is somebody behind you somebody in front of you.

While Alf is talking about his own watch, he is also describing the reality of how most firefighters informally organize at work. An effective unit is one where there is an informal rank ordering of firefighters, everyone gets along, all are in agreement, and everyone has a place in that hierarchy. It is important to note that for Alf, misfits are not those who lack skill, but those with outspoken personalities—something that is not addressed in the formal codes of conduct. Historically, men—especially those in military and paramilitary organizations (Barrett 1996)—have organized in this way, and the fire service is no exception.

This informal ranking is linked to "time served." Those with the most time served are granted the greatest authority and undertake the duties of policing those beneath them. There is no formal procedure that allows this, nor one to say how it should be done. Thus, the rites of passage to the informal hierarchy vary from one watch to another as older firefighters dominate younger ones to "give probies the benefit of their experience." Duke is one of those experienced firefighters, someone whom probies will be advised to approach for advice:

> You are not an individual; you are coming in straight away to be part
> of a team: a team that hopefully know what they are doing with
> regard to, first of all, to safety. And you have got to come in and just
> accept, whatever age you are, however clever you are, that you have
> got to start and em, em, and absorb, absorb that knowledge and that.
> You have just got to fit in with them haven't you?

Duke's argument emphasizes probies' relative unimportance. Duke's advice discourages any effort to understand the rationale behind practice or to challenge it. Duke speaks about the need for unconditional acceptance as though it is a safety requirement. In reality, the trust is more about accepting that Duke has the right to lead; he is the custodian of the informal rites of passage to fitting in. Many firefighters would agree with Duke's assertion that the need to fit probies in is a matter of safety. They would also agree with Christian: "Well it's the tradition. They need to be able to fit in, without being leery and start telling you how to do it. If they have got a good idea, I listen. But I don't like people who come along and tell me. Yunnoo, very loud and trigger-happy." Ian, however, was more direct: "keep your head down and your gob shut." Thus, whether or not the expectations of total deference make sense or not, probies are warned against questioning the authority of traditional views in the fire service.

From the experienced firefighter's standpoint, one of the most critical tasks of a probationary firefighter is to find a way to fit into the day-to-day behavior and work routines. Elder firefighters take the task of fitting probationers into their watch very seriously. Because it is an informal process, how they line probies up with *their* watch is prescribed largely by how they were themselves socialized into it. It is not necessarily those with the best firefighting skills that have the greatest authority with probies. More likely it is those who have excelled at (informally) leading the watch for the longest period of time. Probies who dare question the authority of their elders, or challenge the rationale of the probationary protocol, risk being labeled as misfits, are marginalized, and are frequently forced to leave.

The way that elder firefighters have always formed up in an informal hierarchy provides some order to their lives. Acceptance of the informal hierarchy also ensures that at emergencies firefighters can work together. But the proven levels of exclusion and harassment in the fire service (Hearn & Parkin 1995) suggest that the way firefighters form up may not always be about operating at emergencies. Being a firefighter is traditionally men's work—an exemplar for masculinity. Therefore, it is likely that firefighters' informal hierarchies are based on traditional patriarchies in which older men instruct younger men (Hartmann 1981:14). To a large extent this is the way that commonsense views about the gender order and the division of labor are developed by all masculinities, not least of all in the fire service (Lipman-Blumen 1976). In such a situation it is possible to see that firefighters are developing their more personal masculine agendas in the shadow of firefighting to ensure that the next cohort of firefighters support their view.

HOW PROBIES FIT IN
Having looked at the views of experienced firefighters, it would be interesting to question what probies think. Not unexpectedly, they

too have expectations and perhaps a little trepidation about fitting in. Jack, who is new to the service, was clear about what is expected: "Keep your head down . . . and . . . and be quiet and what have you, and then gradually. Yunnoo like . . . that . . . yunnoo, you feel allowed to be yourself a bit more and more." Jack is fitting in pretty well. He accepts his subordinate status and trusts without question that doing so will eventually lead to his deference being rewarded. Richard expressed a very similar understanding to Jack, but he understands that fitting in is not just about firefighting. Richard explained that fitting in takes some effort:

> I have been biting my tongue with a lot of it while I am on probation; I think it is a requirement. Em, you just take it and say nothing. One, I don't want to make it worse for myself and two, I think it is a bit of respect for the blokes who have been in The Job longer than I have. Em . . . but eh . . . after a while, especially after I have done my probation, finished that . . . then . . . maybe—if I think that something needs saying then I will probably say it, but at the moment I am quite happy with, eh, quite happy with not saying anything. There is a lot of stuff that is a bit unfair, but that is the way it is. I would like to think I would like to treat someone slightly better than I would be treated myself. Not that I have been badly treated.

What is important to note is that Richard considers the socialization process to be unfair and perhaps not altogether necessary, despite the fact that he still trusts the process. Both Jack and Richard expect that if they bide their time they will be allowed to ease their way into the hierarchy—expecting a point to be reached where their views will be listened to.

Because Ken is younger than Jack and Richard and has less experience doing paid work, I expected him to report greater difficulty finding his proper place within firefighters' hierarchy. Instead, Ken seems to be fitting in quite well.

> What they are saying is keep your nose, keep your head down, keep enthusiastic, ask questions and be busy. And that, and that is what I

am doing and I spoke to the leading firefighter who I am following everywhere. If we get called to a job I am going to be backing him up, always getting to go in. I was chatting to him and he says that, at the moment, I seem to have the right attitude; doing really well.

Like Jack and Richard, Ken accepts the rites of passage without question. These men apparently already know how to behave amongst elder men. This is not so much about learning to be a firefighter; the situation would be repeated in any male industry (Collinson 1992, Cockburn 1991a). Men know that if they prove their allegiance to the masculine hierarchy, eventually they will be allowed to climb the ladder and participate in (even lead) it. Fitting in also means that firefighters learn how to protect their job from others.

Although strict deference is demanded, resistance is the norm. Few probationers acquiesce completely. Most regularly test the limits of acceptability. And while measured resistance is tolerated, the risk is in knowing when you have gone too far. It is common for the watch to expect probies to wait silently until they are granted a voice in the hierarchy. Jack's evidence indicates that not all firefighters just accept this situation: "I just started sticking my head up a bit earlier. . . . You see what you can get away with and you take it from there. If they say to you 'you're getting a bit too, a bit too game.'" Jack's resistance appears measured: a test to find out the extent of the boundaries the informal hierarchy lays down for his behavior. When senior members cautioned him for being too familiar, he accepted their authority. But this might not continue for much longer: "Once the probation is over you can do what you like, but you don't want to start standing up to people while you are in your probation." Jack's willingness to openly discuss his occasional resistance hints at the possibility that not all probies keep their resistance to the informal hierarchy private. Yet, most keep their thoughts and feelings to themselves, perhaps because a primary mandate is silent obedience. Roger, for example, described his strategy for surviving the probationary period: "Kept me mouth shut, kept me head down sort of thing; tried to get on with my work and that and do what ever I was told by the senior members. You just have to fit in with them, haven't you?" When asked why he had to fit in, Roger was clear: "Yeah, you have heard stories and that, of people who come in and mouth off and that and so. You never really shake that. Once you get known as a tosser." Roger may be explaining what Richard meant by "make it worse for myself." He suggests a watch may actually "enforce" their hierarchy by simply threatening to attach the label *tosser* to anyone who does not keep his "head down" and who "mouths off." The term *wanker*[1] or *jerkoff* might easily have been used. The circulation of cautionary tales about what *could* happen when one goes too far (and is labeled a misfit) appears to be an effective way to keep probies in their place. Individuals' attempts to avoid such negative labels are a powerful social process (see Goffman 1997).

At first glance the way these probationary firefighters talk about how they fit in seems innocent enough. Ken's acceptance of the informal hierarchy is automatic, Richard and Jack's respect is equivocal, and Roger is reminded of his place in the hierarchy. Through acts of measured resistance, probies discover the limitations and are told what happens when you transgress the boundaries laid down by the watch. Despite no formal requirement for the hierarchy or for fitting probies into it, they readily do so. Although in no way part of their genetic makeup, before their socialization into the watch, these men appear to understand how to behave. There is little room for argument here. None of the probies worked with Ian, but all would understand his (earlier) requirement "keep your head down and your gob shut."

It may be that male firefighters' understandings have their origins in the much wider set of relationships between men. While at school, particularly through play, boys learn about the power of informal hierarchies (Prendergast & Forrest 1998). It is, of course, exactly this early learning about how power is transmitted through hierarchies that underpins a great many patriarchal and homosocial relations. The subtlety of these processes makes them seem natural or in men's genes, but what seems automatic is not. Men invest considerable effort in making their hierarchies work. In the case of firefighters, they do so because lining up in their informal hierarchy is seen as a matter of safety. However, "safety" shadows a secondary agenda—the accomplishment of traditional forms of male domination.

FITTING WOMEN PROBIES IN

Firefighting is a team effort, and effective firefighting depends upon the ability to trust one another. By submitting to their own and the watch's gaze, probies prove to the informal hierarchy that they can be trusted around the station. But is this trust to prove that they are reliable firefighters or good blokes? Evidence that they will comply with informal protocol for being a good bloke can then be taken as "proof" that they can be trusted at a fire. Such arrangements favor patriarchal men by measuring their firefighting ability according to informal male standards about hierarchies. Any change in formal protocol—especially efforts to integrate the watch—puts at risk the age-old rite of passage through which older men maintain male domination by requiring younger men's deference before handing on their skills.

This leaves a situation whereby any new firefighters might disrupt these understandings, endanger the team, and be liable to upset firefighters' image if they fail to accept the authority of patriarchal leaders. Such a situation may be particularly difficult for female probies, whose lifelong experience outside male hierarchies provides them with little knowledge of how to operate within them.

Thus, finding a way to properly socialize women probies into the male hierarchy requires extra effort on everyone's part. Because the initiation protocol for probies is understood by firefighters to be more about safety than male bonding, firefighters who have not yet had to serve with women are naïve about the challenge. The expectation is that new probies will be men; the thought that a proby could be female is for many unspeakable. For example, in describing how a new proby will be treated by his watch, Dominic explained: "If a bloke joins a watch, obviously everyone is looking at him. Whether he has come from training school or another station/watch. Everyone is looking at him consciously, or not. They're sussing out his good points, his bad points." Dominic's language suggests he anticipates a "bloke" and has not considered that any newcomer would be a woman. Without even realizing it, Dominic contributes to the notion that women do not fit. Firefighters' persistent refusal to give up the term *fireman* is one way they do this. Although firefighters would say that the way they speak is habit or institutional behavior, this resistance to the use of the term *firefighter* and their unwillingness to give up the term *fireman* demonstrate the extent to which women challenge their image of themselves.

When a woman, rather than the man Dominic expects, arrives at the station, then firefighters are confused about how to behave. The protocol for initiating male probies is no longer appropriate. Terri described her reception:

> *Terri:* It was awful actually, the first couple of weeks, 'cos they hadn't had a girly on this station. They were all pussyfooting around, "don't swear; don't do this; don't get undressed." You know things like this, "Terri is about" and then three or four weeks into it they all realised I was one of them and did the same as them, it was good.
>
> *DB:* What did you feel would have happened if you hadn't?
>
> *Terri:* What if I didn't fit in with them? I'd been miserable.

Terri's account suggests two things about women probies: first, that women can fit in, and second, that the initiation protocol is not as necessary as some might assume. Terri was fortunate to meet a "sympathetic" watch, but if Terri had not proved "she was one of them," their behavior would soon change. "Pussyfooting around" was more likely an artificial environment that male firefighters would not sustain. Terri's colleagues played a waiting game; as soon as they realized they could impose their will on her, they treated her just like any other proby.

Just like their male counterparts, women find the probationary process challenging. Those who succeed in surviving do so by recognising what men like Ian require—"keep your head down and your gob shut." As Sue explained, you "just get on with the job and fit in with your watch." And like her male counterparts, Jayne questioned the necessity of the methods used to fit them in: "A long hard tough way of doing it. I don't regret it now, but it should have been easier, a less outgoing person would have given up." Jayne and Sue's comments are hardly different from Jack's or Roger's. What is different is that throughout their life Jack and Roger have been prepared for this type of behaviour. Jack and Roger are unlikely to complain, choosing the fire service as an occupation because they enjoy working in male hierarchies. Aware of the manoeuvres and behaviours that they must follow to ensure they are allowed to step into line with older men, Jack and Colin recognise that there is a dividend for complying with a system that has given order to their lives since at least their school days (Prendergast & Forrest 1998, Connell 2000).

These accounts suggest that the women who succeed are more motivated to fit into the existing hierarchy than to dismantle it (Chetkovich 1997). They just want to find their place in the watch. However, that does not mean that the behaviour they "have" to adopt and the treatment they receive is ideal, or their first choice.

Firefighters do not publicly acknowledge that their relations are patriarchal or their informal hierarchy. However, this apparent non-recognition is part of the notion of trust that exists between firefighters. Firefighters who fit in have proved that they can keep quiet about the way they are persuaded to step into line. Snitching about any bad treatment is also something that men quickly learn not to do. Women quickly recognize this, and to be accepted they must prove they will keep the processes of their acceptance hidden, and this includes remaining silent about harassment.

Proving you can be trusted is a rite of passage. Terri suggested that she was able to fit in and was glad when she was trusted and the pussyfooting stopped. Terri may have been fortunate, because other women have had to endure varying types of harassment before they either left the fire service or fitted in with the patriarchal relations on a station. The following example indicates how easily firefighters can let women know they are not wanted:

> *Toni:* We all have a good giggle and then it goes too far and they say "you are in a male environment and if you don't like it stick your fingers in your ears." They thought the problem was with the "c" word, but when it slips out they apologise, OK. But when they talk about women they have been "down on" and what "it" looks like, I don't want to hear the graphic detail.

This is a typical example of how some firefighters will remind women of their place. When Toni challenged them about their behavior the sexual harassment against her increased; yet she did not make a complaint.

Fortunately for Toni, the fire service that employed her was forward-thinking enough to set up a support network. Toni was advised to confront her harassers. She prevailed by reminding her harassers of the possible outcomes if she were to go public. Toni's harassers then left her alone, which indicates just how unnatural their treatment of her was. Toni was then happy to do as men do and, like Terri, fitted in with the ways of the male hierarchy.

Sadly, accounts from other women firefighters—especially from black women in the United States—suggest that Toni's success may be rare (see Yoder & Aniakudo 1995, 1996, 1997). Race complicates the fitting-in process. Black women in the United States find it harder to fit in than their white counterparts (Yoder & Aniakudo 1995, 1996, 1997). Perhaps because the history of racism in the United States makes it more important for black women to make a stand, they do so. Rather than take the abuse or become a "tosser," a significant number of black women (quite rightly) choose to break trust with their male counterparts and file complaints. And while they may win the legal right to serve, they are (currently) foreclosing on the opportunity to fit in.

Official practice in the fire service is to stop all forms of harassment—to welcome women. Senior officers and the Fire Brigades Union have taken positive action to break the spiral of harassment that informal hierarchies use to discourage women. There are also attempts to reduce the heavily masculinized image of the firefighter as someone who only saves lives *at* the fire. It has been recognized that lives can better be saved by carrying the safety message to the community. Some male firefighters have accepted this approach as positive. However, the good done by providing a more caring fire service is easily undone by those firefighters who cannot fit women into the image they have of themselves. Community fire safety requires the softer skills that women are stereotyped as having, and it serves the men in the fire service to prevent contamination of their work by challenging women. It only takes one incident of sexual harassment to remind women that the fire service is not a safe place for them. In a similar fashion to how fear of rape can keep women off the streets (Brownmiller 1975, Dworkin 1981) and men's violence teaches women their place (Hearn 1998), knowing that they may be sexually harassed in the fire service is enough to keep most women away.

Recognizing that they are unlikely to flourish when they are subjected to ongoing harassment and marginalization, women in the United Kingdom are not following the lead of their black sisters in the United States. They rarely directly confront firefighters' misogynist gatekeeping practices. Notwithstanding the difficulties they experience and how they overcome them, women firefighters have shown that given the necessary support (and often without it), like-minded women can fight fires in similar ways and with similar effect as their male counterparts (Baigent 2001a).

CONCLUSION

On September 11, 2001, 340 U.S. firefighters lost their lives while rescuing the victims from the terrorist attacks on the World Trade

Center. It was the greatest number of firefighters' lives ever lost to a single fire. None of them were women. To the media and its public, the fact that not a single woman's name appears on the Wall of Honor is inconsequential. The fact that those who lost their lives were referred to by the media as fire*men* and not firefighters has also been overlooked. No one blinked when the firefighters publicly referred to each other as "brothers." The way that women were marginalized in the title of Rob Picciotto's (2002) account of the events at the World Trade Center, *Last Man Down: The Fireman's Story*, goes unnoticed. It is as if women firefighters were not at that fire (and they were). As in so many other cases, women were once again robbed of their place in history. The subtle way that women's presence was marginalized makes it seem almost disrespectful to question the sexist language and their innocent omission by almost all the media reporting of this event. Why were women not part of one of the greatest moments in firefighting history? The analysis in this chapter suggests that despite sweeping changes at the formal level, at the informal level, the notion of women fighting fires still does not fit into society's picture of firefighting.

Other celebrated masculinized professions—medicine, law, and even to an extent, the military—have responded to the mandate to integrate. Yet, the fire service appears impervious—doubly dominated by (white) men—even trebly so, given the expectation of heterosexuality. Focused observation of the process of fitting probationers into the watch has revealed how patriarchal practices are normalized and sustained. The data show that, without any official authority to do so, elder firefighters act as gatekeepers to an informal hierarchy of men. Fitting probies into this hierarchy demands deference. Those with the authority to demand it do so because in the past they have earned the right by fitting in themselves. They are now the custodians of the hierarchy. Regardless of what policy dictates, they initiate their probies as they themselves were socialized. Harassment is part of this process, but few complain because to do so breaks trust, and they recognize that censure and exclusion can then follow.

Rites of passage into the informal hierarchy controlling social behavior at the fire station conflate the need for safety with the need for homosociality (see Lipman-Blumen 1976). Demonstrating you can be a "good bloke" is as important as establishing your proficiency at fighting fires. Because fitting in requires unquestioned acceptance, few firefighters recognize or are willing to notice the connection between male domination and safety protocols.

It is more difficult for women to become "good blokes" than it is for men. They lack the socialization that men receive as schoolboys. The harassment they experience is often sexualized, and because they are women, the impact is different on them than if they were men. Fitting women in requires a greater effort on everyone's part—women in the fire service also spoil the image of the firefighter as white knight and the patriarchal dividends that go with it (Connell 1995). The women who succeed keep their harassments a secret and are more motivated to fit in than to challenge the status quo. Despite women's wish to "just fit in," some men are more committed to preserving traditional male domination than finding a place on their watch for women.

The fire station where firefighters live remains a "secret garden": a place from where a powerful, high-profile group of people emerge amid a cacophony of lights and noise, hurry to do their work, and then return to the fire station, closing the doors firmly behind them. Occasionally there is some glimpse provided of life behind the closed doors where they work. This comes mostly from mass media profiles that elevate firefighters to celebrity status. Gaining access to firefighters' hidden life behind the closed doors of a fire station may only be possible if an insider first makes the invisible visible. When viewed through the I/eye of a pro-feminist autocritique, it is possible to suggest that fitting in is a contrived arrangement whereby older men ensure that each cohort of firefighters follow in their footsteps to serve the public *and* firefighters' masculine image. This is not surprising, since the workforce within the fire service is so over-whelmingly male. It is also something that the types of men who join the fire service like to do: a behavior that those choosing the next generation of firefighters look for in their recruitment process. Nor is it surprising that experienced firefighters organise informal hierarchies to hand on their firefighting skills. This too has been the way amongst men that has given order to their lives for a long time (Lipman-Blumen 1976, Cockburn 1991b).

This chapter contributes to the mission of this collection by fo-cusing its analytic eye not so much on sexual harassment or upon male domination, but on an informal socialization process that links the two together. With respect to firefighting, earlier studies have documented the harassment of women firefighters and how they experience it (for example, see Yoder & Aniakudo 1995, 1996, 1997, Baigent 2001b). But how their harassers accomplish it and then ra-tionalize it has remained a mystery. In these pages I have sought to reveal how the socialization and initiation of probationers make firefighting nearly impervious to formal efforts to integrate the ranks and eliminate harassment.

My observations of this process underscore the power of informal processes. So subtle is the process through which firefighters step into line with each other that it can appear as the way that fire-fighters evolve naturally. When this process extends to teaching younger males about how to preserve their masculine image as fire-fighters, it also leads to them joining in on the direct and vile harass-ment that males use against women (Hearn & Parkin 2002). Al-though this behavior is hidden behind the term *institutional sexism*, it is in effect a sophisticated selection underpinned by sexual harass-ment to remind women of their place as the people firefighters res-cue, not as the rescuers.

NOTE

1. This derogatory term for men who masturbate, or women who do it for them, is typical of language used by males to feminize and thus subordi-nate other males by suggesting they cannot get proper sex.

REFERENCES

Baigent, D. 1996. *Who rings the bell? A gender study looking at the British Fire Service, its firefighters and equal opportunities.* www.fitting-in.com/diss.

———. 2001a, April. Firefighting: A masculinity in crisis. Paper presented at the British Sociological Association Annual Conference, Manchester.

———. 2001b. *Gender relations, masculinities and the fire service: A qualitative study of firefighters' constructions of masculinity during firefighting and in their social relations of work.* D.Phil. thesis, Department of Sociology and Politics, Anglia Polytechnic University, Cambridge.

Baigent, D., and R. Hill. 2003. *Sunrise: Training firefighters today as emergency service workers for tomorrow.* Cambridge: Anglia Polytechnic University.

Barrett, F. J. 1996. The organizational construction of hegemonic masculinity: The case of the U.S. Navy. *Gender Work and Organisation* 3 (3): 129–142.

Brownmiller, S. 1975. *Against our will: Men, women and rape.* New York: Simon and Schuster.

Chetkovich, C. 1997. *Real heat: Gender and race in the urban fire service.* Piscataway: Rutgers University Press.

Cockburn, C. 1991a. *Brothers: Male dominance and technological change.* London: Pluto.

———. 1991b. *In the way of women.* London: Macmillan.

Collinson, D. 1992. *Managing the shopfloor: Subjectivity, masculinity and workplace culture.* Berlin: de Gruyter.

Connell, R. 1995. *Masculinities.* Cambridge: Polity.

———. 2000. *The men and the boys.* Cambridge: Polity.

Cooper, R. 1986. Millais' *The Rescue:* A painting of a "dreadful interruption of domestic peace." *Art History* 9 (4): 471–486.

Dworkin, A. 1981. *Pornography: Men possessing women.* London: The Women's Press.

Goffman, E. 1997. Self-presentation: From the presentation of self in everyday life. In *The Goffman reader,* ed. C. Lemert and A. Branaman. Oxford: Blackwell.

Hartmann, H. 1981. The unhappy marriage of Marxism and feminism: Toward a more progressive union. In *Women and revolution: A discus-*

sion of the unhappy marriage of Marxism and feminism, ed. L. Sargent. London: Pluto.

Hearn, J. 1994. Research in men and masculinities: Some sociological issues and possibilities. *Australian and New Zealand Journal of Sociology* 30 (1): 40–60.

———. 1998. *The violences of men.* London: Sage.

Hearn, J. and W. Parkin. 1995. *"Sex" at "work": The power and paradox of organization sexuality.* Hertfordshire: Prentice Hall/Harvester Wheatsheaf.

———. 2002. *Gender, sexuality and violence in organizations.* London: Sage.

Her Majesty's Chief Inspector of Fire Services (HMCIFS). 2002. *Report of Her Majesty's Chief Inspector of Fire Services England and Wales: Statistical Annex.* London: Office of Deputy Prime Minister.

Industrial Tribunal (IT). 1995. *Clayton v. Hereford and Worcester Fire Brigade; Sub Officer Ronald East; Sub Officer Gordon Perkins, Case no. 27856/ 93.* London: Her Majesty's Stationary Office.

Lipman-Blumen, J. 1976. Homosocial theory of sex roles. In *Women and the workplace,* ed. M. Blaxall and B. Reagan. London: University of Chicago Press.

Martin, S., and N. Jurik. 2000. *Doing justice, doing gender.* Thousand Oaks, Calif.: Sage.

National Fire Protection Agency (NFPA). 2001. *Fire analysis and research division: Trends in firefighting and fire prevention occupations by women by race.* www.nfpa.org.

Picciotto, R. 2002. *Last man down: The fireman's story.* London: Orion.

Prendergast, S., and S. Forrest. 1998. Shorties, lowlifers, hardnuts and kings: Embodiments and emotions in school. In *Emotions in social life: Critical themes and contemporary issues,* ed. G. Gendelow and S. Williams. London: Routledge.

Yoder, I., and P. Aniakudo. 1995. The responses of African American women firefighters to gender harassment at work. *Sex Roles: A Journal of Research* 32 (3/4): 125–138.

———. 1996. When pranks become harassment: The case of African American women firefighters. *Sex Roles: A Journal of Research* 35 (5/6): 253–238.

———. 1997. Outsider within the firehouse: African American women firefighters. *Gender and Society* 11 (3): 324–346.

4 | SEXUALIZATION OF WORK ROLES AMONG MEN MINERS

Structural and Gender-Based Origins of "Harazzment"

Kristen Yount

In the twenty-first century, men continue to dominate waged labor. Despite numerous efforts to close it, the gender gap in wages remains remarkably stable. In 2000, for example, female workers were still earning less than $.75 of a male worker's dollar (U.S. Census Bureau 2002). This gap is largely the result of a continued concentration of women in traditionally female occupations. In lieu of substantial wage increases in jobs sex-typed as women's work, the prospect of income parity for women depends on their integration into higher-paying, traditionally male jobs.

In rural areas, opportunities for earning living wages are especially scarce. In communities where coal production is the primary industry, underground mine work provides the greatest opportunities for earning high wages. Coal mining is also one of the most male-dominated occupations in the United States today. In 2002, for example, nearly 94 percent of all coal mine workers were men (U.S. Bureau of Labor Statistics 2002a).[1] While a coal miner on a production crew in 2000 earned $17 to $19 per hour, typical rural working-class women's jobs such as waitressing, grocery store cashiering, and hotel house cleaning paid from $6 to $7 per hour (U.S.

Bureau of Labor Statistics 2002b). Work in a coal mine thus was an attractive option, since a woman could more than double her wages there. Women entering the mines, however, faced resistance from male colleagues that often took the form of sexual harassment.

The analysis presented here, based on field research with miners, was designed to investigate processes affecting the integration of women workers into the coal industry. In the early stages of the study, two basic points became apparent. First, while the majority of women miners were generally satisfied with their relations with most coworkers, a significant minority of women reported harassment as a source of emotional distress that impaired their job performance. The form of harassment they identified as the most prevalent, and thus the most problematic, fell within the context of a larger category of behaviors that I refer to as "harazzment," a term that is meant to include both *harassment*, or hostile behaviors, and *razzing*, or more teasing, playful exchanges. Second, harazzment of both an asexual and sexual nature occurred, not only between men and women, but among male workers as well. Indeed, this type of behavior constituted an important binding element in the culture of miners. My premise is that the tenacious character of harazzment and the dilemmas women face contending with it cannot be adequately understood without an assessment of the ways in which the mode of interaction is established among men in the workplace.

The discussion explores harazzment as a means of exerting male domination and offers a contribution toward understanding how this type of behavior comes to prevail in certain types of work settings. I argue that, while the behaviors are manifestations of masculinity brought into the workplace, they also have emerged because they help workers to manage emotional states that arise in response to their conditions of production. Further, a mutually causal relationship exists between gender and work-emergent traits and behaviors. That is, gender roles originate from the positions women and men have held historically within the division of labor. Elements of masculinity, such as those displayed by harazzment, are associated with men because men have predominated in occupations entailing physical labor, danger, and interdependence. This relationship between gender and work roles is revisited at the end of the chapter.

I begin by describing my data collection methods. This section is followed by a discussion of the properties of harazzment and a brief commentary on literature relevant to the concept. The main body of the chapter consists of an examination of the structural determinants of harazzment among men miners and a discussion of the debilitating effects the forms of interaction have on women workers. I end by elaborating on the implications of the analysis for furthering research on sexual harassment and for understanding the social construction of masculinity in the larger culture.

DATA COLLECTION

My primary sources of data consist of field notes and transcripts from seventy-two in-depth interviews with employees from eight mines in two western states. The interviews lasted about three hours each and included 10 supervisors, 25 men miners, and 37 women miners. Six group discussions with workers were also tape-recorded; two of these focused on harazzment. I also spent some forty-four hours observing interactions in mines, spending much of this time in the eating area, where the caustic, jocular interactions I discuss here were common. In addition, I interviewed other persons involved with mining (e.g., miners' spouses and union officials) and attended four national conferences of women miners, where I recorded short interviews, group discussions, and workshops, several of which dealt with sexual harassment.

In total, I spent five months living in two rural mining communities, interacting in my role as a researcher, observing, and conducting conversational interviews at various social events such as evenings in bars, private parties, baseball games, and company picnics. This participation as a peripheral member of miners' social worlds helped me to develop rapport and familiarity with them, and at several private gatherings I was given permission to tape-record their conversations. In short, through a variety of means, I compiled a collection of in situ and recounted instances of harazzment upon which the following analysis is based.

THE CONCEPT OF HARAZZMENT

Behaviors that I refer to as harazzment were described by miners as razzing, ragging, thrashing, abuse, giving someone a hard time, or simply harassment. The category includes physical horseplay, practical jokes, and verbal banter (e.g., impromptu teasing and cutting retorts, memorized jokes, the use of epithets, and swearing). Although many of the exchanges pertained to work performance, the content frequently contained sexually explicit references. Both women and men miners deemed these interactions to be problematic as well as enjoyable aspects of work life. Indeed, the same behaviors were variously used for malicious and benevolent purposes. Moreover, multiple meanings were embedded in harazzing encounters that were consequently ambiguous to those involved. At times, there were discrepancies between the reported intentions of initiators and the interpretations of the behaviors by recipients and audience members. Behaviors reported as friendly by initiators sometimes distressed and were described as harassment by targets. Conversely, recipients were sometimes not offended, but the initiators characterized their intentions as hostile. For example, miners sometimes feigned friendliness to disliked miners. The joke lay in the shared knowledge that targets were being duped into thinking that others liked them while initiators were signifying their exclusion.

I use the term *harazzment* to capture the ambiguity of these interactions and to describe their range along a continuum encompassing friendly, razzing exchanges and aggressive, harassing behaviors. Both razzing and harassment involved potentially derisive, embarrassing, and/or intimidating behaviors designed to fluster or distress a target. Razzing, however, had a playful character, always involved what the actor believed to be an element of humor or amusement, and was kept at a level considered tolerable to the recipient. In contrast, harassment was intended to exceed the target's threshold of manageable distress and/or to designate the person as an outgroup member. Harassment in coal mines was an extension of, and cannot be understood independently from, razzing.

PERSPECTIVES ON HARAZZMENT

Discussion of behaviors associated with harazzment can be found in literature on the male gender role, humor, and sexual harassment. Research on masculinity indicates the centrality of the joking relationship among boys (Fine 1980) and men (Lyman 1987, Swain 1989) as a means of generating comradeship and negotiating latent tensions. Studies of humor point to a multiplicity of purposes accomplished by humorous interactions (Zijderveld 1983). Psychological analyses focus on joking and laughter as regulating mechanisms for anxiety and aggression (Freud [1905] 1960) and as vehicles for self-esteem enhancement (La Fave, Haddad, & Maesen 1976). More sociological analyses emphasize, on the one hand, the ways in which joking maintains cultural boundaries and hostilities between groups (Burma 1946, Kanter 1977). On the other hand, joking facilitates cohesion within groups by providing a safety valve for antagonisms (Cheatwood 1983), a tool for communicating norms and enforcing conformity (Khoury 1985, Stephenson 1951), and a method of negotiating shared meanings (Fine 1984). In short, jokes can be used to include and to exclude individuals. Moreover, the same humorous interaction may contain elements of both aggression and amiability. As Radcliffe-Brown noted, "the joking relationship is a peculiar combination of friendliness and antagonism" (1940:196).

Although harazzment, as I conceive it here, includes both asexual (e.g., work-related) and sexually suggestive interactions, the category encompasses what researchers of sexual harassment have operationalized as abusive language and sexual teasing, jokes, remarks, comments, and touching (Gruber 1989a). Efforts to explain sexual harassment in the workplace are largely based on two perspectives specified by Tangri, Burt, and Johnson (1982) as the sociocultural and organizational models. The sociocultural framework emphasizes the impact of gender socialization of women and men outside the workplace and asserts that sexual harassment is a manifestation of male dominance that reflects and sustains status differences existing between the sexes in the larger society. The organizational model focuses analysis on characteristics of the work setting. Variation in the prevalence of harassment among work sites is linked to factors including the numerical distribution of the sexes and the existence of an "unprofessional" or "sexualized" social ambience character- ized by swearing, sexual jokes, and so forth. A contribution toward integrating these approaches is offered by Gutek (1985) and her col- leagues, who develop the concept of sex-role spillover, or "the carry- over into the workplace of gender-based roles that are usually irrele- vant or inappropriate to work" (Gutek & Morasch 1982:56). Their survey research supports the hypothesis that when one sex domi- nates numerically, aspects of that sex role spill over and shape social interactions on the job. According to this approach, then, harazz- ment in mines stems from the high proportion of men behaving in a typically male way.

In the present analysis, harazzing behaviors among men miners are understood as dually established, both by gender conformity pressures and by the requirements of the work role. For the most part, however, my analysis extends the organizational model of ha- rassment by focusing on the ways in which harazzing social con- texts—or unprofessional and sexualized atmospheres—are shaped by the labor and conditions of production in a mine. Factors deter- mining harazzment in a workplace are (a) a high proportion of men, (b) physically strenuous work, (c) danger, and (d) a high degree of interdependence for production, safety, and morale. As I discuss in the concluding section, my framework also offers contributions to the sociocultural model in that it holds implications for understand- ing the relationship between the workplace structure and gender socialization outside the workplace.

A basic conceptual difference between my framework and the sociocultural/spillover models is that both of these imply that harazzing behaviors penetrate or are infused into the work role. The correspondence between sex-typed behaviors and work behaviors in jobs numerically dominated by one sex is attributed primarily to the influence of gender, rather than conformity to the demands of the work setting. In contrast, I share the position asserted by many miners in my study that harazzment was an integral aspect of the work role itself. The basic proposition I develop is that the nature of the productive activity and the characteristics of the work environment in coal mines generated certain types of distress (anxiety, fear, frustration, threats to self-esteem) and also limited the strategies workers employed to regulate their emotions. This created a situation in which harazzment emerged as a valuable means of emotion management. In the following sections, I discuss how harazzment served this end, beginning with the razzing end of the spectrum. Note that, although many of the interactions involved sexual content, I reserve discussion of this phenomenon for a special section.

RAZZING

Coal mines have considerable potential for generating fear and anxiety. The environment is damp, dark, and alien; the popping and rumbling of the mountain as it cracks and shifts provide a continual reminder of the existing hazards. Unpredictable accidents can come from any direction (cave-ins, upheavals, exploding methane gas, heavy equipment).

To contend with these conditions, miners employed a number of strategies to limit the hazards around them (e.g., discussing safety factors in production decisions). Most miners reported, however, that supervisors pressured them to work at a pace that jeopardized safety; strict adherence to safety regulations slowed production and jeopardized profits. Thus, miners often anticipated retaliation if they refused particularly unsafe conditions or persisted in pressing safety issues. Consequently, they relied heavily on cognitive maneuvering that reduced distress by giving them a sense of efficacy and security. In essence, the methods entailed sustaining a definition of the physical surroundings as relatively benign and a definition of themselves as individuals exceptionally suited to mastering danger and difficulty.

Tough Self-Presentations. To a large extent, feelings of mastery over the environment were conveyed through "tough" self-presentations characterized by assertiveness, confidence, competence, and stoicism (cf. Haas 1977). While these qualities are associated with masculinity, the interdependence and danger in mines encouraged their positive valuation. Because miners worked in close cooperation, individual expressions of distress were contagious and disruptive. The morale of the group depended on each miner's ability to manage a self-presentation in response to stressful encounters. In short, emotion management was not an individual accomplishment but a collectively constructed and enforced effort that required support from each individual.

Razzing played a central role in sustaining tough self-presentations, constituting what Hochschild (1979) refers to as "emotion work," or efforts to change the degree or quality of emotional experiences through suppression of undesired feelings and evocation of desired emotions. Joking and laughter served as a tension release that cloaked fear and allowed nervous energy to be vented, diminished the degree of perceived threat in the environment by providing a means of avoiding thoughts of existing hazards, and curbed the spread of fear by deflecting serious discussion that engendered anxiety.

Group Cohesion and Affection. Group cohesion also was central to the regulation of miners' emotional states. Conceiving of themselves as valued members of a capable and mutually protective group rather than lone individuals helped workers feel they had the resources to control hazards and the support they needed in the event of accidents. Razzing helped to perpetuate a sense of mutual caring among workers by providing an acceptable vehicle for conveying tempered expressions of affection (cf. Swain 1989). While direct and unambiguous expressions of caring signified emotional vulnerability and excessive intimacy, facetious put-downs communicated warmth and familiarity while preserving tough self-presentations.

Team Spirit. Jocularity also contributed significantly to another important basis of morale, that is, the feelings of pride and exhilaration that came from working together as a team. As in Burawoy's (1979) factory setting, the production process in a mine assumed the form of a game: the work was frequently characterized by miners as a team sport in which crews competed with each other for production levels. As a number of miners noted, the euphoric atmosphere created by jocular interactions energized and animated the group, fostering a state of enthusiasm that facilitated the team spirit. First-line supervisors generally encouraged the banter because it evoked emotional states conducive to production and often relied on razzing themselves to get workers "pumped" or "psyched" for work.

Managing Antagonisms. While coal mines had potential for generating feelings of belonging and affection, the difficult physical environment and interdependent nature of the labor also generated interpersonal tensions and frustration that threatened group cohesion. Hostility had an exceptional propensity to spread and to disrupt not only morale but safety and production as well. Thus, although many miners described themselves as internally volatile, self-control or an easygoing stoicism was valued and was facilitated by jocularity.

Razzing, for example, broke tensions when interactions verged on open hostility; a joke redefined the situation as a friendly one by changing the topic or belittling the importance of the source of anger. As most scholars of humor note, joking provides a means of tempering expressions of hostility. Kidding another miner about irritating behavior allowed the actor to vent frustration and communicate the problem while, at the same time, signaling the desire for continued friendly relations. Expressing anger in this way minimized the possibility of antagonistic responses from the target because the initiator could take recourse to joking intentions, leaving the recipient in the uncomfortable position of being perceived as the agent of conflict by responding in an unambiguously hostile manner.

Self-Esteem Enhancement. In a coal mine, a worker's tough social identity was threatened by the difficult and hazardous nature of the work and the interdependent character of coal mining, which created a situation in which workers vied for recognition under the constant observation and assessment of each other. Other researchers have found that threats to the self-concept encourage comparison processes that increase self-esteem (Crocker et al. 1987) and, long ago, Hobbes ([1651] 1958) suggested that joking serves actors by creating a sense of their own superiority at the expense of the target. In mines, derisive jokes provided a vehicle for exerting power and enhancing self-esteem through social comparison processes. Jokes designed to fluster a recipient allowed initiators to assess their own coolheadedness in a favorable light. Hence, those who expressed distress were likely targets. Moreover, the self-esteem of the actor was bolstered by the applause of the audience to the jokes. As displays of creativity and intellectual prowess, razzing allowed actors to best others and situate themselves in a dominant position. As one male miner observed, "When they find out that something's offensive to you, they just keep going and going and going. The best thing to do is just ignore it and not let them know it offends you. . . . If you're the one who's continually putting a person into that state, it makes you feel superior because you have power over them."

Testing and Socializing. Newcomers to a crew most often encountered "heuristic" hazing that was instructive for all parties. That is, it permitted others to assess the target's threshold for distress and general suitability as a team member. It also taught the target to manage a tough self-presentation—to appear calm, confident, and undaunted. For example, practical jokes such as chaining newcomers to equipment or jumping out from the dark replicated the most common stressors in a mine by creating physical discomfort, fear, and frustration. The razzing was directed most intensely toward those who expressed distress and was continued until the miners either left the workplace or learned to participate in the collective effort to regulate emotional states. Heuristic razzing tested the character of targets and also extended an opportunity to them to win acceptance and respect. Accomplishing this required the newcomer to respond to the interactions as challenges and to synchronize with the rhythms of the banter by mastering a repertoire of cutting remarks and quick comebacks.

HARASSMENT

During the normal flow of interactions among miners, targets were sometimes distressed by instances of razzing not meant by initiators to be harassment; most miners reported that, on occasion, the teasing "got to them." Among accepted crew members, these episodes passed and were not exceptionally troublesome. Provocations directed toward some men, however, were clearly meant to exceed their thresholds of tolerable distress. As one male boss noted, "Sometimes kidding around isn't kidding around any more; it becomes damn serious." Usually, this type of harassment assumed the form of collaborative ostracism campaigns that severely impaired targets and often led them to quit their jobs. Two avenues led to this situation.

First, harassment was directed toward men who failed to affect a tough self-presentation and appeared consistently distressed by the teasing. Men who openly objected to the jibes were subjected to large doses of harassment. Miners who appeared to be emotionally vulnerable were likely to acquire labels such as *wimps*, *wusses*, and *faggots*. These men presented both a threat and an opportunity; that is, their inclusion threatened the group's tough identity while their presence offered the chance for others to compare themselves favorably, vent frustrations, and reassert qualities that defined accepted crew members.

A second but not mutually exclusive route to ostracism involved harassment designed to purge individuals defined as impediments to production. As one miner put it, "If a guy's not doing his job, he'll get weeded out. . . . We ride him, harass him, give him a bad time. . . . Our crew can eat up anybody. We get rid of the dead weight." Acquiring a reputation as "dead weight" depended upon a man's own attitudes and behaviors. However, elements of prejudice on the part of others were often involved (e.g., a high proportion of ostracized men were ethnic minorities). In many cases, these men were subjected to discriminatory treatment, including assignment to low-prestige, isolated work that did not allow them to develop skill or demonstrate abilities. This treatment provided perceived validation of preexisting prejudicial beliefs about them that allowed colleagues to justify the harassment directed toward the men during ostracism campaigns.

THE SEXUAL CONTENT OF HARAZZMENT

The topic of sexuality permeated work life in mines. Men swore, told "dirty" jokes and tales of sexual adventure, teased each other about sexual abilities, touched in suggestive ways, and "propositioned" each other. As one man described it, "The dirty jokes never end. It's like a gross-out contest. . . . When I first got hired, I had a hard time adjusting to it. . . . Sexual stuff—I've heard it all underground. Everybody gets into it because it's part of the job." In general, the work-role scripts were characterized by a sexual readiness or self-perpetuating propensity to assign sexual meanings to relationships, interactions, and inanimate objects.

While these behaviors reflected conformity to the male role and were acquired by most men prior to entering the workplace, conditions in a mine provoked sexualized interactions. As a number of men noted, talking about sex provided a pleasurable uplift that attenuated distress. Intimate disclosures involved in sexual talk also indicated trust and thus facilitated group cohesion. Further, the behaviors helped miners to manage tough impressions; sex was a highly preoccupying subject that assisted in avoiding thoughts of omnipresent dangers. The objectification of women reflected in some of the jokes also signified a man's toughness; that is, by indicating that he objectified women, a man discounted an image of himself as someone who was capable of affection and, therefore, emotionally sensitive and vulnerable.

Underlying the sexualized milieu in mines was a current of competition surrounding heterosexual prowess or the ability to engage in frequent sexual activity with women and to secure exclusive sexual rights to women defined as desirable. This value was reflected in men's razzings about sexual competence and physique, in an emphasis on male sexual performance in the majority of memorized jokes, and in jokes that denigrated both women and men's capacity to control them, for example: "You have any pictures of your wife in the nude? You want to buy some?" or "Did you hear the story of Susie Brown? She said no man could lay her down. When over the hill came Piss-Pot Pete with forty pounds of swinging meat."

The preexisting valuation of heterosexual prowess was exacerbated by two dilemmas that confronted miners. First, they faced a cooperation-competition bind; while they were required to cooperate and felt pressures to present themselves as individuals who put the team's interests above their own, they also stood in competition with each other for job security, promotion, and the esteem of colleagues. This situation encouraged emphasizing alternate bases of competition that did not directly pertain to job tasks—primarily wit and sexual performance. Competition in these arenas allowed miners to enhance their self-esteem while maintaining self-presentations as team-serving individuals.

A second important structural basis for the valuation of heterosexual prowess in mines stemmed from the potential for intimacy and affection to develop among men miners and the resulting anxieties concerning their own homosexual tendencies. Regardless of theoretical orientation, there is a consensus among students of joking that humor and laughter express and provide a release for tensions not always explicitly recognized or acknowledged by the individuals involved. For example, in his examination of joking among college fraternity men, Lyman (1987) notes the high proportion of denigrating, sexual jokes about the young men's mothers. Drawing on Chodorow's psychoanalytic approach (1978), he explains the phenomenon, in part, as a manifestation of early childhood repression of attachment to the mother. In my collection of miner's jokes, however, the mother does not appear. Rather, both memorized and impromptu jokes pertained, in general, to heterosexual prowess and, more specifically, to homosexual encounters:

Man miner: Let's say your donkey eats both feet off of my rooster. What do you have? Two feet of my cock in your ass.

Man miner: One time this guy says, come up here, we need you to do something for us. So we climb up about 100 feet, huffing and puffing, and he goes, would you give me a blow job? That was all he wanted. And the other guy says, how about if I just blow in your ear and work on your ass for a while?

Homosexual themes were also manifested in much of the physical horseplay, including hugging a man from behind and "humping" him, parading and judging penises, and "greasing," which involved stripping a man and covering his genitals with equipment grease. In their study of miners, Vaught and Smith (1980) also report the prevalence of "penis games" among groups of men, including the practice of holding a man down and masturbating him. Like several miners in my study, who characterized these encounters as cases of degradation and domination, the authors see the games as ritualistic forms of humiliation. Applying a functionalist analysis, they argue that the rites increase mechanical solidarity by testing a man's willingness to abandon his identity outside the mine and to submit to the will of the group. Their analysis, however, is problematic in that they discount the possibility that any real sexual content can be attributed to the encounters. Indeed, debates among investigators of rape (Berger & Searles 1985) emphasize the difficulties of disentangling sexuality and dominance, leading some to argue that male sexuality and domination are inextricably entwined (MacKinnon 1979).

An alternate explanation for sexual harazzment among men miners is that the episodes were simultaneously acts of degradation and also reflections of homosexual impulses and tensions. Homophobic fears were exacerbated by conditions in mines in the following ways. As I noted, maintaining a strong sense of group cohesion was central to the emotion-management strategies miners employed. The reliance of workers on each other for protection created emotional ties that were particularly strong (e.g., "I've known guys for years that I'm not as close to as guys at the mine. . . . There's just something that's there. You tend to get very close" [man miner]). Men's studies scholars posit, however, that homophobia permeates and limits close relationships among men so that feelings of closeness and sexuality easily become confused (Lehne 1976, Lewis 1978). Moreover, the physical, dangerous, and exploitative nature of the labor generated a collective and erotic state of excitement among miners. And, as several miners noted, mines are "sexy" places in that they are dark, hidden, and isolated from the community ("When you're down in that dirty, dark hole, it just fits in to talk dirty" [man miner]). Thus, the setting suggested the lifting of censorship regarding sexual behavior, and a code of silence existed among miners regarding behaviors that occurred on the job. Further, while sexual talk was employed to evoke and suppress emotional states, preoccupation with the subject can itself engender sexual arousal. Finally, and significantly, homophobic anxieties were intensified by the sex ratio in the work setting, where men experienced extended interaction with each other. During the day, men worked, ate, showered, and drove long distances to and from the mine together. Single workers in particular also spent most of their leisure time together, drinking in bars and playing sports. Thus, in lieu of women miners, it was likely that sexual arousal would occur in the presence of other men and become associated with them.

To contend with tensions stemming from homophobia, miners first of all rejected their own homosexual tendencies by denigrating homosexuality and harassing men thought to be gay. Second, they asserted and extolled their heterosexual prowess by, for example, providing elaborate accounts of their sexual encounters with women. Doing so gave indication of their sexual orientation and also allowed them to associate sexual feelings with women rather than men. Third, they permitted sexual impulses to occur among men but defined and legitimized the instances as joking around:

Woman miner: Men act like freaks underground. Like gay-bees. They grab a man from behind and hump him, you know?

Man miner: A lot of that's joking.

Woman miner: It degrades the man, but it's a joke to him, too.

Man miner: Yeah, it's just a big joke. All it is, is a joke.

Interviewer: Does that happen very often?

Man miner: Oh yeah, a lot. It happens quite a bit. It's just their way of getting along.

Woman miner: They're nasty! Is what it is, man! [laugh]. See, underground they can cut loose.

Man miner: Yeah, it's a place you can cut loose, do whatever you want. But it's just joking. Most of it's just joking.

WOMEN WORKERS AND HARAZZMENT

How, then, does this workplace culture affect women miners? As I have discussed elsewhere (1991), different types of women encountered different amounts and types of harazzment and experienced different levels of distress from it, depending on the social identity they sought to establish (e.g., as "ladies" versus "tomboys"). There was also considerable variation in terms of hostile or friendly intentions on the part of men; by razzing women, many men were extending an invitation to them to become group members. A highly vocal minority of men, however, were strongly opposed to women as miners, particularly on the production crews that operated the equipment used to dig and haul the coal.

Harazzment of women miners must be understood as embedded within the context of this hostility within the workplace and also within relations of sexuality and dominance between the sexes in the larger culture. Because of these factors, significant shifts in the meanings attributed to harazzing episodes occurred when women were involved. While many harazzing episodes were nebulous with respect to friendly or hostile and asexual or sexual content, the interactions were more likely to be imbued with a hostile and sexual meaning when women were targeted. For example, a man could usually razz a male coworker with impunity by asking the man to give him a "blow job." This same remark directed to a woman was more likely to be interpreted by all parties involved as a deliberately offensive sexual encounter. In short, behaviors objectively identical to those addressed to men often lost their razzing character and took the form of harassment of women because initiators were aware of the potential for the episode to exceed a woman's threshold of tolerable distress.

For the most part, men either refrained from or modified the roughhousing of women (e.g., some women were greased but the grease was smeared on their clothing in a playful manner). One woman, however, was stripped and greased, an event that led her to leave her job and to seek counseling. Several other women encountered and were highly distressed by sexually suggestive touching such as hugging and humping. Furthermore, the lewd and collective character of verbal harazzment was often intimidating for token women in groups of men because it raised the specter of rape. Women were also frequently exposed to jokes that assumed a shared perspective of women as sexual objects. Some women were offended by the vulgarization of sexuality because reproductive functions were central to their female identity and sense of worth. Even if sexual comments were not directed toward a woman, they were often sent and/

or received as such. Because of its effectiveness in humiliating and flustering women, antagonistic men used sexual harassment to degrade, dominate, and define a woman as an outsider. Men who were supportive of women were highly reluctant to stand up for them because, by doing so, they jeopardized their workplace relations in a setting where the ability to get along was crucial.

Moreover, women faced critical dilemmas in responding to sexual harazzment. If they objected, they positioned themselves as interlopers and, like men, were subjected to intensified harazzment (cf. Enarson 1984). Despite the shifts in meaning that occurred, women were still bound by the rules of joking relations in which "one is by custom permitted . . . to tease or make fun of the other, who in turn is required to take no offense" (Radcliffe-Brown 1940:195). Although interviews reflected miners' awareness that meaning transformations took place in the presence of women, the accounts many men gave of women objectors conspicuously omitted reference to these shifts; initiators were most often exonerated on the grounds of their joking intentions and the normative character of their interactions (cf. Martin 1980). If women labeled the behaviors as sexual harassment, they characterized their own workplace relations in sexual terms and brought their sexual reputations to the fore as a public issue. Moreover, by drawing attention to the sexual character of an interaction, women presented threats to men miners because they exposed the sexual content of men's relations with each other. Indeed, it is when a joke fails to be humorous that the tensions underlying it are revealed (Emerson 1969).

The effects of work-related harazzment must also be viewed in terms of women's status both as tokens and as women (cf. Zimmer 1988). For example, the stereotype of women as incompetent rendered them likely candidates for male/female comparison processes affected by razzing; beliefs that women were easily distressed made them tempting targets for pranks and teases. Because some men resisted their presence, women were often moved from crew to crew and thus were vulnerable to the heuristic razzing given to newcomers. Razzing compounded the lack of confidence attendant on women's visibility as tokens and their lack of experience in performing job tasks. As a result, women, more than men, became disconcerted and preoccupied with harazzment, often at the expense of their work performance—particularly those who came from traditionally female jobs that had not provided experience contending with jocular jibes.

In general, women miners whom I refer to as "Tomboys" were more likely to be harazzed, but they maintained a higher sexual harassment threshold or degree of vulgarity necessary to distress them. Like most men, their basic strategy of adaptation was to maintain a tough, assertive self-presentation and to make use of the comeback or caustic retort that outwitted and embarrassed the initiator. This was reported by a number of women to be a gratifying means of emotion management and status maneuvering and was appreciated by both male and female coworkers. As Fine (1987) argues, participation in sexual banter helps women to win acceptance in male groups. However, this proposition needs to be refined to take into account the shifts in meaning I have discussed and the degree of obscenity considered appropriate in a setting. Use of the comeback was precarious in a mine, where abrasive and highly explicit interactions were the norm. Women who reciprocated the same level of vulgarity and aggressiveness typical among men violated both the sexual double standard and dominance relations between the sexes and ran the risk of igniting an escalation of harazzment by some men into behaviors that severely distressed them (e.g., in the case of the woman who was stripped and greased). Pursuing harassment charges was then particularly problematic, not only because the women feared job-related retaliation, but also because they risked their sexual reputations as others sought to justify the harassment by claiming the women to be willing agents in creating the situation. In short, women, unlike men, were constrained in the extent to which they could use sexual harazzment as a tool for exercising interpersonal power.

Lady miners had a lower sexual harassment threshold and were less likely to encounter harazzment. The strategy employed by many of these women was to strive to establish lady/gentlemen relations in the workplace and to disengage from the interactions, that is, to ignore harazzment or use a "passive" response (Gruber & Bjorn 1986). While this approach was more workable on labor crews that performed supportive tasks such as delivering supplies, the method was difficult, if not impossible, on production crews. Compared to labor work, production involved more danger and interdependence and thus exacerbated harazzment. Moreover, there was more resistance to women in higher-prestige production positions. Consequently, many women who relied on a disengagement strategy chose to stay on supportive crews. Indeed, harazzment played a significant role in perpetuating a sex-based division of labor in which women miners were concentrated in lower-paying positions within the mines.

Furthermore, even friendly razzing that did not necessarily distress women played a role in perpetuating negative stereotypes of women. For example, razzing spotlighted women at moments when they made mistakes; competent performance did not provide humorous material. Rather, others were alert to women's transgressions that could be celebrated. Because razzing won initiators' esteem, the episodes often involved a number of peers and became centerpieces of interaction that increased the conspicuousness of instances of women's incompetence and rendered the instances highly memorable to colleagues.

Finally, I emphasize the pivotal role of first- and second-line supervisors in harassing situations that created the highest levels of distress for women, most severely impaired their ability to work, and frequently led them to resign. For example, a substantial minority of bosses, especially on production crews, sought to expel women through excessive and publicly administered reprimands because they felt women jeopardized production levels on which the bosses' own job security depended. Harassing women also helped them to solidify a gender-based affinity with male workers opposed to women miners (cf. Hartmann 1976).

In addition, some women were targeted by coworkers for ostracism campaigns that were legitimized by a social definition of the women as exceptional threats to production. This legitimation was largely contingent on the training, assignments, and public evaluations a supervisor gave a woman (cf. Deaux & Ullman 1983, Martin 1980). A supervisor could undermine a woman's reputation by giving her easy assignments that led her peers to conclude she used her gender to obtain preferential treatment. Or, a boss could give her the appearance of incompetence by assigning her difficult tasks and withholding the instruction she needed. In other words, harassment must be analyzed within the context of other forms of discrimination women face.

Because of their power, bosses could curtail or encourage ostracism efforts. In some cases, the supervisor's harassment of a woman designated her as an appropriate target for hostilities. In other cases, bosses circumvented the possibility of discrimination charges by instigating a campaign carried out by coworkers. In sum, supervisors played an orchestrating role in shaping coworker definitions of women and determining harassing versus razzing interactions with them.

DISCUSSION

The framework presented here offers an understanding of the tenacity of harazzing behaviors in coal mines. They were valued because they signaled membership in the community of men. They were not, however, simply a case of sex-role spillover (Gutek 1985). Tough self-presentations and the jocular, sexualized banter and roughhousing that facilitated them emerged from miners' efforts to manage their emotional states.

While harassment occurs in every type of workplace, the analysis implies that certain forms of harassment are more problematic within certain types of work settings. That is, more instances of sexually explicit, collective, and physical forms of what I call harazzment should be associated with occupations entailing the conditions specified earlier—a high proportion of men, strenuous labor, danger, and a high degree of interdependence. As Gruber (1989a, 1989b) discusses, efforts to compare harassment across work settings are hampered by diversity among researchers in categorizations of harassment, inconsistent time frames, and inadequate indicators of severity. In addition to the need for more standardized and contextualized measures, the present analysis indicates that an understanding of the pervasiveness, content, and forms of harassment needs to be grounded in an examination of the physical and social conditions of production that exist in a workplace and the nature of the productive activity (e.g., physical, intellectual, socioemotional). Variation in harassment among occupations can be more accurately predicted by aggregating jobs not only according to the sex ratio and/or broad Census Bureau categories, but also according to these factors.

In closing, I would like to return to a discussion of the interrelated effects of gender and structure on employees' workplace behavior. While the sociocultural approach to sexual harassment emphasizes the impact of gender on work life, the present perspective also draws attention to ways in which the work life of women and men produces gender. The Marxist proposition concerning the significance of productive and reproductive activities in shaping ideology and behaviors (Marx & Engels [1846] 1976) may be extended to explain attributes associated with sex. This effort requires, however, that emotion management be elevated to a more central theoretical position, a neglected emphasis in most analyses of the labor process and consciousness (e.g., Kohn & Schooler 1983, Schwalbe 1986). That is, masculine and feminine qualities are largely rooted in individuals' efforts to evoke emotions conducive to their work and to regulate the distress generated by their labor and work setting.

Elsewhere (1986) I argue that gender roles and stereotypes ultimately originate from and reflect the positions of women and men in a sex-segregated workforce and in the home (cf. Eagly 1986).

Women, for example, are thought to be nurturing because they play expressive roles in these spheres. Harazzing behaviors are associated with men because men have predominated in occupations such as construction work, police work, and the military, which entail physical labor, danger, and interdependence. The military is particularly important in terms of creating the cultural association between work role and masculine traits, since a large proportion of men, particularly blue-collar men, are socialized by the institution.

Once animated by the division of labor, gender expectations assume a life of their own. They exert pressures on adults to conform to male/female roles across situations and also propel patterns of childhood gender socialization that, in turn, contribute to the perpetuation of a sex-based division of labor. Children not only self-select but are channeled into sex-typed play activities because parents and others want them to acquire skills and attitudes appropriate to their sex and also want to prepare them for the types of positions women and men hold in the labor market. Boys are encouraged to participate in team sports such as football that are characterized by the conditions that generate harazzing interactions and other behaviors associated with masculinity. Indeed, studies reflect the extent to which the childhood play of boys is sex-segregated and team-oriented and involves physical play and risk-taking or rule-breaking behaviors (Fine 1980, Thorne & Luria 1986).

While feminist psychoanalytic theories (e.g., Chodorow 1978) help us to understand the early childhood roots of the male role, a historical, social structural analysis is required to explain the particular configurations of various forms of masculinity. To understand the reification of gender as it develops through the interaction of internal, psychodynamic, and external, institutional factors, it is necessary to further specify the structural consistencies of the primary arenas in which boys and men are socialized and to elaborate the mutually causal relationship between the division of labor and gender roles.

NOTE

1. Coal mining has always been dominated by men. In 1977 women constituted 2.8 percent of all coal-mining employees (U.S. Bureau of Labor Statistics 2002a). This number is somewhat misleading because it includes office workers and other support-related jobs as well as those that involve mining. In 1978, lawsuits filed against 153 coal-mining companies resulted in settlement agreements to encourage the hiring of women miners. By 1985, the proportion of women miners more than doubled—to a whopping 5.5 percent. Nearly twenty-five years later, the proportion of women miners continues to hover around 5.5 percent.

REFERENCES

Berger, Ronald J., and Patricia Searles. 1985. Victim-offender interaction in rape: Victimological, situational, and feminist perspectives. *Women's Studies Quarterly* 13:9–15.

Burawoy, Michael. 1979. *Manufacturing consent.* Chicago: University of Chicago Press.

Burma, John H. 1946. Humor as a technique in race conflict. *American Sociological Review* 11:710–715.

Cheatwood, Derral. 1983. Sociability and the sociology of humor. *Sociology and Social Research* 67:325–328.

Chodorow, Nancy. 1978. *The reproduction of mothering: Psychoanalysis and the sociology of gender.* Berkeley: University of California Press.

Crocker, Jennifer, Leigh L. Thompson, Kathleen M. McGraw, and Cindy Ingerman. 1987. Downward comparison, prejudice, and evaluations of others: Effects of self-esteem and threat. *Journal of Personality and Social Psychology* 52:907–916.

Deaux, Kay, and Joseph C. Ullman. 1983. *Women of steel: Female blue-collar workers in the basic steel industry.* New York: Praeger.

Eagly, Alice H. 1986. *Sex differences in social behavior: A social role interpretation.* Hillsdale, N.J.: Erlbaum.

Emerson, Joan P. 1969. Negotiating the serious import of humor. *Sociometry* 32:169–181.

Enarson, Elaine P. 1984. *Woods-working women: Sexual integration in the U.S. Forest Service.* Tuscaloosa: University of Alabama Press.

Fine, Gary A. 1980. The natural history of preadolescent male friendship groups. In *Friendship and social relations in children*, ed. Hugh C. Foot, Antony J. Chapman, and Jean R. Smith. New York: Wiley.

———. 1984. Humorous interaction and the social construction of meaning: Making sense in a jocular vein. *Studies in Symbolic Interaction* 5:83–101.

———. 1987. One of the boys: Women in male-dominated settings. In *Changing men: New directions in research on men and masculinity*, ed. Michael S. Kimmel. Beverly Hills, Calif.: Sage.

Freud, Sigmund. [1905] 1960. *Jokes and their relation to the unconscious*. London: Hogarth.

Gruber, James E. 1989a. *Sexual harassment research: Problems and proposals*. Paper presented at the annual meeting of the American Sociological Association, San Francisco, California.

———. 1989b. *Sexual harassments: Types and severity*. Paper presented at the annual meeting of the Society for the Study of Social Problems, Berkeley, California.

Gruber, James E., and Lars Bjorn. 1986. Women's responses to sexual harassment: An analysis of sociocultural, organizational, and personal resource models. *Social Science Quarterly* 67:814–826.

Gutek, Barbara A. 1985. *Sex and the workplace: The impact of sexual behavior and harassment on women, men, and organizations*. San Francisco: Jossey-Bass.

Gutek, Barbara A., and Bruce Morasch. 1982. Sex ratios, sex-role spillover, and sexual harassment of women at work. *Journal of Social Issues* 38:55–74.

Haas, Jack. 1977. Learning real feelings: A study of high steel ironworkers' reactions to fear and danger. *Sociology of Work and Occupations* 4 (2): 147–169.

Hartmann, Heidi. 1976. Capitalism, patriarchy, and job segregation by sex. In *Women and the workplace: The implications of occupational segregation*, ed. Martha Blaxall and Barbara Reagan. Chicago: University of Chicago Press.

Hobbes, Thomas. [1651] 1958. *Leviathan*. New York: Bobbs-Merrill.

Hochschild, Arlie R. 1979. Emotion work, feeling rules, and social structure. *American Journal of Sociology* 35:551–573.

Kanter, Rosabeth M. 1977. *Men and women of the corporation*. New York: Basic Books.

Khoury, Robert M. 1985. Norm formation, social conformity, and the confederating function of humor. *Social Behavior and Personality* 13:159–165.

Kohn, Melvin L., and Carmi Schooler. 1983. *Work and personality: An inquiry into the impact of social stratification.* Norwood, N.J.: Ablex.

La Fave, Lawrence, Jay Haddad, and William A. Maesen. 1976. Superiority, enhanced self-esteem, and perceived incongruity humor theory. In *Friendship and social relations in children,* ed. Antony J. Chapman and Jean R. Smith. New York: Wiley.

Lehne, Gregory K. 1976. Homophobia among men. In *The forty-nine percent majority: The male sex role,* ed. Deborah S. David and Robert Brannon. New York: Random House.

Lewis, Robert A. 1978. Emotional intimacy among men. *Journal of Social Issues* 34:108–121.

Lyman, Peter. 1987. The fraternal bond as a joking relationship: A case study of the role of sexist jokes in male group bonding. In *Changing men: New directions in research on men and masculinity,* ed. Michael S. Kimmel. Beverly Hills: Sage.

MacKinnon, Catharine A. 1979. *Sexual harassment of working women: A case of sex discrimination.* New Haven, Conn.: Yale University Press.

Martin, Susan E. 1980. *Breaking and entering: Policewomen on patrol.* Berkeley: University of California Press.

Marx, Karl, and Frederick Engels. [1846] 1976. *The German ideology.* Moscow: Progress Publishers.

Radcliffe-Brown, A. R. 1940. On joking relationships. *Africa* 13:195–210.

Schwalbe, Michael L. 1986. *The psychosocial consequences of natural and alienated labor.* New York: State University of New York Press.

Stephenson, Richard M. 1951. Conflict and control functions of humor. *American Journal of Sociology* 56:569–574.

Swain, Scott. 1989. Covert intimacy: Closeness in men's friendships. In *Gender in intimate relationships: A microstructural approach,* ed. Barbara J. Risman and Pepper Schwartz. Belmont, Calif.: Wadsworth.

Tangri, Sandra S., Martha R. Burt, and Leanor B. Johnson. 1982. Sexual harassment at work: Three explanatory models. *Journal of Social Issues* 38:33–54.

Thorne, Barrie, and Zella Luria. 1986. Sexuality and gender in children's daily worlds. *Social Problems* 33:176–190.

U.S. Bureau of Labor Statistics. 2002a. *National employment, hours, and earnings, Series Id: EEU10120001(n)*. Washington, D.C.: U.S. Bureau of Labor Statistics. http://data.bls.gov/servlet/SurveyOutputServlet (Accessed February 15, 2003).

U.S. Bureau of Labor Statistics. 2002b. *Occupational employment statistics (OES) survey: 2000 OES industry-specific estimates 3-digit SIC Industry Groups*. Washington, D.C.: U.S. Bureau of Labor Statistics. http://www.bls.gov/oes/2001/oes_ooal.htm (Accessed February 15, 2003).

U.S. Census Bureau. 2002. *Historical income tables—people, Table P-40. Women's earnings as a percentage of men's earnings by race and Hispanic origin: 1960–2001*. Washington, D.C.: Bureau of the Census. http://www.census.gov/hhes/income/histinc/p40.html (Accessed February 15, 2003).

Vaught, Charles, and David L. Smith. 1980. Incorporation and mechanical solidarity in an underground coal mine. *Sociology of Work and Occupations* 7:159–187.

Yount, Kristen R. 1986. A theory of productive activity: The relationships among self-concept, gender, sex-role stereotypes, and work-emergent traits. *Psychology of Women Quarterly* 10:63–88.

———. 1991. Ladies, flirts, and tomboys: Strategies for managing sexual harassment in underground coalmines. *Journal of Contemporary Ethnography* 19:396–422.

Zijderveld, Anton C. 1983. The sociology of humor and laughter. *Current Sociology* 31:1–103.

Zimmer, Lynn. 1988. Tokenism and women in the workplace: The limits of gender-neutral theory. *Social Problems* 35:64–77.

5 RECOGNITION PROCESSES IN SEXUAL HARASSMENT, BULLYING, AND VIOLENCE AT WORK

The Move to Organization Violations

Jeff Hearn and Wendy Parkin

This chapter examines sexual harassment and male domination in two main ways. First, we place the practices of sexual harassment into the context of and in relation to bullying and physical violence and to violation more generally in organizations in terms of the social and historical processes of recognition. Second, we argue that while gender and sexuality have been relatively neglected in mainstream organization studies (Hearn & Parkin 1987, 1995), in relation to harassment, bullying, and physical violence, more have been even further marginalized, and these conditions have themselves constructed and constrained the field of sexual harassment and its study. We examine sexual harassment, bullying, and violence in organizations through the analytical lens of violation in organizations. Most literature and policy on harassment, bullying, and violence at work tends to compartmentalize each area and to define violence only in terms of physical violence, with little evidence of insight from one area influencing another. These three behaviors are still generally perceived as separate and nongendered. Organizational policies often deal with harassment, bullying, and violence as separate categories with little attempt to recognize links and no overall framework. Rather than making simple differentiations between the three forms, we view harassment, bullying, and physical violence as all violations to the person, with similar processes of recognition, silencing, and their interconnections. Accordingly, we have developed the concept of *organization violations* to encapsulate all these forms of violence to and violation of the person. Thus, our aims in this chapter are (1) to review the research and policy weaknesses that stem from the treatment of sexual harassment, bullying, and physical violence as separate phenomena; and (2) to use the concept of organization violations to develop a theoretical and practical framework for integrating these areas.

The historical and contemporary domination of organizations by men, along with the gendering and sexualing (giving meaning in terms of sexuality) of organizations, provides the context for an analysis of harassment, bullying, and violation. Sexual harassment, bullying, and physical violence do not "just happen." They occur within definite, yet changing, historical social relations. They are formed within complex organizational processes of recognition and response, as part of the wider politics of, and struggles for, recognition in contemporary political movements (Honneth 1995, Fraser 1997). Usually men perpetrate sexual harassment; most physical violence in and around the workplace is by men. Statistics on bullying indicate that men and women are both involved in bullying, but this fact cannot be understood outside the gendering, particularly the masculinization, of most organizations and management.

There is now considerable research and literature on the gendering of organizations, strongly influenced by debates within feminism. Organizations are often doubly gendered, in their structures and processes, and more contextually through the domination of the public over the private domains. Although sexuality has not been a central concern in studies of gender and organizations, there has been increasing research and theorizing on sexuality and organizations, arising partly from the concerns of second-wave feminism about women's control over their bodies and sexuality (Farley 1978,

MacKinnon 1979). The concept of *organization sexuality* (Hearn & Parkin 1987, 1995) addressed the ways in which organizations and sexuality simultaneously construct each other. This occurs through social processes such as movement and proximity, feelings and emotions, ideology and consciousness, and language and imagery. If gender and sexuality have been neglected in organization theory, then violence has been even more so.

Constructions of victims and survivors of sexual harassment, bullying, and physical violence occur in a variety of discourses. Though the term *victim* has been critiqued as implying lack of agency, its abandonment can divert attention from the complex, persistent, and long-term effects of receiving violence and being violated. Victims have often been individualized, even in much policy and research debate, though there is now in the United States (e.g., class action lawsuits), but rarely elsewhere, a trend toward collective claims against corporations for groups of victims. Harassment is often seen as being "asked for." Bullying, often constructed as something to be ashamed of or hidden, especially for men, is typically individualized, even though bullying "cultures" are recognized. Being a victim of physical violence tends to attract the most sympathy. Constructions of physical violence often invoke criminality (unlike sexual harassment and bullying) and make specific links to "high-risk" organizations, situations, and clienteles. Different "constituencies" or "communities," or lack thereof, of victim and survivors are constructed for each. In none of these cases has there been a clear social movement of those with similar experiences, as with, say, the disability, antiracist or women's movements.

The concept of *organization violations* reveals the relationships between harassment, bullying, and physical violence as violations to the person. Before setting out the organization violations framework, we briefly explore each issue separately, partly to reflect on the time scales by which each has been recognized on organizational agendas.

SEXUAL HARASSMENT

Sexual harassment is the most explicitly gendered and sexualed of the three forms; it includes both physical and nonphysical violations. The recognition of sexual harassment was part of, and led to, the understanding of organizations as gendered and sexualed. Although the concept of sexual harassment is very recent, dating from the 1970s, it is of course not new throughout history. We could take examples from past millennia, but let us briefly consider three from the Industrial Revolution. Though there are documented examples of both sexual harassment and intervention against it in the eighteenth century (e.g., see McKendrick et al. 1983:61), it was not until the middle and late nineteenth century when there was a more established organizational concern about sexuality, sexual impropriety, sexual violence, and sexual harassment in workplaces.

By the 1840s and 1850s the mixing of women and men in British workplaces was subject to challenge. Walby's (1986:115–116) examination of the patriarchal nature of the dominant discourse, especially the male bourgeoisie's stance on female sexuality, shows that these men publicly condemned nonmarital sexuality, particularly for women. Conditions in paid work were held to encourage female sexual activity and so were especially condemned. Factories were believed to encourage sexual contact between female operatives and male operatives and masters. Women's wages were believed to encourage "immorality" such as drunkenness. The conditions in the mines particularly horrified the British parliamentary commissioners in 1840–1842. They were obsessed with the sexual conduct of the colliery women. Drunkenness, immodesty, and profanity were held to indicate likelihood of promiscuity. With their continual references to the state of undress of the male and female workers, they focused on this aspect of women's work rather than on other more serious issues such as physical suffering.

The debate on women's sexuality and harassment of women by men was also conducted in relation to the growing bureaucracies. Aron (1987) has documented in detail a U.S. example. In 1864, three years after women had been appointed as clerks in the U.S. Treasury Department, a special congressional committee was instituted to investigate "certain charges against the Treasury Department." A report that charged that some men supervisors had sexually harassed and propositioned women clerks fed contemporary fears that it was such employment that corrupted women. According to the book *The Sights and Sounds of the National Capital,* published in 1869 by John Ellis, "The acceptance of a Government Clerkship by a woman is her first step on the road to ruin."

A final example is from an 1892 case at a Lancashire weaving mill involving the "immoral proposals" and "indecent language" of an overlooker, Houghton Greenwood. His actions as well as those of other men at the mill were the subject of a committee of inquiry consisting of local clergy. Their report condemned his and other men supervisors' actions and stressed the employer's responsibility to protect women employees, though it is unclear what exactly happened regarding punishment or other intervention (Fowler 1985).

Sexual harassment, and even awareness of and action against it, are thus not new. That this is still an ongoing problem for organizations, and a contradictory process is shown by the increasing recognition of sexual harassment through tribunals and other legal avenues at the same time that it is still a hidden process with a continuing lack of recognition. Though definitions vary widely, there is now a proliferation of discourses on sexual harassment: organizational, managerial, policy, trade union, feminist, quantitative, and so on. It has also been argued that all women experience sexual harassment during the course of their employment (Wise & Stanley 1987). Despite this, the dominant discourse is still that of the isolated harasser and the isolated victim. The experience is dominantly constructed as an intermittent harassment act rather than a process that is developed and sustained over time. It is seen more as the act of the occasional "bad apple" rather than the result of the more general exercise of male power in organizational structures. The harassed person, usually a woman, is not generally constructed as a victim or survivor, as is the case with other forms of sexual violence. There is still a stigma, sometimes couched in such spoken or unspoken questions as "Did she encourage him?" or "Was she unable to take a joke?" These constructions inhibit the formation of explicit collectivities of survivors, especially since the victim is more likely than the perpetrator to be sexualized.

Since the late 1970s and 1980s, however, analyses of sexual harassment have frequently placed it within a broader framework of gendered power relations. MacKinnon (1979:1) defines sexual harassment in terms of its links to the power of men's heterosexuality: "sexual harassment . . . refers to unwanted imposition of sexual requirements in the context of a relationship of unequal power. Central to the concept is the use of power derived from one social sphere to lower benefits or impose deprivations in another . . . when one [social sphere] is sexual, the other material, the cumulative sanction is particularly potent." Sedley and Benn (1982) emphasize that "sexual harassment is to do with men exercising power over women in the workplace. This is a reflection of our male dominated society." These general features are more specifically seen in sexual harassment in police, army, business, and legal organizations, which give a picture of severe and continuing harassment possibly being more evident in such traditionally male-dominated organizations (Hearn & Parkin 2001).

BULLYING
Thought on bullying, beginning in the late 1970s, concentrated on the school as a locus of such activities. The recognition of the problem of workplace bullying is relatively recent. There is an increasing awareness of the effects of bullying at work with debate as to whether it is an isolated act or a more integral part of organizational culture and management. As with sexual harassment, it is difficult to define; definitions range from a couple of sentences on a fact sheet (IPD 1998) to six pages. Field (1996:41–46), for instance, presents examples that include people being constantly scrutinized, found fault with,

undermined, overruled, marginalized, isolated, excluded, threatened, humiliated, belittled, or patronized. Quine (1999) provides a summary and analysis of policy development and suggests that

> most definitions of workplace bullying share three elements that are influenced by case law definitions in the related areas of racial and sexual harassment. First, bullying is defined in terms of its effect on the recipient not the intention of the bully; thus it is subject to variations in personal perception. Second, there must be a negative effect on the victim. Third, the bullying behavior must be persistent. (1999: 229)

Web sites (e.g., Bully OnLine) provide definitions and assist emerging virtual communities. As with sexual harassment, it is unwanted behavior that the recipient finds intimidating, upsetting, embarrassing, humiliating, or offensive.

The recognition of bullying has arisen in a number of contexts, from personal accounts and campaigns, particularly through the Internet, to trade unions (TUC 1998a, 1998b, NATFHE 1998) and employer organizations, tribunals, and the media. Many respondents from these sources suggested that bullying was commonplace in their organizations and occurred at all levels, with the majority being bullied by someone more senior. Even if not directly involved, many senior managers condoned bullying, leaving victims with little option but to cope on their own. Other organizations denied it was a problem, making it difficult for victims to complain. Some models of bullying (e.g., Field 1999) focus on the psychological profile of bullies but also point to changes in organizations that increase pressure and workload, and thus contribute to pressure on individuals. Hickling (1999) argues that the widespread portrayal of the bully as a psychopath has distracted researchers from exploring organizational environments, structures, and cultures. Also, a focus on the psychological profiling of bullies generally ignores the fact that bullying is an integral part of some organizations and their violations. Perhaps more importantly, the context and processes of bullying are rarely recognized as manifestations of male power within organizations.

There is a fine line between managers taking a "strong managerial line" and bullying (Andrea Adams Trust n.d.). Corporate pride in strong management can encourage bullying as part of company culture in order to achieve high levels of performance and productivity. Bullying thrives when it is normative or taken for granted across management hierarchies, especially in highly competitive environments where individuals regularly use bullying to motivate staff. The problem of management failure to act or management participation is quite common. The organizational setting is still, however, frequently analyzed in terms of outcomes—such as loss of productivity and stress—rather than in terms of processes such as harassment and violence.

Cary Cooper suggests that bullying accounts for between a third and a half of all employment-related absences due to stress (TUC 1998a:4) and says it leads to suicide and a range of other problems, such as major breakdowns, loss of confidence, loss of self-esteem, and underachievement. Bullying, like harassment, has often been taken for granted, ignored, or defined as "initiation" or "horseplay." The denial and complicity of management make it difficult to complain when management is directly involved. Moreover, when bullying occurs, it may also involve sexual harassment. Together, they may create an especially stressful and perilous environment, as some recent examples from the British military suggest. Dyer (1997a, 1997b) reports on two cases where women military personnel were incapacitated after enduring years of sexual assaults and physical and emotional intimidation. One case involved a woman in the Territorial Army who, after experiencing ongoing verbal abuse and ostracism from her male peers for three years and being raped by one of the officers, was unable to work after she left the army. Boseley (1997) describes another incident in which a wren was paid substantial compensation after she became bulimic and had to be winched off a Royal Navy ship to undergo psychiatric treatment because of a sustained campaign of harassment and bullying by sailors. She suffered such severe trauma that she had to retire on medical grounds after twelve years of service, and she was on antidepressants two years after leaving. In these examples, the problems of harassment and bullying are both implicated. Bullying *and* harassment are cited but not addressed as violence, despite the long-term physical and mental health damage. The combination of bullying and harassment creates a more serious situation than only "harassment." These examples give an indication of the grading and ranking of harassment and bullying experiences that diminish harassment unless it is combined with bullying. This could result in neither being recognized as "part of the continuum of men's violence towards women" (Kelly 1988).

PHYSICAL VIOLENCE

If bullying is a recent addition to organizational analysis, then physical violence is even more so. There has been growing recognition of workplace violence in the last two decades. Violence and safety at work have recently become a separate area of policy and research, distinguishable from harassment and bullying. This has often been in response to well-publicized attacks on members of organizations by clients or the public, as in shootings in schools. As with bullying, this violence is not specifically gendered, nor is it sexualed within a limited set of discourses. Victims and survivors may identify as crime victims rather than have anything to do with the organizational setting. The predominant discourse on physical violence detracts attention from other organization violations, including bullying and harassment.

An increasing concern with violence in and around organizations has been led by policy rather than based on research and has focused on single issues such as threats to employee safety, employers' preventive measures, or the personal impact of violence. U.K. research and policy interventions have often been within a "personal safety" or "health and safety" frame. The prominent policy, practice, and, to some extent, research organization, the Suzy Lamplugh Trust (1994), has promoted the centrality of safety at work, emphasizing what workers can do to maximize their own safety, rather than focusing on the perpetrators of violence and links with male domination. This is a complex policy agenda, in which the responsibility of potential victims is stressed. The *Review of Workplace-Related Violence* (Standing & Nicolini 1997) is an important document summarizing research and highlighting methodological and policy issues. It develops Poyner and Warne's (1986) model of violence in workplaces by distinguishing between incidents involving (1) "agents with no legitimate nexus to the organization"; (2) agents who are "the receiver[s] of some service of the organization"; and (3) agents who are "in some form of employment relationship (past or present) with the affected organization." Though this is a useful development, it tends to reify the organization and not deal with violence by organizations as agents. Also, its focus is on violence that is *unexpected and incidental* to work rather than *part* of work.

Discussions of physical violence typically focus on certain organizational sectors and factors that are usually regarded as indicators of high-risk conditions: those who handle money, valuable goods, and goods with street value; those in authority; lone workers; providers of care, advice, education, and service; and those working with people who have been or are potentially violent people (Poyner & Warne 1988, Cardy 1992, Woods et al. 1993). The emphasis on these sectors or factors alone fails to address the wider picture of organization violations. In addition, most research definitions of "violence at work" fail to consider critical factors like whether it is violence at the physical workplace itself or when working away from the workplace or traveling to work (crucial for some workers), as well as violence by relatives or partners who may be coworkers. Because there is a tendency to reduce violence to physical violence, some forms of bullying and harassment are ignored entirely. Also, as is often the case with men's accounts of violence, the violent incident is described in relative isolation from its context and social life more generally (Hearn 1998).

Research finds that physical violence and threats in and around work organizations are relatively common: 10 percent of Finnish government workers reported experiencing "psychological molestation" (being bullied at least once a week for at least six months); a quarter of Swedish health care workers were afflicted by physical violence or threats at least twice a month (Toomingas & Nordin 1995); and three-quarters of 130 Swedish medical staff in old-age nursing wards were threatened by physical violence in the course of a year (Bergström 1995). A particular concern is the rapid increase in reports of violence at work. The 1992 British Crime Survey indicated that about a quarter of violent assaults at work involved other workers and the remainder involved members of the public, including members of other organizations. There is evidence to suggest that a rapid increase has occurred in reports of such violence in recent years, even though there is still probably considerable underreporting. This increase may be due to both actual increases in violence and to greater consciousness of violence at work. The annual rate of reported violent assaults doubled in the United Kingdom in 1981–1991 (Loss Prevention Council 1995) and in Finland in 1980–1993 (Lehtiniemi & Palmu 1995). Further large increases are reported from the 1995 British Crime Survey, along with increases in repeat victimization, though much of this increase may be due to respondents defining more experiences as violence. Homicide is now the second most common cause of death in U.S. workplaces (Vanden-Bois & Bulutao 1996). Thus, it appears that some forms of violence are increasing, as is the recognition of some acts as violence.

Recently, discussions of the factors and sectors involved in violence have increased recognition further because of heightened attention from the media and greater public concern. Three environments are especially prominent: schools and institutions for older children and young people; sports organizations; and transport organizations. These organizational settings have some common elements: all are heavily gender coded and often spatially male domains; they operate with a complex mix of rules and constraints and "unrestrained" physical movement; they are relatively "enclosed" corridors within society; and they pose complex uncertainties around limits of organizational and managerial authority over violence within those organizational worlds. The September 11, 2001, terrorist attack on the World Trade Center can itself be understood as a huge, profoundly gendered violence perpetrated through transport organizations. The possibilities for such large-scale violence follow from the use of aircraft technology as weapons. This is again overwhelmingly an activity of men, especially young men.

There are, however, larger areas still where recognition of violence is only now beginning to occur. According to the International Labor Organization, 1.1 million people, including 12,000 children, are killed at work every year. The figures are especially high in developing countries, where the death rate in the construction industry is more than ten times that in industrialized countries. The International Labor Organization estimates that 160 million people develop occupational diseases and 250 million suffer workplace injuries every year (Di Martino 2000). Historically, demonstrating "corporate intentionality" or even negligence with regard to accidents and manslaughter has been difficult, particularly because of the problem of identifying accountability within hierarchical chains of command; however, this is changing. The number of manslaughter prosecutions against company directors is rising. In 1996, against the backdrop of growing disquiet at this lack of corporate accountability for a series of major disasters in the United Kingdom (e.g., King's Cross, Pipa Alpha, Clapham Junction, Zeebrugge), the Law Commission proposed a new offense of "corporate killing." A death is regarded as a company's responsibility if it is caused by failure in the way the company's activities were managed or organized to ensure the health and safety of persons employed in or affected by these activities.

RELATIONSHIPS BETWEEN SEXUAL HARASSMENT, BULLYING, AND PHYSICAL VIOLENCE: TOWARD ORGANIZATION VIOLATIONS

The relationships between gender, sexuality, harassment, bullying, violence, violation, and power are complex. It is important to recognize both the special features of sexual harassment, bullying, and physical violence and their differences. Definitions of sexual harassment and bullying differ significantly. The former emphasizes sexual advances, touching, jokes, pornography, and sexist language and implies men's power over women. Lists of bullying behaviors are usually much more work orientated, with unwanted behavior focusing on the work task and emphasizing stress and loss of productivity. Such formulations are more subtly gendered. Both academic and policy discussions of physical violence are not usually gendered and usually focus on physical attacks and behaviors that are not usually assumed to be associated with workplaces, but with "violent settings" such as prisons.

In making comparisons between harassment, bullying, and physical violence, there is a danger of presuming a linear progression from one to the other and then ranking them with physical violence at the "top," more likely to be perceived within a criminal framework. Sexual harassment is the most explicitly gendered, and also the least criminalized. It is often seen as not as severe as physical violence, thus preventing it from being perceived as violence. Joking about sex or race might be falsely described as "mild" and may seem far removed from physical violence. Seeing each as a separate category compartmentalizes them and detracts from addressing their interconnections with gender, sexuality, and organizational power.

All the phenomena discussed here are violations of the person. They violate "human dignity," a concept that needs to be gendered to fully comprehend the male-dominant and heterosexist nature of most violations. Focusing on violence as violation brings together debates on different forms of violence that have usually been kept separate. While the conceptual framework of "organization violence" (Hearn 1994) has been used, we consider the term *organization violation* as analytically more useful because it includes not only what is recognized as harassment, bullying, and physical violence (each of which is still generally seen as something contrary to the ordinary life of the organization), but also other violations, whether mundane or structural. In indicating that each form of "violence" violates and damages the person, the concept of *organization violation* contradicts any presumed linearity.

While notions of a continuum or continua of violence are useful, they need to be treated with caution. Their overly behavioral focus may neglect experiences of violation and play down both more structural relations of oppressions and mundane experiences of violation in organizations that would not usually be labeled harassment, bullying, or even sometimes physical violence.

In organizations, heterosexuality is embedded within gendered language within gendered organizations. In business there is talk of "penetrating" markets (Hearn & Parkin 1987, 1995, Collinson & Hearn 1996). In military organizations recruits are encouraged to be more "masculine" or derided by superiors as "poofs" or "women" (Addelston & Stiratt 1996). The language of male control merges with the language of men's domination within organizations. Violations occur in routine organizational processes, in managerial and work cultures, in the ordinary enactment of authority, and in the very existence and ordinary functioning of organizations whereby certain people are demeaned. Structural relations of oppression and mundane experiences of violation are not mutually exclusive; they may violate without resort to physical violence. *Organization violation* refers to the simultaneous structural presence, operation, and social enactment of organization and violation.

There are clear overlaps between sexual harassment, bullying, and physical violence. Not all bullying is sexual harassment, though arguably most or even all sexual harassment is a form of bullying and violence to the individual. Bullying and violence are not just "associated with" sexual harassment; rather, harassment is a form of bullying and violence linked with the male gendering of organizations. Behaviors and actions that may be defined as physical violence, such as an assault by a man on a woman colleague following a sexual relationship, may not be defined as sexual harassment by researchers or policy analysts even though the woman involved clearly experienced it as such. In situations where sexual harassment (e.g., sexual advances) is not the problem but gender-related issues are the concern, the term *gender harassment* may be a more suitable concept. With bullying, some of the behaviors included in definitions may seem "mundane" or as an inevitable part of organizational life. Being persistently ignored, being given unmanageable workloads, and being constantly denigrated to other colleagues are examples of behavior often perceived by recipients as bullying. Similarities between sexual harassment, bullying, and physical violence—such as physical or psychological harm, intimidation, persistence, and unwantedness—need to be recognized. All appear endemic in many workplaces, though unrecognized in most organizational analyses. The processes through which each has been named and voiced are also similar in that they involve being voiced and being silenced and kept unspoken. Naming and voicing do not automatically lead to policies and practices that could create less violent working environments. Many remain silent because they fear losing their jobs, they have little confidence in management, or they face difficult legal procedures or further intimidations.

Sexual harassment, bullying, and physical violence are to be understood in the context of the gendering and sexualizing of organizations. Since this is only acknowledged for sexual harassment, the gendering of bullying and violence is usually ignored. For example, Field (1999) suggests that bullying is not a gender issue, even though women are more likely than men to admit to being bullied. His argument is that women as well as men are bullies and that bullying occurs where there is a higher incidence of female managers, such as in teaching, nursing, and social work. Similarly, Cardy (1992:2) considers "aggression and violence in the workplace as a people problem not a gender problem." He supports this claim by stating that twice as many men as women suffer from assaults at work. However, such claims oversimplify understandings of gender power relations in organizations and need to be set alongside studies on bullying, harassment, and physical violence in predominantly male organizations and organizational cultures, of, say, firefighters, policemen, and armed services personnel (Gregory & Lees 1999).

ORGANIZATION VIOLATIONS AND MALE DOMINATION

In general, nongendered approaches have several shortcomings. First, most targets of sexual harassment are women. Second, violence by men toward men or between men is related to the social construction of men and masculinities. With bullying and physical violence, the ways in which organizations are constituted through gender make it impossible for bullying to be understood outside this gendering. Finally, these claims ignore the masculinism of most organizations and management. Even when an organization is not obviously male dominated, masculine norms or structural power by males is often the case.

In contrast to both Field and Cardy, and contrary to the interpretations of some commentators, the most important general conclusion of studies of sexual harassment, bullying, physical violence, and organizations is the continuing significance of gender relations. Swedish (Statistics Sweden 1995) and Finnish (Ministry of Foreign Affairs 1993, Ministry of Social Affairs and Health 1995, Veikkola & Palmu 1995) official victim statistics indicate that more women report "job-related violence" than men do, as Field suggests they do with bullying. The 1993 Statistics Finland surveys showed violence at work as the most common form of violence for women and the most rapidly increasing category of violence. Aromaa (1993:10) notes that "survey research indicates that women are very seldom in a position in which they psychologically harass, violate or 'mob' men in the workplace." He continues that research results show that "for women the experiences of work-related violence—physical violence or threats implicating violence—have increased." This theme has also been explored by Haapaniemi and Kinnunen (1997:57); they comment that "one explanation for the increase in violence and threats of violence at work, concerning mainly women, is the rapid expansion of occupations in the health and social service sectors and other service occupations." The TUC (1999) report *Violent Times: Preventing Violence at Work* found that young women were twice as likely to be attacked at work than their male counterparts. Almost a quarter of women in the 25 to 34 age group had been threatened with violence at work, and 11 percent had been attacked, compared with 6 percent of men of the same age.

There are at least five ways in which this male domination operates. First, there is the obvious clear perpetration of sexual harassment, bullying, and physical violence by men, individually or in groups. Second, we can point to male domination in the nature of men's reactions to sexual harassment, bullying, and physical violence, whether formally in policies or more informally in terms of collusion, avoidance, or other responses. Third is the dominance of male presence throughout organizations and their hierarchies, such as in business, governments, the police, the judiciary, the church, the armed forces, and so on. Fourth, many organizations and professions that are seen as predominantly female still have male management either directly or at a distance, as in residential care organizations. This is also apparent in midwifery, where it is overwhelmingly women who care for women at the same time that the profession is controlled by the male medical discourse. Moreover, just because an organization is not obviously male dominated does not mean that men's power is not being exercised. There are clearly gendered hierarchies of occupations, professions, and organizations, such as doctors over nurses, lawyers over social workers, and so on. These are relevant to both the contextualization and practice of harassment, bullying, and physical violence, facilitating some forms of behavior and constraining others.

Finally, and more subtly, there are powerful assumptions about what constitutes management, with "strong," "macho" environments still being seen as desirable (Collinson 1988, Einarsen & Raknes 1997). Whatever the gender, such a culture of management is imposed on personnel regardless of their gender, but with women having to comply in order to progress and men having to comply to avoid being seen as "soft" or "feminine." The reluctance of men to complain about bullying can also be perceived as the unwillingness of men to present other than a so-called macho coping image. Some men accept the "all's fair in business" thinking so much that they suppress their reactions and refuse to label negative experiences as bullying or violation (Wright & Syme 1997). Not being able to handle negative experiences may thus be experienced as a sign of weakness on their part. Wright and Syme (1997) also identify three kinds of what they call "corporate abuse": extremely competitive win/lose corporate cultures in which people strive against their colleagues rather than with them; blaming cultures in which people are frightened to step out of line; and sacrifice and overwork cultures, which involve people putting their jobs and their work above their personal and social lives and well-being to the extent that they become ill (see Johnson 1986). On the other hand, this emphasis on "strong management" contrasts with "weak" management and leadership regimes, where harassment, bullying, and even physical violence may not be intervened against (Einarsen et al. 1994, Leymann 1996). As Brodsky (1976:83) noted, "for harassment to occur, harassment elements must exist within a culture that permits and rewards harassment." Accordingly, Salin (2002) suggests that, "if there is no policy against bullying, no monitoring policy, and no punishments for those who engage in bullying, it might be interpreted as if the organization accepts it, and a possible perpetrator may perceive the costs and dangers of bullying as very low." These various very grounded ways of understanding management are themselves typically marginalized from mainstream debates on management, both practically and academically. The organizational context of pressure from above is thus an important issue in analyzing harassment and bullying, as well as physical violence. A central theme for all analyses of organization violations is hierarchical and managerial power. Since men still dominate management, their opportunities to exercise power in negative, violating ways are greater than those of women, as is their ability to silence complaints. Some women are accessing higher positions, bringing opportunities to exercise power negatively, as suggested in some bullying surveys. Men have dominated hierarchies in organizations throughout history. There are a growing number of studies of powerful male cultures and women's consequent difficulties (e.g., French 1995, Collinson & Hearn 1996). The masculinization of workplaces sets the norms by which women who seek to join must behave; hence the phrase "becoming one of the boys" (Wadjman 1998). This may be essential to survive in an environment where the greatest insult to a man would be to be seen in any way "soft" or "like a woman." For men, to point the finger at women who bully and harass is convenient in distracting attention from masculinist environments and their responsibilities. When we started giving presentations on sexuality in organizations in the early 1980s, we grew to expect that the first question or comment would be from a man giving an example of a woman who harassed or asking us to comment on women who do. This is not to deny the possibility of harassment, bullying, and violence by women; this may even be an important issue in workplaces dominated by women and for some women in especially ruthless work environments.

CONCLUSION: TOWARD VIOLATION-FREE ORGANIZATIONS
Though there is a growing recognition of sexual harassment, bullying, and physical violence in and around contemporary organizations, it cannot be concluded that there is more such violation in an absolute sense. In organizations, as elsewhere, the doing of violation affects its construction, recognition, and what counts as sexual harassment, bullying, and physical violence in the first place. The more that violation is done, the greater its intensity, and the more that it is likely to be taken for granted. As more violation is done, the threshold of what counts as violation rises. Violation can easily become normalized in organizational and management practices in the name of "strong" management. With more violation, less awareness of violation is likely as violation becomes normalized. On the other hand, doing violation may be followed by its initial recognition,

complaints, and contests over the complaints, including further dynamics of violation and further processes of recognition.

The analysis of organization violations cannot ignore wider theoretical and political changes. Organizations and work are located in time and space, are gendered, sexualized, and violent and violating, and provide the context for the structural power of heterosexual men. Often defined in terms of a fixed place, organizations and work have become increasingly diffuse in time and space, since they have expanded and changed in character. Organizations range from tiny groupings to virtual organizations to those huge concentrations of resources in international corporations valued at more than the gross national product of many poorer countries (Bannerjee & Linstead 2001, Hearn & Parkin 2001). What constitutes an organization in an increasingly global world where national boundaries and policies diminish alongside the huge global power of multinationals is increasingly difficult to specify.

Debates on postmodernity and globalization raise contradictory possibilities for the movement toward violation-free organizations. The idea of postmodern organizations as leaner, less hierarchical, and more decentralized might offer a way forward in focusing on the structures of power that maintain abusive relationships. On the other hand, these processes of globalization give rise to the exploitation of less industrialized countries and their labor power, while at the same time the abuse of international travel and information and communication technologies for sexual purposes is increasingly widespread.

Increasingly, organizations and the violations that occur within them are characterized by contradictory combinations of possibilities for violation, organizational control thereof, self-surveillance by managers, and resistance to organizational control and controls of violation. The social trajectory of organization violation is slowly becoming a more explicit part of contemporary organizational life. The developing politics of organization violations is necessary and urgent.

In the face of all this, the concept of a violation-free organization or workplace may seem idealistic and utopian. Nevertheless, we see this as a necessary organizational state to work toward. Ishmael (1999:147) suggests the creation of "positive work environments" and believes it is possible to have a "harassment-free" work environment. This is achieved, she argues, by auditing the organization's culture and managing the outcomes in a range of ways. Key to the success is consideration of leadership and management styles. This approach links with the "Dignity at Work" movement. The concept of a violation-free organization allows violation to be voiced and dealt with explicitly. Independent social auditors or agencies outside the organizational hierarchy could deal with contentious situations and prevent people from having to complain through the very structures that harass them in the first place (Collier 1995). There is a major need for greater expertise in organization violations. This may be partly accomplished by broad education in schools, organizations, management, professions, and so on, though independent "auditing" specialists, both internal and external, are also needed. Furthermore, a wider societal perspective is especially important with the increasing interlocking of organizations in networks or sets of interorganizational relations. Important as policies and practices that reduce discrimination are, they are limited in their ability to create a violation-free environment. Even in a supposedly postfeminist world, the power of gender cannot be disregarded because male domination of organizations still frequently underpins their cultures, as both the context for organization violations and forms of practice of organization violations.

REFERENCES

Addelston, J., and M. Stiratt. 1996. The last bastion of masculinity: Gender politics at the Citadel. In *Masculinities in organizations*, ed. C. Cheng, 54–76. Thousand Oaks, Calif.: Sage.

Andrea Adams Trust. n.d. *Workplace bullying*. Hove, UK: Andrea Adams Trust.

Aromaa, K. 1993. Survey results on victimization to violence at work. In *OECD panel group on women, work and health. National report: Finland,* ed. K. Kauppinen, 136–148. Helsinki: Ministry of Social Affairs and Health.

Aron, C. S. (1987). *Ladies and gentlemen of the civil service: Middle class workers in Victorian America.* Oxford: Oxford University Press.

Bannerjee, B. S., and S. Linstead. 2001. Globalization, multiculturalism and other fictions: Colonialism for the new millenium? *Organization* 8 (4): 683–722.

Bergström, A. M. 1995. Threat and violence against health care personnel. In *Research on violence, threats and bullying as health risks among health care personnel,* ed. R. Bast-Pettersen, E. Bach, K. Lindström, A. Toomingas, and J. Kiviranta, 17–20. Copenhagen: TemaNord.

Boseley, S. 1997, February 8. Navy counts the cost of a culture of sexual abuse. *The Guardian:* 8.

Brodsky, C. M. 1976. *The harassed worker.* Toronto: Lexington Books/D.C. Heath.

Bully OnLine. 1999. timfield@successunlimited.co.uk.

Cardy, C. 1992. *Training for personal safety at work.* Aldershot: Gower.

Collier, R. 1995. *Combating sexual harassment in the workplace.* Buckingham and Philadelphia: Open University Press.

Collinson, D. L. 1988. "Engineering humor": Masculinity, joking and conflict in shopfloor relations. *Organization Studies* 9:181–199.

Collinson, D. L., and J. Hearn, eds. 1996. *Men as managers, managers as men: Critical perspectives on men, masculinities and managements.* London: Sage.

Di Martino, V. 2000. *Violence at the workplace: The global challenge.* Geneva: International Labor Organization.

Dyer, C. 1997a, June 24. Damages for wren made ill by sex harassment. *The Guardian:* 4.

———. 1997b, July 7. Woman raped and bullied in Territorial Army job. *The Guardian:* 6.

Einarsen, S., and B. I. Raknes. 1997. Harassment in the workplace and the victimization of men. *Violence and Victims* 12:247–263.

Einarsen, S., B. I. Raknes, and S. Matthiesen. 1994. Bullying and harassment at work and their relationships to work environment quality: An exploratory study. *European Work and Organizational Psychology* 4 (4): 381–401.

Farley, L. 1978. *Sexual shakedown: The sexual harassment of women on the job.* London: Melbourne House.

Field, T. 1996. *Bully in sight: How to predict, resist, challenge and combat workplace bullying.* Didcot, UK: Success Unlimited.

———. 1999. *Those who can, do. Those who can't, bully.* Bully OnLine. http://www.successunlimited.co.uk/bully/worbal.htm.

Fowler, L. 1985. *Women and work: Sexual harassment, patriarchy and the labor process.* Unpublished Master of Science thesis Industrial Sociology, University of Bradford, Bradford.

Fraser, N. 1997. *Justice interruptus: Critical reflections on the "Postsocialist" condition.* New York and London: Routledge.

French, K. 1995. Men and locations of power: Why move over? In *Gender, culture and organizational change: Putting theory into practice,* ed. C. Itzin and J. Newman, 54–67. London and New York: Routledge.

Gregory, J., and S. Lees. 1999. *Policing sexual assault.* London and New York: Routledge.

Haapaniemi, M., and A. Kinnunen. 1997. Muuttunut työtilanteiden väkivalta 1980–1993 (Changes in violence at work 1980–1993). *Työ ja ihminen* 1:14–23.

Hearn, J. 1994. The organization(s) of violence: Men, gender relations, organizations, and violences. *Human Relations* 47 (6): 707–730.

———. 1998. *The violences of men: How men talk about and how agencies respond to men's violence to women.* London: Sage.

Hearn, J., and W. Parkin. 1987. *"Sex" at "work": The power and paradox of organization sexuality.* Brighton: Wheatsheaf; New York: St. Martin's.

———. 1995. *"Sex" at "work": The power and paradox of organization sexuality,* rev. ed. Hemel Hempstead: Prentice Hall/Harvester Wheatsheaf; New York: St. Martin's.

———. 2001. *Gender, sexuality and violence in organizations. The unspoken forces of organization violations.* London: Sage.

Hickling, K. 1999. *Harassment at work: A general population study.* Master's thesis, University of Huddersfield, Huddersfield.

Honneth, A. 1995. *The struggle for recognition: The moral grammar of social conflicts.* Cambridge, Mass.: MIT Press.

Institute of Personnel and Development (IPD). 1998. *Harassment at work: Key facts.* London: IPD.

Ishmael, A., with B. Alemoru. 1999. *Harassment, bullying and violence at work*. London: The Industrial Society.

Johnson, R. 1986. Institutions and the promotion of violence. In *Violent transactions*, ed. A. Campbell and J. J. Gibbs, 181–205. Oxford: Blackwell.

Kelly, L. 1988. *Surviving sexual violence*. Cambridge: Polity.

Lehtiniemi, A., and T. Palmu. 1995. Health. In *Women and men in Finland*, ed. E.-S. Veikkola and T. Palmu, 19–30. Helsinki: Statistics Finland.

Leymann, H. 1996. The content and development of mobbing at work. *European Journal of Work and Organizational Psychology* 5 (2): 165–184.

Loss Prevention Council. 1995, February. *Technical briefing note for insurers*. London: Loss Prevention Council.

MacKinnon, C. A. 1979. *The sexual harassment of working women*. New Haven, Conn.: Yale University Press.

McKendrick, N., J. Brewer, and J. H. Plumb. 1983. *The birth of a consumer society: The commercialization of eighteenth century England*. London: Hutchinson.

Ministry of Foreign Affairs. 1993. *CEDAW convention: Second periodic report by Finland*. Helsinki: Tabloid.

Ministry of Social Affairs and Health. 1995. *Violence against women in Finland*. Helsinki: Ministry of Social Affairs and Health.

NATFHE. 1998. *Advice for NATFHE branches: Whistleblowing*. London: National Association of Teachers in Further and Higher Education (NATFHE).

Poyner, B., and C. Warne. 1986. *Violence to staff: A basis for assessment and prevention*. London: Tavistock Institute of Human Relations/Health and Safety Executive.

———. 1988. *Preventing violence to staff*. London: Tavistock Institute of Human Relations/Health and Safety Executive.

Quine, L. 1999. Workplace bullying in NHS Community Trust: Staff questionnaire survey. *British Medical Journal* 3 (18): 228–232.

Salin, D. 2002. *Ways of explaining workplace bullying: A review of enabling, motivating and precipitating structures and processes in the work environment*. Unpublished manuscript. Helsinki: Swedish School of Economics and Business Administration.

Sedley, A., and M. Benn. 1982. *Sexual harassment at work*. London: NCCL Rights for Women Unit.

Standing, H., and D. Nicolini. 1997. *Review of workplace-related violence.* Contract Research Report 143/1997. London: Health and Safety Executive (HSE).

Statistics Sweden. 1995. *Living conditions report No 88: Victims of violence and property crime 1978–1993.* Stockholm: Statistics Sweden (National Council for Crime Prevention-Brå).

The Suzy Lamplugh Trust. 1994. *Violence and aggression at work: Reducing the risks.* London: The Suzy Lamplugh Trust.

Toomingas, A., and H. Nordin. 1995. Reports of violence and threats against Swedish health care personnel. In *Research on violence, threats and bullying as health risks among health care personnel,* ed. R. Bast-Pettersen, E. Bach, K. Lindström, A. Toomingas, and J. Kiviranta, 11–13. Copenhagen: TemaNord.

Trades Union Congress (TUC). 1998a. *Beat bullying at work: A guide for trade union representatives and personnel managers.* London: TUC.

———. 1998b. *Bullied at work? Your guide to tackling workplace bullying.* London: TUC.

———. 1999. *Violent times: Preventing violence at work.* London: TUC.

VandenBois, G., and E. Bulutao, eds. 1996. *Violence on the job: Identifying risks and developing solutions.* New York: American Psychological Association.

Veikkola, E.-S., and T. Palmu, eds. 1995. *Women and men in Finland.* Helsinki: Statistics Finland.

Wadjman, J. 1998. *Managing like a man.* Cambridge: Polity.

Walby, S. 1986. *Patriarchy at work.* Cambridge: Polity.

Wise, S., and L. Stanley. 1987. *Georgie Porgie: Sexual harassment in everyday life.* London: Pandora.

Woods, M., and J. Whitehead with D. Lamplugh. 1993. *Working alone: Surviving and thriving.* London: IPM/Pitman.

Wright, L., and M. Syme. 1997. *Corporate abuse.* New York: Simon and Schuster.

6 THE SEXUAL HARASSMENT OF MEN
Articulating the Approach-Rejection Theory of Sexual Harassment

Margaret S. Stockdale

Sexual harassment is a problem rooted in male dominance. Men who harass use their social, economic, organizational, and physical power to define how gender is to be structured in an organizational setting. Sexual harassment is a tool to maintain a masculine hierarchy that rewards men who possess the requisite masculine traits. Women are in a double bind in situations controlled by men with a propensity to harass. If they attempt to break traditional female gender roles, such as entering traditionally male occupations, they may be targeted for harassment as a means of dissuasion. If they conform to traditional feminine gender roles, such as dressing in feminine ways or occupying traditionally female jobs, they may evoke sexual attention, which shifts attention from their worker status to a sexual playmate status. Both forms of harassment against women serve to maintain the status quo of male dominance. This chapter aims to show that sexual harassment of men also perpetuates male dominance by promoting a masculine ethic. The motives of masculine superiority and feminine subordinance apply when men harass men as they do when men harass women.

With the U.S. Supreme Court's decision in *Oncale v. Sundowner*

Offshore Services, Inc. (1998), in which sexual harassment of men by men was found to be actionable as a form of sex discrimination, theory and research on men's sexual harassment experiences have begun to emerge (Berdahl, Magley, & Waldo 1996, DuBois et al. 1998, Foote & Goodman-Delahunty 1999, Franke 1997, Stockdale, Wood, & Batra 1999, Waldo, Berdahl, & Fitzgerald 1998). Examination of men's sexual harassment experiences is important not only to address under-researched concerns of sexual harassment of men, but to also shed light on a broader theory that explains the sexual harassment of both men and women.

This paper discusses the development and validation of a new theory of sexual harassment. Although the theory should apply to all forms of harassment, it has been developed and tested on men's sexual harassment experiences because this context helps us more clearly understand the approach-rejection distinction that is central to the theory. After briefly reviewing theories of why sexual harassment is a form of sex discrimination, I discuss, in the context of men's sexual harassment experiences, the distinction between sexual harassment that is motivated by sexual (albeit misguided) interests versus that which is motivated by a desire to maintain masculine dominance. Following a brief review of extant statistics on men's sexual harassment experiences, I discuss recent research aimed at testing tenets of the approach-rejection theory. Specifically, I critique existing measures of sexual harassment with regard to their ability to capture men's sexual harassment experiences, and I discuss the development of measures that more specifically address the sexual harassment of men and sexual harassment intentions. Furthermore, I provide evidence to support the nomological network of men's harassment experiences. Finally, I attempt to show how the approach-rejection theory can more fully explain the wrongness of sexual harassment against both women and men.

THEORIES OF THE WRONGNESS OF SEXUAL HARASSMENT

Generally, there are three theories to explain why sexual harassment is a form of sexual discrimination and therefore illegal (Franke 1997).

The inequality theory is the underlying basis for Title VII of the Civil Rights Acts of 1964 and 1991 because sexual harassment constitutes non-work-relevant conditions that a person experiences because of his or her gender. A prima facie question is "But for the plaintiff's sex, would the harassment have occurred?" The sex-is-sexism theory, articulated by Susan Estrich (1991), claims that sexual matters objectify women more so than men and therefore debase women. The antisubordination theory extends Estrich's sex-is-sexism theory by stating that sexual harassment is a means by which men continue to dominate and exploit women physically, economically, and personally (MacKinnon 1979). Sex is a means of exerting power over women because it reifies the historical context in which women's sexuality has been used as a means of subordinating them.

Each of these theories provides a compelling explanation of the wrongness of sexual harassment. The inequality theory remains the dominant legal theory. The logic is simple—sexual harassment is non-work-relevant, harmful behavior aimed disproportionately at women. An employer who requires female employees to endure his unwanted sexual advances but leaves male employees alone is discriminating against women. "But for" the employee's gender, she would not have been subjected to such treatment. This theory often holds for opposite-sex sexual harassment because it is assumed or demonstrated that harassers only harass those of the opposite sex (usually men harassing women), and by logical extension, homosexual harassers would only harass those of the same sex. Although the "but for" test explicitly tests whether the harassing treatment violates Title VII's equality principle, it implicitly perpetuates the myth that sexual harassment arises only from sexual motives. In opposite-sex sexual harassment cases, the "but for" test is an expeditious way for plaintiffs to prove sex discrimination; however, in same-sex sexual harassment, only harassment by homosexual perpetrators appears to pass the test.

The inequality theory also creates difficulty for perpetrators who harass both male and female targets, so-called equal opportunity harassers. For example, in *Chiapuzio v. BLT Operating Corp.* (1993), the harasser was sexually licentious toward female employees while also using sexually loaded behavior to mock and ridicule male employees. It appears that the inequality theory is sufficient for establishing that some (perhaps much) sexual harassment is discriminatory, but it leaves other forms unexplained.

The sex-is-sexism theory goes farther in explaining the harm of sexual harassment, but some commentators do not agree that all forms of sexual expression in the workplace or other organizational settings are harmful to women (Lobel 1993, Williams, Giuffre, & Dellinger 1999). The antisubordination theory also more fully recognizes the wrongness of sexual harassment than does the inequality theory, but like sex-is-sexism theory, it does not provide an adequate basis for understanding men's sexual harassment experiences. According to inequality theory, only sexual harassment of men by women or homosexual men fits the inequality definition, and neither sex-is-sexism nor antisubordination theory explains why sexual harassment can be harmful to men.

Inasmuch as a technology is a collection of techniques and processes that help social groups achieve certain goals, Franke (1997) and Stockdale et al. (1999) proposed that sexual harassment is wrong because it perpetuates a "technology of sexism" that enforces heterosexist, hypergender standards in the workplace. According to Franke (1997:745), what makes sexual harassment sex discrimination is "not the fact that the conduct is sexual, but that the sexual conduct is being used to enforce or perpetuate gender norms and stereotypes."

The following section presents statistics on the sexual harassment of men and argues that men's harassment experiences fall into two broad categories of motives: approach-based harassment, in which sexual attention is the primary motive, and rejection-based harassment, in which humiliation or debasement is the primary motive. Rejection-based harassment, in particular, serves to maintain male dominance by perpetuating hypermasculine, heterosexist gender norms.

STATISTICS ON SEXUAL HARASSMENT OF MEN

Although many surveys assessing the prevalence of sexually harassing behavior or events have been conducted in the past two decades (for review and critique, see Arvey & Cavanaugh 1995), they all have been developed from an understanding of female sexual harassment. Nonetheless, three surveys conducted by the U.S. Merit Systems Protection Board (USMSPB 1981, 1988, 1995) on the federal workforce, and studies in the U.S. military generally (Department of Defense: Martindale 1991, Edwards et al. 1997), provide some of the few broad assessments of sexual harassment for both women and men (see also Gutek 1985). Table 6.1 outlines the measures used in several of these studies. According to the USMSPB surveys, 42 to 44 percent of women and 14 to 19 percent of men in the federal workforce had experienced at least one sexually harassing experience within two years. Moreover, the types of experiences remained relatively stable over the fourteen-year span of these studies. Most women and men who were harassed experienced unwanted sexual teasing and jokes. Next most common were unwanted requests for dates and unwanted calls and letters. Relatively few harassed women and men experienced requests for sexual favors and attempted or actual assault and rape.

One striking difference between men's sexual harassment experiences and women's experiences was the gender of the initiator. According to the USMSPB, while 21 percent of men were harassed by other men (same-sex sexual harassment: SSSH), only about 2 percent of women experienced SSSH. Men are much more likely to experience SSSH than are women; thus, a closer examination of SSSH harassment is needed to better understand sexual harassment of men.

My colleagues and I (Stockdale et al. 1999) recently examined the prevalence of men's sexual harassment experiences ascertained by the 1995 Department of Defense survey on gender issues (SEQ-DoD, Edwards et al. 1997). Table 6.1 outlines this scale. We examined differences between men who experienced SSSH ($n = 780–781$) vs. other-sex sexual harassment (OSSH) ($n = 462–463$). Experiences more likely to be perpetrated by women (OSSH) than by men (SSSH) tend to belong to the categories of sexual hostility and unwanted sexual attention (i.e., being treated differently because of one's sex, being put down because of one's sex, being whistled at in a sexual away, attempts to establish a sexual relationship, being stared at sexually, repeated requests for dates, being touched in a way that made one feel uncomfortable, and receiving unwanted kissing. Comparatively, SSSH experiences were various forms of sexist hostility (i.e., unwanted crude offensive remarks, repeated sex stories and jokes, and being shown sexist, suggestive materials).

These findings are consistent with those reported by DuBois et al. (1998) in their reanalysis of the Department of Defense 1988 Survey of Sex Roles in the Active Duty Military[1] (Martindale 1991). Among female respondents who reported at least one episode of unwanted social-sexual experience in the military in the preceding twelve months (and who reported sufficient information for analysis), only 0.9 percent experienced SSSH. Comparatively, SSSH characterized the experience of 35 percent of men who reported at least one episode of unwanted social-sexual experience. Among harassed male respondents, uninvited, unwanted sexual teasing, jokes, remarks, or questions were the most common types of experiences (58 percent), but these behaviors were even more prevalent among those experiencing SSSH (73 percent). Men experiencing SSSH were also more likely than men experiencing OSSH to report rape (3.2 percent vs. 0.8 percent, respectively). Men experiencing OSSH were more likely than SSSH men to experience unwanted sexual touching, cornering, pinching, or brushing against, as well as unwanted sexually suggestive looks, gestures, or body language. For women, the pattern of experiences did not differ as a function of the gender of the harasser.

Finally, to show that these differences in men's OSSH and SSSH experiences are not limited to military settings, Waldo et al. (1998) examined three samples of men in nonmilitary settings: a large public utility ($n = 378$), faculty and staff at a midwestern university ($n = 209$), and a western agribusiness food-processing plant ($n = 420$). Rates of experiencing at least one unwanted social-sexual experience from a male perpetrator (SSSH) were 37 to 42 percent, whereas rates of OSSH were 26 to 46 percent. However, there were clear distinctions in the types of behavior constituting SSSH vs. OSSH. In all three samples, those experiencing SSSH were significantly more likely than those experiencing OSSH to be the object of lewd comments, and in two of the three samples, more likely to be the object of behaviors and actions that enforced the male gender role. Those experiencing OSSH, on the contrary, were more likely than those experiencing SSSH to be the object of unwanted sexual attention (in one sample), or to be the object of negative remarks about men (in all three samples).

A TYPOLOGY OF SEXUAL HARASSMENT EXPERIENCES:
SAME VS. OTHER GENDER INITIATOR
AND APPROACH VS. REJECTION MOTIVES

Men's OSSH and SSSH appear to clearly delineate two broad classes of motives for sexual harassment. Approach-based SH consists of unwanted sexual advances or sexual attention, and although these events can be motivated by power and dominance motives (see Bargh & Raymond 1995), they tend to imply sexual attraction. In the survey research cited above, with the exception of rape, these were the typical forms of experiences by men who reported unwanted social-sexual OSSH experiences (DuBois et al. 1998, Stockdale et al. 1999, Waldo et al. 1998). The rare, but nonetheless egregious, same-sex rape experiences reported in DuBois et al. (1998) may have been typical of sexual assaults of men that occur in sex-segregated institutions, which are committed not as acts of sexual attraction but as acts of domination (e.g., Cotton & Groth 1982, Nacci & Kane 1983;

see also Stermac et al. 1996 for a discussion of motives behind same-sex assault against men).

Rejection-based SH consists of behaviors that imply a desire to humiliate, punish, and otherwise drive away the target. Rejection behaviors can range from "bullying" behaviors such as ridiculing a person for not being able to "get sex" to sexual assault, as in the same-sex rape incidents noted above. Joseph Oncale, the offshore oil-rig worker whose sexual harassment case against his coworkers and supervisor was the first male SSSH case heard in the U.S. Supreme Court (*Oncale v. Sundowner Offshore Services, Inc.* 1998), experienced rejection-based SH. In addition to constant ridicule and derision by his coworkers, Oncale was sodomized in the locker room with a bar of soap. In *Polly v. Houston Lighting & Power Co.* (1993), the defendant claimed that his male workers sexually harassed him because he would not engage in "dirty" conversations and because he disapproved of their use of profanity. In both *McWilliams v. Fairfax County Board of Supervisors* (1996) and *Goluszek v. H. P. Smith* (1988), the defendants were both described as men who were perhaps developmentally delayed.[2] The defendants' male coworkers relentlessly taunted these men with comments about having sex, exposed them to sexual stimuli on the job (e.g., putting a condom in their food), and in the case of McWilliams, simulated sex acts upon him.

My colleagues and I (Stockdale et al. 1999, Stockdale, Gandolfo, et al. 2003) argue that rejection-based sexual harassment is conducted to enforce preferred heterosexist, hypermasculine gender-role behavior. Men who do not live up to their tormentors' masculinity standards are targeted for harassment. For example, men who appear to be effeminate, gay, or in other ways not sufficiently masculine (e.g., young and inexperienced) are likely targets for rejection-based SSSH. Rejection-based sexual harassment is sexist because it serves to exalt hypermasculinity and diminish femininity.

Hypermasculinity is a rigid male sex-role stereotyped identity composed of calloused sex attitudes toward women, a conception of violence as manly, and a view of danger as exciting (Mosher & Sirkin 1984). Relatedly, heterosexism is an ideological system in which non-hetereosexual persons, forms of behavior, relationships, or communities are denied, denigrated, and stigmatized (Fernald 1995, Herek 1990). Research has shown that individuals expressing hypermasculine or heterosexist behavior do so to bolster their image among others. For example, Herek (1986) has shown that expressing antigay attitudes is positively associated with other men's perceptions of one's masculinity. Expressions of hypermasculinity may confer similar benefits. Quinn (2002) found that men who engage in various forms of gender harassment do so not simply to harm their targets, but to enhance their masculine image among other male onlookers. Wade and Brittan-Powell (2001) found that men holding traditional masculine ideologies (similar to hypermasculinity) collect their identity by associating themselves with similar others and are considered to have a gender-role self-concept that is externally defined, stereotyped, conformist, and rigid. Furthermore, such attributes are associated with a proclivity to sexually harass (Wade & Brittan-Powell 2001). Thus, rejection-based same-sex sexual harassment may represent an extension of hypermasculine, heterosexist behavior that perpetuates a masculine ideology by not only punishing male gender deviants, but by also bolstering the masculine perception of the initiator.

For women, the lines between rejection and approach-based harassment are less distinct. Unwanted sexual attention toward women can involve both approach and rejection motives. As Estrich (1991) notes, sexual behavior toward women reifies women's subordination. A boss or a coworker who views his female colleague as a sexual object implicitly devalues her professional worth. Therefore, initiators may repeatedly request dates from female colleagues or touch them in unwanted ways because the initiators are sexually attracted to their female colleagues or employees. But such initiators also send a rejection message that women are not valued as colleagues, just as hanging pornography and polluting the work environment with sexist jokes and comments serves to reject women's presence in the workplace. For men, however, rejection and approach motives are more clearly delineated. With the exception of homosexually inclined initiators, SSSH against men is typically of the rejection form. Rejection-based OSSH harassment by women may be used to poke fun at men (e.g., saying the men "only have one thing on their minds") but doesn't have the insidious effects as rejection-based OSSH against women. Similarly, men may experience discomfort and in some cases serious consequences from approach-based OSSH, but it typically does not perpetuate the reproduction of masculine hegemony as do rejection-based SSSH against men and all sexual harassment against women.

MEASURES OF SEXUAL HARASSMENT OF MEN

There have been a number of self-report instruments of sexual harassment experiences developed in the past decade. The Sexual Experiences Questionnaire (SEQ; Fitzgerald, Gelfand, & Drasgow 1995) is arguably the most widely used measure of sexual harassment. The original version was based on Till's (1980) unpublished report of a nonrepresentative sample of people who provided examples of sexual harassment they had experienced, observed, or heard about in postsecondary educational institutions. Fitzgerald et al. (1988) developed behavioral examples of sexual harassment based on the Till report to create items for the SEQ, which they administered to samples of undergraduate women and men, graduate women at two universities, and female faculty, staff, and administrators at one university. Over 800 undergraduate men responded to the survey, and although their incidence for endorsing any SEQ item was generally less than women's incidence rates, they reported fairly high rates of most examples of gender harassment (e.g., suggestive stories or offensive jokes, crudely sexual remarks, use of sexist or pornographic teaching materials, being treated differently due to gender, and sexist remarks about career options; incidence rates were 12.44–36.30 percent).

The authors of the SEQ have created many versions for different types of settings, such as agribusiness (Glomb et al. 1997), public utilities (Fitzgerald et al. 1995), and the military (SEQ-DoD, Edwards et al. 1997), as well as many educational settings; however, most of the SEQ versions have been tested only on women. Berdahl et al. (1996) suggested that sexual harassment falls under a broader phenomenon of negotiations of gender, that is, attempts to define and redefine what constitutes appropriate behavior and roles for men and women. They stated that men will feel harassed by behavior that challenges current constructions of masculinity as a domain of characteristics reserved for men (e.g., dominance, privilege, and success in the workplace), whereas women feel harassed by behavior that equates femininity with subordinance in the workplace. Waldo et al. (1998) culled responses from the few samples of men that had been collected by Fitzgerald and her team, as well as previously unpublished qualitative responses from men in a couple of their samples, to critique the usefulness of the SEQ for measuring men's sexual harassment experiences. They concluded that previous versions of the SEQ did not adequately represent men's sexual harassment experiences, and they developed additional items designed more specifically for men. These items were combined with several previous items from other versions of the SEQ to create the Sexual Harassment of Men (SHOM) Scale.

Janice Motoike and I (Stockdale & Motoike 2000) expanded on the SHOM to develop a scale titled "Men's Sexual Harassment Experiences" (MSHE) that would more fully incorporate the approach and rejection forms of harassment. Table 6.1 summarizes the pool of 63 items measuring the various forms of nonconsensual sexual behaviors that men might experience. Of these, 25 items were from the SHOM (and of these, about 19 were based on the SEQ; Fitzgerald & Shullman 1985). Additional items were created from examining the legal cases of sexual harassment against men and extracting examples of sexually harassing behaviors that were reported in the case law (e.g., others exposed their anatomy to me; someone left a condom or other sexually related object for me to find). Hazing research was also examined, and behavioral examples were extracted as items (e.g., I have been the object of sexually explicit jokes; I have had to endure talk about perverse sex acts). Finally, our research team brainstormed a number of items based on the theoretical underpinnings guiding our research (e.g., I experienced threats to my masculinity; I was questioned about my manhood). We eliminated 12 items from the original set that were poorly worded, redundant, or double-barreled, leaving a final set of 51 items included on the survey. An additional item, "Were you sexually harassed?" was added as a validity item.

Initial psychometric analyses on the MSHE with a sample of 347 college men at a midwestern university yielded a 31-item scale with four orthogonal factors. Coercive Sexual Advances ($\alpha = .73$) is a 9-item scale (including 5 SEQ items) that includes both quid pro quo forms of behavior as well as unwanted sexual attention (refer to Table 6.1 for sample items and response format). Men who endorsed items on this subscale were more likely to experience such behaviors from women (37.5 percent) or both genders (29.7 percent) than from men alone (6.6 percent). The average level of response was quite low.[3] Experiences of coercive sexual advances were modestly correlated with self-reports of academic ($r = .21$, $p < .05$) and emotional deterioration ($r = .23$, $p < .05$) (Stockdale & Motoike 2000).

Masculinity Teasing ($\alpha = .79$), the second factor, contained 9 items (2 from the SHOM) reflecting experiences of being teased, insulted, or threatened because of not conforming to masculine standards. Men were more likely to experience such behaviors from other men (27.1 percent) or from both genders (36.3 percent) than from women alone (5.3 percent). The average level of such experiences was also relatively low ($M = 0.45$, $SD = 0.47$), and they were correlated with self-reports of emotional ($r = .29$, $p < .05$) but not academic deterioration ($r = .06$, $p < .05$).

Crude Sexual Display ($\alpha = .76$), the third factor, contained 5 items (1 from the SEQ) reflecting exposure and sexual come-ons.

Women were more likely to commit such acts toward men (55.5 percent) than were men alone (2.3 percent) or both genders (17.6 percent). The average level of experiences was somewhat higher than the two previous forms (M = 0.79, SD = 0.68) but very modestly correlated with academic and emotional deterioration (r's = .14 for each, $p < .05$).

Sexualized Environment (α = .74) was the fourth factor. It contained 7 items (2 from the SHOM and 1 from the SEQ) measuring the extent to which the respondent was exposed to dirty jokes and comments or was put down because he was a man. Male respondents were most likely to experience such behaviors from both genders (70 percent) than from just men alone (6.3 percent) or women alone (9.2 percent). The average level of these experiences was higher than for the other forms of sexual harassment that men experienced (M = 0.91, SD = 0.60), and they were moderately correlated with emotional (r = .22, $p < .05$) but not academic deterioration (r = .06, ns).

The MSHE as well as the SHOM show that while women and men's experiences overlap, some are unique to men, such as masculinity teasing. Furthermore, these experiences seem to be reliably measured and show modest association with important outcomes. However, since neither the MSHE nor the SHOM has received extensive research attention, further work is needed to determine the validity of these scales in a variety of settings. Some concern has been raised about whether behavioral-type scales such as the MSHE, SHOM, and SEQ adequately measure sexual harassment experiences (Arvey & Cavanaugh 1995, Wiener & Hurt 2000). None of these measures assess the EEOC definition of sexual harassment, nor do they incorporate aspects of case law that have shaped the court's understanding of illegal sexual harassment. For example, behavioral measures do not necessarily capture the severity and pervasiveness components that are critical to the legal definition. The MSHE, for example, measures behaviors that men may potentially construe as

Table 6.1

Sexual Harassment Surveys: Instructions, Scales, and Response Items

	Merit Systems Protection Board & Department of Defense (1988)[a]	Department of Defense Sexual Experiences Questionnaire (SEQ–DoD)[b]	Sexual Harassment of Men Scale (SHOM)[c]	Men's Sexual Harassment Experiences Scale (MSHE)[d]	Experiences of Sexual Harassment Scale (ESH)[e]	Sexual Harassment Intentions Scale[d]
Instructions	In the past [12 or 24 months] have you experienced any of the following, uninvited, unwanted sexual attention:	How often during the past 12 months have you been in situations . . . where one or more individuals . . . of either gender:	During the past 2 years at work, have any of your supervisors or co-workers:	Not including sexual behavior in a consensual relationship . . . in the past 24 months, I have:	At any time while you have been employed:	To what extent do you believe that the person(s) involved in this event:
Subscales and/or Sample Items	Whistles, calls, hoots, or yells? Sexual teasing, jokes, remarks, or questions? Sexually suggestive looks, gestures, or body language? Letters, telephone calls, or materials of a sexual nature? Pressure for dates? Sexual touching, cornering, pinching, or brushing against?	*Gender Harassment: Sexist Hostility* (e.g., repeatedly told sexual stories or jokes that were offensive to you?) *Gender Harassment: Sexual Hostility* (e.g., whistled, called, or hooted at you in a sexual way?) *Unwanted Sexual Attention* (e.g., made unwanted	*Gender Harassment: Lewd Comments* (e.g., often told offensive or dirty stories or remarks?) *Gender Harassment: Negative Remarks About Men* (e.g., said things to put men down [for example, that men don't make good supervisors?]) *Gender Harassment: Enforcing*	*Coercive Sexual Advances* (e.g., been criticized for refusing sexual advances) *Masculinity Teasing* (e.g., been questioned about my manhood) *Crude Sexual Display* (e.g., had someone expose their genitals to me) *Sexualized Environment* (e.g.,	*Quid Pro Quo* (e.g., have you ever been expected to engage in sexual relations or participate in any other sexual behavior in order to get or keep a job?) *Hostile Work Environment* (e.g., have you ever been subjected to unwelcome sexual advances, requests	*Rejection* (e.g., was trying to insult you?) *Sexual Attraction* (e.g., wanted to establish a sexual relationship with you?) *Joking* (e.g., was having a good time without any bad intent?) *Masculinity Socialization* (e.g., was teaching you a lesson about being a

Attempts to promote participation in sexually oriented activities? Pressure for sexual favors? Actual or attempted rape or sexual assault?	attempts to establish a romantic sexual relationship with you despite your efforts to discourage it? *Sexual Coercion* (e.g., made you feel like you were being bribed with some sort of reward or special treatment to engage in sexual behavior?)	*the Male Gender Role* (e.g., insulted you by saying you were a "fag" or "gay"?) *Unwanted Sexual Attention* (e.g., tried to get you to talk about personal or sexual things when you did not want to?) *Sexual Coercion* (e.g., hinted you might be treated poorly for not doing something sexual?)	been the object of sexually explicit jokes)	for sexual favors, sexual comments, jokes, innuendos, letters, sexually demeaning language, or other kinds of sexual behavior that were severe and pervasive enough to create an intimidating, hostile, or offensive work environment for you?)	man?) *Friendship Socialization* (e.g., considered you to be a close friend?)
Response Scale 1 = never 2 = once 3 = once a month or less 4 = 2–4 times a month 5 = once a week or more	1 = never 2 = once or twice 3 = sometimes 4 = often 5 = very often	1 = never 2 = once or twice 3 = sometimes 4 = often 5 = most of the time	0 = never 1 = once 2 = more than once	0 = no 1 = not sure 2 = yes	1 = not at all 2 = small extent 3 = moderate extent 4 = large extent 5 = very large extent

a Martindale 1991, USMSPB 1995.
b Edwards et al. 1997.
c Waldo et al. 1998.
d Stockdale & Motoike 2000.
e Gutek et al. 2002.

harassing, but high scores do not necessarily indicate that respondents have experienced illegal sexual harassment.

To summarize, extant measures of sexual harassment do not adequately measure the kinds of experiences that men construe as sexually harassing. The SHOM and the MSHE help to bridge that gap, but both rely on behavioral experience methods, like the SEQ, which do not directly assess the important legal requirement of severity and pervasiveness (Weiner & Hurt 2000). Other approaches to measuring sexual harassment that do not rely on behavioral experiences may reveal other understated but important qualities of sexual harassment that are critical to men's as well as women's sexual harassment experiences. Two such approaches, Gutek's Experiences of Sexual Harassment Scale and my team's Sexual Harassment Intentions Scale, are discussed below.

To help reconcile sexual harassment measurement with the legal definition of sexual harassment, Barbara Gutek and her colleagues recently developed a short, 5-item measure that closely parallels the EEOC definition called "Experiences of Sexual Harassment" (Gutek, Stockdale, et al. 2002; see ESH in Table 6.1). Preliminary research using this scale reveals that it produces lower prevalence rates than the SEQ and SHOM, that the gap between ESH scores and labeling one's experiences as sexual harassment is smaller than the gap between SEQ and SHOM scores and labeling; and that the gender difference in ESH scores is larger than the gender difference on the SEQ and SHOM. All these findings are in line with the hypothesis that the ESH is a more accurate measure of "real" sexual harassment experiences than the SEQ or SHOM (and by extension, the MSHE).

Because of the limitations of the SEQ and its progeny in measuring sexual harassment of men, another approach to measuring the dimensions of men's sexual harassment experiences has been developed to measure targets' perceptions of the motives behind the harassment experienced. Stockdale and Motoike (2000) developed a 23-item scale called the Sexual Harassment Intentions Scale, asking respondents (347 college-age men) to rate their perception of the perpetrator's intentions. These questions were in reference to the event the respondent felt had the greatest effect on them (see Table 6.1). Principle Components Analysis (PCA) with Varimax rotation revealed a five-factor solution accounting for 66.8 percent of the variance. The resulting scales were labeled Rejection (a = .94), Sexual Attraction (α = .95), Joking (e.g., α = .83), Masculinity Socialization (α = .77), and Friendship Socialization (e.g., α = .78).

The structure of the Sexual Harassment Intentions Scale supports the notion that men perceive different motives for experiencing harassing behaviors, some of which are benign, such as joking and friendship socialization, and others of which reflect the approach-rejection distinction articulated earlier (i.e., sexual attraction vs. rejection and masculinity socialization). Although men endorsed friendship socialization (M = 2.02, SD = 1.22) and sexual attraction (M = 2.16, SD = 1.29) motives for their harassment experiences more than rejection (M = 0.52, SD = 0.87) or masculinity socialization (M = 0.52, SD = 0.79), the latter two scales were more strongly correlated with academic deterioration (r = .35; r = .45, respectively) and emotional deterioration (r = .41; r = .30, respectively) than any of the other intention scales (the next highest correlation was r = .14 between sexual attraction and academic deterioration) or between any of the MSHE scales and these outcomes (reported earlier). Thus, negative consequences to men only occurred when they had experienced rejection-based forms of sexual harassment.

Further analyses (Stockdale & Gandolfo 2001) revealed that men who had experienced harassment that they considered to be motivated by rejection experienced greater academic deterioration if they actively complained about the harassment (e.g., made a complaint or told the person to stop) than if they did nothing. This finding lends credence to the idea that rejection-based harassment is used as a tool to punish male sex-role deviance and to shape men's masculine behavior. Men who complained about being harassed may have been further ridiculed for not being able to put up with the teasing and taunting, which then may have led to greater academic deterioration. This, however, is only speculation because the data do not clearly reveal what happened to men who complained about being harassed.

THE HARM OF SEXUAL HARASSMENT AGAINST MEN

Previous research has tended to conclude that men do not suffer from unwanted social-sexual experiences (sexual harassment) nearly to the extent that women do. Gutek (1985), in her community study of Los Angeles County residents, for example, reported that men who indicated having such experiences initiated by women mostly dismissed them as trivial or funny. In one of Fitzgerald's first comprehensive surveys of sexual harassment using an early version of the SEQ (Fitzgerald et al. 1988), on 15 of 20 items that could be analyzed, women were significantly more likely than men to have had an unwanted social-sexual experience. The items that produced no gender differences were either rare experiences (such as being rewarded for sexual cooperation) or gender harassment experiences. The authors concluded that men are quite unlikely to be harassed—a conclusion reached by almost all other sexual harassment survey researchers (e.g., USMSPB 1981, 1988, 1995). Finally, using sophisticated statistical techniques, Donovan and Drasgow (1999) found that men do not experience the kinds of gender harassment that women experience, such as "being treated differently because of your sex," "experiencing offensive sexist remarks," "putting you down or being condescending to you because of your sex," and "being stared at, leered at, or ogled in a way that made you feel uncomfortable," even if they are harassed in other ways.

I do not refute these findings or interpretations of them; instead, I raise two seemingly contradictory possibilities. First, men's sexual harassment experiences and the resulting damages may have been underestimated, especially when research procedures rely on female-centered instruments, such as the SEQ. Rejection behaviors or intentions, especially those likely to be committed by other men, can more fully account for men's sexual harassment experiences and consequences. Second, even if men's harassment experiences are more accurately assessed, I would argue that the harm to men, on average, will not be as bad as the harm of sexually harassing experiences to women. This argument is stipulated on the context of male dominance and the general prevalence of sexism and violence toward women—a system that in general is oppressive to women.

Two interesting empirical studies showcase the harm that women suffer from gender harassment or from merely being in a potentially harassing environment. Parker and Griffin (2002) surveyed 262 female and 315 male police officers in the United Kingdom about their experiences with gender harassment, perceptions that women police officers are not accepted, and experiences of work-family conflict. Among women, each of these stressors was significantly related to psychological distress. Furthermore, for women the pressure to overperform in their jobs fully mediated the relations between gender harassment and perceptions of nonacceptance with psychological distress. In other words, women who experienced behavior and attitudes that were rejecting of their presence in the police force felt the pressure to overperform in their jobs in order to "prove" themselves. This, in turn, increased psychological distress. Men's experiences of gender harassment were moderately lower than women's[4] but were only slightly correlated with overperformance demands ($r = .12$, $p = .05$) and not correlated with psychological distress. Thus, gender harassment did not produce the same level of harm in men as it did in women.

Researchers at the University of Illinois (Glomb et al. 1997) examined the effect on women of being in a work environment where other women were sexually harassed. The authors adopted the term *ambient sexual harassment* to describe the indirect effect that harassment of other people has on women themselves. After accounting for other forms of stress and any individual harassment participants experienced, ambient sexual harassment had detrimental influences on both job satisfaction and psychological well-being. The authors did not include men in their research, so it is uncertain whether ambient sexual harassment has similar effects on men. Nonetheless, this study makes clear that the damages of even subtle sexual harassment are far-reaching for women. Furthermore, it seems doubtful that men would suffer these same effects.

DISCUSSION

The approach-rejection theory of sexual harassment posits that sexual harassment is a function of sexism that operates to maintain a system of masculine dominance and feminine subordinance. Harassers have two broad ways to achieve their goals: reducing employees to sexual objects (approach harassment) or using sexually enriched behavior to police objectionable gender behavior (rejection harassment). Rejection-based harassment closely parallels the concept of gender harassment. Arguing that power holders (i.e., men) resist the expansion of traditional gender roles or the intrusion of women or feminine attributes into masculine domains, such as women moving into male-dominated occupations, but also fear repercussions from engaging in blatant sexual harassment, Miller (1997) found that men in traditionally masculine occupations (e.g., the military) engage in a wide variety of covert forms of gender harassment to dissuade women from moving into these roles. Miller also referred to instances of men using these tactics against other men who displayed undesirable gender qualities, such as being weak. Both approach and rejection harassment are harmful to women and are often conflated, but against men, these forms are more distinct. Focusing on sexual harassment of men elucidates the distinction between approach and rejection harassment and contributes to the literature showing that sexual harassment does not have to involve sexual intent in order to be harmful, discriminatory, and sexist (e.g. Gutek 1985, Parker & Griffin 2002).

The research that my colleagues and I have conducted, albeit exploratory, demonstrates that the unwanted social-sexual experiences of men fall within these two broad categories. When both same- and other-gender harassment is assessed and the survey instruments adequately measure both rejection and approach forms of harassing behavior, it becomes clear that men can be the victims of sexual harassment (particularly gender harassment) that, like women's sexual harassment experiences, enforces male dominance. We found that same-sex, rejection-based harassment of men consisted of behaviors that either ridicule, demean, and punish men who appear to violate desired masculine gender expressions, or that socialize men to adopt hypermasculine, heterosexist gender-role identities. Furthermore, male targets who believed that their perpetrators had such motives experienced worse emotional and academic outcomes than did men who believed their perpetrators had sexual attraction motives (or other motives). Although more research is needed to examine the validity of the scales that were introduced in this chapter (MSHE and Sexual Harassment Intentions Scale), as well as to further explore the conditions that facilitate sexual harassment of men, we believe this research should be guided by the approach-rejection theory.

FUTURE RESEARCH

The approach-rejection theory and the study of men's sexual harassment experiences in general have many fruitful avenues for future research. Psychometric research to develop and validate inclusive measures of sexual harassment is needed. The SEQ and its progeny have stimulated considerable research on the nature of sexual harassment experiences, but it remains problematic for measuring men's sexual harassment experiences, as well as for distinguishing illegal sexual harassment from other forms of social-sexual behavior in the workplace (Gutek et al. 2002). Furthermore, Gutek, Doumba, and Murphy (2002) have raised several concerns about the utility of the SEQ, noting that its developers frequently change features of the scale, such as the wording and number of items, the item stem (which brackets the time frame respondents use to assess the amount of unwanted social sexual behavior they have experienced), and the item response scale (e.g, from a two- or three-point response scale to a five-point scale).

More research is also needed to examine the type of harm—if any—and the mechanisms that create harm to men who experience either approach or rejection forms of sexual harassment. If gender harassment causes psychological distress for women because it creates a demand to overperform in their jobs (Parker & Griffin 2002), what harm do harassed men experience and why? Gender harassment pressures women to overperform because they are being tested in a work environment where they perceive they are not welcomed. Men are not likely to feel unwelcome in a work environment, especially if it is a male-dominated environment, but they may feel pressured to conform to hypermasculine, heterosexist norms that may conflict with their gender role or values. Therefore, it is possible that measures of role conflict may mediate the association between rejection-based harassment and psychological distress for men. Similarly, efforts are needed to explore the impact that approach-based harassment has on men. I suspect that the degree and type of harm vary sharply by whether the approach harassment is committed by women or by men, since many men fear and abhor even mild forms of homosexual advances (Fernald 1995).

CONCLUSION

Sexual harassment is a "technology of sexism" perpetuating masculine hegemony. This chapter demonstrates that sexual harassment can be more fully understood if the concepts of approach- and rejection-based harassment are distinguished. Furthermore, it suggests that men co-opt other men to this hegemonic system through acts of rejection-based sexual harassment. Future research needs to develop further and validate measures of the approach-rejection theory with regard to men's sexual harassment experiences, and to test hypotheses that derive from the approach-rejection theory.

Practically, I call for sexual harassment trainers, policy makers, and human resource professionals to recognize both the variety and sources of sexual harassment against both men and women and to understand how the approach-rejection distinction helps to particularly reveal the nature of same-sex sexual harassment that is particularly onerous for men. Finally, I call upon researchers, practitioners, and policy makers to understand that male dominance and masculine hegemony remain the root cause of sexual harassment for both women and men.

NOTES

1. This was a random survey of military personnel, with $N = 20,249$.
2. McWilliams had a learning disability and arrested cognitive and emotional development, and Goluszek had lived his entire life with his mother, had little to no sexual experience, and blushed easily at sexual comments.
3. $M = 0.39$, $SD = 0.41$, on a scale from 0 (never) to 2 (more than once).
4. The effect size, D, for the difference in women's and men's mean gender harassment scores was .22, which is considered to be a small effect size (Lipsey 1990).

REFERENCES

Arvey, R. D., and M. A. Cavanaugh. 1995. Using surveys to assess the prevalence of sexual harassment: Some methodological problems. *Journal of Social Issues* 51:39–52.

Bargh, J. A., and P. Raymond. 1995. The naïve misuse of power: Nonconscious sources of sexual harassment. *Journal of Social Issues* 51:85–96.

Berdahl, L., V. Magley, and C. Waldo. 1996. The sexual harassment of men? Exploring the concept with theory and data. *Psychology of Women Quarterly* 20:527–547.

Chiapuzio v. BLT Operating Corp. 826 F. Supp. 1334, 1337–38 (D. Wyo. 1993).

Cotton, D. J., and A. N. Groth. 1982. Inmate rape: Prevention and intervention. *Journal of Prison and Jail Health* 2:47–57.

Donovan, M. A., and F. Drasgow. 1999. Do men's and women's experiences of sexual harassment differ? An examination of the differential test functioning of the Sexual Experiences Questionnaire. *Military Psychology* 11 (3): 265–282.

DuBois, C., D. Knapp, R. Faley, and G. Kustis. 1998. An empirical examination of same- and other-gender sexual harassment in the workplace. *Sex Roles* 39:731–749.

Edwards, J. E., T. Elig, D. Edwards, and R. Riemer. 1997. The 1995 armed forces harassment survey: Administration, datasets, and codebook (Report No. 95–015, DTIC/NTIS No. AD A323 945). Arlington, Va.: Defense Manpower Data Center.

Estrich, S. 1991. Sex at work. *Stanford Law Review* 43:813–860.

Fernald, J. L. 1995. Interpersonal sexism. In *The social psychology of interpersonal discrimination*, ed. B. Lott and D. Maluso, 80–117. New York: Guilford.

Fitzgerald, L. F., M. Gelfand, and F. Drasgow. 1995. Measuring sexual harassment: Theoretical and psychometric advances. *Basic and Applied Social Psychology* 17 (4): 425–445.

Fitzgerald, L. F., and S. Shullman. 1985. *The development and validation of an objectively scored measure of sexual harassment.* Paper presented at the annual meeting of the American Psychological Association, Los Angeles, California.

Fitzgerald, L. F., S. Shullman, N. Bailey, M. Richards, J. Swecker, Y. Gold, M. Ormerod, and L. Weitzman. 1988. The incidence and dimensions of sexual harassment in academia and the workplace. *Journal of Vocational Behavior* 32:152–175.

Foote, W. E., and J. Goodman-Delahunty. 1999. Same-sex harassment: Implications of the Oncale decision for forensic evaluation of plaintiffs. *Behavioral Sciences and the Law* 5:123–139.

Franke, K. M. 1997. What's wrong with sexual harassment? *Stanford Law Review* 49:691–772.

Glomb, T. M., W. Richman, C. Hulin, F. Drasgow, K. Schneider, and L. Fitzgerald. 1997. Ambient sexual harassment: An integrated model of antecedents and consequences. *Organizational Behavior and Human Decision Processes* 71:309–328.

Goluszek v. H.P. Smith. 697 F. Supp. 1452 (N.D. Ill. 1988).

Gutek, B. A. 1985. *Sex and the workplace: Impact of sexual behavior and harassment of women, men, and organizations.* San Francisco: Jossey-Bass.

Gutek, B. A., B. Doumba, and R. Murphy. 2002. *A review and critique of the Sexual Experiences Questionnaire (SEQ).* Submitted for publication.

Gutek, B. A., M. Stockdale, R. Done, and S. Swindler. 2002. *The Experiences of Sexual Harassment Scale: A short measure of sexual harassment based on a legal definition.* Submitted for publication.

Herek, G. M. 1986. The social psychology of homophobia: Toward a practical theory. *Review of Law and Social Change* 14:923–934.

———. 1990. The context of anti-gay violence. *Journal of Interpersonal Violence* 5:316–333.

Lipsey, M. W. 1990. *Design sensitivity: Statistical power for experimental research.* Newbury Park, Calif.: Sage.

Lobel, S. A. 1993. Sexuality at work: Where do we go from here? *Journal of Vocational* Behavior 42:136–152.

MacKinnon, C. 1979. *Sexual harassment of working women.* New Haven, Conn.: Yale University Press.

Martindale, M. 1991. *Sexual harassment in the military: 1988 report.* Arlington, Va.: Defense Manpower Data Center.

McWilliams v. Fairfax County Board of Supervisors. 72 F.3d 1191 (4th Cir.), cert. denied, 117 S. Ct. 72 (1996).

Miller, L. L. 1997. Not just weapons of the weak: Gender harassment as a form of protest for army men. *Social Psychology Quarterly* 60:32–51.

Mosher, D. L. and M. Sirkin. 1984. Measuring a macho personality constellation. *Journal of Research in Personality* 18:150–163.

Nacci, P. L., and T. Kane. 1983. The incidence of sex and sexual aggression in federal prisons. *Federal Probation* 47:31–36.

Oncale v. Sundowner Offshore Services, Inc. 118 S. Ct. 998 (1998).

Parker, S. K., and M. Griffin. 2002. What is so bad about a little name-calling? Negative consequences of gender harassment for over-performance demands and distress. *Journal of Occupational Health Psychology* 7: 195–210.

Polly v. Houston Lighting and Power Co. 825 F. Supp. 135 (S. D. Tex. 1993).

Quinn, B. A. 2002. Sexual harassment and masculinity: The power and meaning of "girl watching." *Gender and Society* 16:386–402.

Stermac, L., P. Sheridan, A. Davidson, and S. Dunn. 1996. Sexual assault of adult males. *Journal of Interpersonal Violence* 11:52–64.

Stockdale, M. S., and C. Gandolfo. 2001. *Men's sexual harassment experiences and the effectiveness of coping strategies.* Unpublished manuscript, Department of Psychology, Southern Illinois University, Carbondale.

Stockdale, M. S., C. Gandolfo, R. Schneider, and F. Cao. 2003. Perceptions of sexual harassment of men. Submitted for publication.

Stockdale, M. S., and J. Motoike. 2000. *The Men's Sexually Harassment Experiences Scale: Development and validation study*. Paper presented at the 2000 meeting of the Society for the Psychological Study of Social Issues. Minneapolis, Minnesota.

Stockdale, M. S., M. Wood, and L. Batra. 1999. The sexual harassment of men: Evidence for a broader theory of sexual harassment and sex discrimination. *Psychology, Public Policy and Law* 5:630–664.

Till, F. J. 1980. *Sexual harassment: A report on the sexual harassment of students*. Washington, D.C.: National Advisory Council of Women's Educational Programs.

U.S. Merit Systems Protection Board (USMSPB). 1981. *Sexual harassment in the federal workplace: Is it a problem?* Washington, D.C.: U.S. Government Printing Office.

———. 1988. *Sexual harassment in the federal workplace: An update.* Washington, D.C.: U.S. Government Printing Office.

———. 1995. *Sexual harassment in the federal workplace: Trends, progress, and continuing challenges.* Washington, D.C.: U.S. Government Printing Office.

Wade, J. C., and C. Brittan-Powell. 2001. Men's attitudes toward race and gender equity: The importance of masculinity ideology, gender-related traits, and reference group dependence. *Psychology of Men and Masculinity* 2:42–50.

Waldo, C. R., J. Berdahl, and L. Fitzgerald. 1998. Are men sexually harassed? If so, by whom? *Law and Human Behavior* 22:59–79.

Wiener, R. L., and L. Hurt. 2000. How do people evaluate social sexual conduct at work? A psycholegal model. *Journal of Applied Psychology* 85: 75–85.

Williams, C. L., P. Giuffre, and K. Dellinger. 1999. Sexuality in the workplace: Organizational control, sexual harassment, and the pursuit of pleasure. *Annual Review of Sociology* 25:73–93.

THE "REASONABLE WOMAN" AND
UNREASONABLE MEN
Gendered Discourses in
Sexual Harassment Litigation

Michael S. Kimmel and Tyson Smith

On October 13, 2002, the cover of the *New York Times Magazine* portrayed a white male corporate executive taunting a fellow male employee: "Hey girlie boy! Too bad you couldn't close that deal. I guess this is a man's job huh? Why don't you just wear a dress to work? You'd sure look cute in one! ha ha ha ha ha ha ha ha ha ha!" At the bottom of the cover page, a box announced the title of the article: "When Men Taunt Men, Is It Sexual Harassment?" (Talbot 2002).

The answer was a qualified maybe. Margaret Talbot, the article's author, is as contemptuous of hypermasculine jerks swaggering through the workplace "bagging" their fellow male employees as she is of overly litigious wimps who might be a little light in their loafers. In her rush to decertify hostile environment claims by men against other men, Talbot conflated peer harassment with harassment of subordinates by their supervisors (all the cases were the latter, although she continually assumed they were the former), and she ignored corporate and white-collar settings to suggest that males who took offense were really bridling at "normal" working-class shop floor antics. (Letter writers to the paper in subsequent weeks both reproduced her myopia and pointed out her blind spots.) "If a guy doesn't want to get goosed or be called a girlie boy, then he shouldn't go to work at an auto dealership or an oil field," wrote one. But another reminded Talbot that sexual harassment is not about sex, but about power; others applied that gender analysis to the problem at hand. "[W]omen know that without sexual harassment laws, the consciousness of the workplace would never have been raised," wrote one woman. "Now men are willing to stand up to the bullies who define masculinity in such a negative way" (Talbot 2002).

Talbot did, however, raise the issue, and she described cases that—were they directed against anyone else (i.e., women, Jews, blacks, ethnic minorities)—would have been immediately apparent as harassment, and the perpetrators subject to harsh penalties.

In that sense, this current discussion eloquently illustrates the case we will make in this essay: harassment of men in the workplace is less visible because the standards used to determine harassment are derived from hegemonic notions of masculinity, and the criteria deployed in the targeting of victims are equally concerned with the maintenance of those hegemonic standards. When men establish a pattern of behavior that ridicules a male coworker for being effeminate or asexual, or even for simply not taking "sufficient" interest in sexually explicit humor or material, it is not simply a case of men behaving badly at work. It is a case of "gender policing"—the deliberate enforcement of gender norms by other men, a means of extracting compliance by targeting those who do not submit. Gender policing is the basis for much of same-sex sexual harassment (Brake 1999).

We argue that laws prohibiting sexual harassment open up opportunities for women to expand the range of behaviors traditionally defined as "feminine"—thus enabling women to enter fields previously closed to them, to be protected from hostile speech or actions, and to be protected from unwanted sexual solicitation. But these same laws that have expanded the range of opportunities for women to be women also narrow the opportunities for men to be men; that is, they replace the particular with the universal, reinscribing one norm of masculinity as the single masculine norm. Although recent court decisions suggest that the gender policing that constitutes much same-sex sexual harassment is finally achieving some legal scrutiny, we believe that the norms against which both male and female behaviors are measured remain unexamined, and therefore problematic.

We believe that this gender myopia results, in part, from the structural problems endemic to a sexual harassment legal code that relies on Title VII as its foundation, but also from the more sociological processes that reproduce privilege by using the particular standards of the privilege as the standards against which all "others" are measured.

SEXUAL HARASSMENT

Initially, sexual harassment cases only involved women being harassed by men. Sexual harassment was seen as adversely affecting women's equality in employment in two ways: (1) through "quid pro quo," in which a woman's employment situation is dependent upon her consenting to sexual activity, or her employment situation is adversely affected by her refusal to do so; and (2) through a "hostile environment," which takes as sexual harassment any set of activities or utterances that constitute a pattern that will adversely affect women's employment situation by making them afraid or uncomfortable. A supervisor typically violated the former provision, thus making sexual harassment an abuse of power. The latter, however, was often undertaken by male colleagues and coworkers who resented the woman's entry into the workforce.[1]

In this chapter we are concerned with the "hostile environment" form of sexual harassment, both for women and for men. While many commentators frame same-sex sexual harassment as an issue about a gay male supervisor harassing a straight or gay subordinate, these cases are rare when compared to same-sex sexual harassment because of gender.

Court adjudication of sexual harassment typically often fell to the plaintiff making a case that her employment situation was adversely affected by the behavior, either from supervisors or from coworkers. Traditionally, the court had applied a "reasonable person" standard to discern whether, in fact, harassment had taken place: would an objective bystander, observing the events, perceive it as harassment? However, a breakthrough circuit court case, *Ellison v. Brady* (1991), found that the "reasonable person" was actually a "gendered" observer and that the gender of the person was a man. Thus the court reasoned that it would use a "reasonable woman" standard: would a woman, similarly situated, perceive the interaction as harassment? As Judge Beezer, the circuit judge writing the Ellison opinion, stated:

> We believe that in evaluating the severity and pervasiveness of sexual harassment, we should focus on the perspective of the victim. If we only examined whether a reasonable person would engage in allegedly harassing conduct, we would run the risk of reinforcing the prevailing level of discrimination. Harassers could continue to harass merely because a particular discriminatory practice was common, and victims of harassment would have no remedy. We therefore prefer to analyze the harassment from the victim's perspective. A complete understanding of the victim's view requires, among other things, an analysis of the different perspectives of men and women. . . . We adopt the perspective of a reasonable woman primarily because we believe that a sex-blind reasonable person standard tends to be male-biased and tends to systematically ignore the experiences of women. (*Ellison v. Brady* 1991)

While this was a breakthrough for women—adjudication of cases would henceforth be based not on the intention of the actor but on the experience of the acted upon—it also enshrined a basic, unalterable difference in the way men and women would likely perceive an interaction. Men, the courts assumed, would not find such behavior to be harassment because they would see it as "natural" or an "inevitable" part of the working relationship (that men would always seek to sexualize any encounter with women) and could therefore not be reasonable enough to perceive it as harassment. By implication, "reasonable" women replaced "unreasonable" men. Men would not see the harassment because, as far as they could see, it was just "normal" masculinity in action. "Men" may be different from "women," the courts reasoned, but all "men" are the same.

Such a move was not without its problems for women. Adler and Peirce (1993) note that such a standard will inevitably shift as societal attitudes about women change. However, since this breakthrough case, sexual harassment cases have continued to be adjudicated according to the reasonable woman standard. In the remainder of this paper, we discuss some of the consequences of this form of adjudication, specifically in assumptions about men.

SAMENESS AND DIFFERENCE

While workplace discrimination cases stem from a definition of equality that requires that we treat those who are alike as if they were alike, sexual harassment proceeds from different assumptions about equality, seeming to recognize essential differences and therefore relying on the notion that equality also requires that we treat "unalikes" as if they were unalike. Many commentators have observed that this dual definition of equality—treating alikes alike, and treating unalikes unalike—has put the target population, the population that is injured by the discrimination, in a certain legal bind. Sometimes they must minimize difference in order to be treated equally, or the same; at other times, they must maximize difference in order to be treated equally, or differently. We are not using the term *equality* as a synonym for *fairness* or *justice,* which are moral and ideological terms. Instead, we are arguing that the meaning of equal treatment with regard to gender is confounded by the fact that the law is unable to account for actual differences between women and men—which would mean that similar treatment might be discriminatory—while at the same time remaining cognizant of the similarities—which would mean that treating them differently would be discriminatory (see Smith & Kimmel 2004).

For example, efforts to gain access to the workplace must emphasize that female workers are no different from male workers, while other cases maintain that pregnant female workers are indeed different from male workers. In either case, sexual harassment perpetuates and reproduces gender inequality; it serves to "perpetuate, enforce, and police a set of gender norms that seek to feminize women and masculinize men" (Frank 1997:696). This has put women—and gays and lesbians—in a difficult position, best expressed in the title of a law review article by feminist theorist Jewelle Gomez: "Repeat After Me: We Are Different. We Are the Same" (Gomez 1986). But rarely, if ever, is the comparative question fully articulated. Different from whom? The same as whom?

The answer is: *men*. In all these cases, men serve as the unexamined norm against which women are measured. Where women have sought access, they are to be treated no differently than men are treated. Where women have sought to acknowledge the specificity of their experiences, they are to be treated differently than men are treated. But how are men to be treated? What are men like in the first place? These questions are assumed, but never answered.

Efforts to end gender discrimination have enlarged the scope of women's activity and successfully replaced stereotypic definitions of femininity with an understanding of variation and diversity among women. The courts have demonstrated in their more recent record of cases related to gender that there are various ways to construe the meaning of womanhood; not all women are mothers, and not all women are workers. Many women are nurturing and caring; however, some are interested in combat and uninterested in having children.

Meanwhile, the courts have stuck to a one-dimensional understanding of masculinity; its definition has been reified into one normative construction, anchored by traditional stereotypes. The gender-neutral standard is a male standard—a hypothetical man who conforms to a "hegemonic" version of masculinity (see Connell 1995). This hegemonic model represents the normative standard, an aggregation of ideal traits, which then becomes the normative standard against which other gender constructions might be measured; it is, in the words of Virginia Woolf, "the perfect type of which all the others are imperfect adumbrations" (Woolf [1938] 1966:142).

Nonhegemonic models of masculinity are thereby problematized, and embedded but unarticulated assumptions about masculinity reproduce both male domination and the domination of hegemonic masculinity over other masculinities. One study by psychologists found that victimized men in same-sex sexual harassment cases do not fit their offenders' gender-role stereotype of "heterosexual hypermasculinity," the exaggerated normative construction (Stockdale, Visio, & Batra 1999). Sexual harassment thus also teaches men what type of man should be at the top of the hierarchy. Men experiencing same-sex sexual harassment tend to be slightly younger, to have less seniority, to be lower paid, and to not hold a supervisory position compared to men who experienced opposite-sex sexual harassment or men who experienced no sexual harassment (Stockdale et al. 1999).

The process by which hegemonic masculinity is reproduced has economic consequences as well as psychological ones. Since both women and men are measured against these standards, the criteria for raises, promotions, and the assignment of important clients or cases will reflect such "gender-neutral" standards for excellence. Performance evaluations, job security, and benefits will all depend on these criteria. Schultz (2001:2), for example, sees that "the day to day interactions through which co-workers create relationships that mark some people as insiders and other people as outsiders are a crucial part of the dynamic that sustains sex segregation and hierarchy in the workplace. Harassment is not always about who is on top and who is on bottom; it is also about who is 'in' and who is 'out.'"

Nor are the consequences—economic or psychological—symmetrical for gender-nonconforming women and gender-nonconforming men. There is differential treatment for men and women who diverge from their gender expectations. This differential treatment—between a man who acts feminine and a woman who acts masculine—"marks the continuing devaluation, in life and in law, of qualities deemed feminine. The man who exhibits feminine qualities is doubly despised, for manifesting disfavored qualities and for descending from his masculine gender privilege to do so. The masculine woman today is more readily accepted. Wanting to be masculine is understandable; it can be a step up for a woman, and the qualities associated with masculinity are also associated with success" (Case 1995:2).

To date, legal reasoning in sexual harassment cases has centered on women's need for protection from men's "natural" predatory impulses. This is typically referred to as the "sexual desire-dominance" paradigm (see, for example, Schultz 1998). Boys will be boys, the thinking goes, but they should not be so when they are around girls. When boys are around other boys, or men around other men (as is the case in *Goluszek*), however, it is a different matter, as we will see.

By examining five pivotal cases in sexual harassment law, we will argue that the courts challenge gender stereotypes for women by disaggregating the definition of femininity, but they rely on a monolithic understanding of masculinity, making it more deeply entrenched as normative and thus, ironically, maintaining the dynamics of male domination that lead to harassment in the first place. Only by disaggregating masculinities can gender discrimination be adequately addressed and adjudicated. We conclude with one hopeful direction that the courts appear to be taking.

STEREOTYPES ABOUT MASCULINITY

Gender discrimination is not permitted when it is based on stereotypes and not on real differences; however, in practice, this mandate appears to apply only to women. When men are considered, the courts often rely on very traditional and stereotypic definitions of masculinity.

This traditional normative construction of masculinity consists of several elements, cleverly codified by Robert Brannon and Deborah David (1975) in the mid-1970s (and barely modified since then). These include (1) "No Sissy Stuff"—the relentless repudiation of the feminine; (2) the "Big Wheel"—masculinity implies wealth, power, and status; (3) the "Sturdy Oak"—emotional impermeability, inexpressiveness, reliability in a crisis; and (4) "Give 'em Hell"—daring, risk taking, and aggression (Brannon & David 1975).

Textbooks on men's lives (see, for example, Doyle 1989) use these elements as organizational framing devices; psychological inventories of gender identity disaggregate them into a series of adjectives associated with masculinity, including *aggressive, ambitious, analytical, assertive, athletic, competitive, dominant, forceful, independent, individualistic, self-reliant, self-sufficient,* and *strong* (see, for example, O'Neil, Good, & Holmes 1995).

At the same time, social scientists have come to think of masculinities in a very different way, based on the differences among men. We understand that what constitutes masculinity varies across cultures, over time, throughout the life course, and among a variety of different groups of men at any one time. The pluralized term *masculinities* has come into use to underscore these differences. (See, for example, Brod 1994, Connell 1995, Kimmel 1994, 1995; but see also Hearn 1996 for a critique of how the "masculinities" may also obscure power dynamics among various definitions.)

Equally important, though, is the understanding that this stereotypic construction does correspond to the hegemonic definition of masculinity (cf. Connell 1995). This hegemonic definition becomes the standard against which all other masculinities are to be measured and evaluated. It is deployed coercively against gender-nonconforming men, and comparatively to maintain socially created differences between women and men as natural, and therefore legitimate. Consequently, by substituting the singular normative definition (hegemonic) for the multiple "normal" distribution, male domination remains unchallenged, both as a model against which women must array themselves and also as the model for all men.

In the cases that follow, we will see how the court's legal reasoning reinscribes each of these normative dimensions of masculinity and applies them to both women and other men. This is not an argument that men are therefore the "victims" of some version of reverse discrimination. In fact, ours is exactly the opposite argument. We maintain that the invisibility of masculinities in legal discourse about gender will reveal how gender-nonconforming men are misunderstood, disregarded, and dismissed, and how the normative standard of masculinity ends up harming both women and men.

Below, we examine several landmark sexual harassment cases. The first of these cases, *Jenson v. Eleveth Mines*, was the first class action sexual harassment case in American history, and it dragged through the courts for twenty-five years. This was in part because no one seemed to agree on the standards to be used in adjudicating it. Our next case, *Bethel School District No. 403 v. Fraser* (1986), concerns protecting women and girls from offensive speech or offensive behavior because women and girls are different from men and boys. The next two cases, *Goluszek v. H. P. Smith* (1988) and *Polly v. Houston Lighting and Power Company* (1993), describe the application of these assumptions to cases of male-male sexual harassment. Implicit are assumptions about men and masculinities that were never addressed—assumptions that turn out to be empirically false. From its earlier decisions that blamed the victims of male-to-male harassment, the court has, since its 1998 landmark decision in Oncale, begun to understand the multiple meanings of masculinities. We conclude with some thoughts on these same-sex sexual harassment cases.

OPPOSITE-SEX SEXUAL HARASSMENT
Jenson v. Eleveth Mines
Lois Jenson worked at *Eleveth Mines* in the northern Minnesota "Iron Range." As soon as she arrived at the plant, crude graphic

pictures and words proliferated; posters and calendars of nude women were hung in plain sight, almost like badges of honor among the men. Verbal teasing became physical contact that increasingly became violent. Other signs ranged from a male pretending to perform oral sex on a sleeping woman coworker to a man touching a woman . . . to women being presented with various dildos, one of which was named "Big Red" (Bingham & Gansler 2002:57–58).

The court concluded that these constituted sexual harassment. In fact, the creation and maintenance of a hostile environment were business as usual at the plant, designed, the court concluded, to "inform women that they were perceived primarily as sexual objects and inferior to men" (Bingham & Gansler 2002:272). The court found the harassment to be so severe that some of the seventeen eventual plaintiffs carried knives to work for self-protection and several were forced to go out on disability because of depression. However, the court awarded only minuscule damages and, in effect, limited the ability of a defendant to obtain emotional distress recovery in a sexual harassment case.

But what did such a view of women imply about men? How were men supposed to behave? By seeking to protect women from such an environment, the court actually reinscribed the behavior as "masculine." Eleveth Mines "is a male dominated environment . . . in terms of the sexualized nature of the workplace. . . . Male-focused references to sex and to women as sexual objects have persisted throughout the time that women have worked [there]" (Bingham & Gansler 2002:271). A later appeals decision found that "for generations the iron mining industry on the Iron Range was dominated by males who were products of a culture"—in other words, this was just men acting like men (p. 351). Permitting women to be "different" from men in the workplace assumed that all men were basically the same as the other harassing men at the plant.

Although the courts were incapable of recognizing this, some of the male workers themselves did. The men described pressure from other men to be aggressive toward the women. "If I walked into a room with four or five guys sitting on chairs and a guy got up and gave me his chair," commented one woman, "one guy would say, 'What are you giving her your chair for? Are you fucking her?' In order to be nice to a woman you had to be fucking her" (p. 57). After the case was formally adjudicated and eventually settled, the men reflected on the verdicts. "A lot of good people's images have been hurt because we were all grouped together in this case as being animals. There were only a select few that treated women that way but we all got the rap for it" (p. 381).

Bethel School District No. 403 v. Fraser

This case involves a high school student in Washington State who made a speech at a voluntary school assembly on behalf of a friend who was running for student body president. The assembly was held during school hours and was attended by approximately six hundred students, many of whom were fourteen-year-olds. During the entire speech, Fraser referred to his candidate in terms of an elaborate, graphic, and explicit sexual metaphor. Some of the students at the assembly hooted and yelled during the speech, some mimicked the sexual activities alluded to in the speech, and others appeared to be bewildered and embarrassed. Among his comments, Fraser said:

> I know a man who is firm—he's firm in his pants, he's firm in his shirt, his character is firm—but most of all, his belief in you, the students of Bethel, is firm. . . . Jeff Kuhlman is a man who takes his point and pounds it in. If necessary, he'll take an issue and nail it to the wall. He doesn't attack things in spurts—he drives hard, pushing and pushing until finally—he succeeds. . . . Jeff is a man who will go to the very end—even the climax, for each and every one of you. (*Bethel* 1986:688)

The morning after the assembly, the assistant principal called Fraser into her office and notified him that the school considered his speech to have been a violation of the school's "disruptive-conduct rule," which prohibited conduct that substantially interfered with the educational process, including the use of obscene, profane language or gestures. After he admitted that he deliberately used sexual innuendo in the speech, he was informed that he would be suspended for three days and that his name would be removed from the list of candidates for graduation speaker at the school's commencement exercises. Fraser filed suit in federal district court, alleging a violation of his First Amendment right to freedom of speech. The court held that the school's sanctions violated the First Amendment, that the school's disruptive-conduct rule was unconstitutionally vague and overbroad, and that the removal of Fraser's name from the graduation speaker's list violated the Due Process Clause of the Fourteenth Amendment. The Supreme Court reversed that decision. The opinion of the Court, delivered by Justice Burger and joined by four other judges, stated: "These fundamental values of 'habits and manners of civility' must, of course, include tolerance of divergent political and religious views, even when the views expressed may be unpopular. But these 'fundamental' values must also take into account consideration of the sensibilities of others, and in the case of a school, the sensibilities of fellow students" (*Bethel* 1986: 678).

Most revealing, however, was Burger's reasoning about why such sexual speech should be curtailed:

> The pervasive sexual innuendo in Fraser's speech was plainly offensive to both teachers and students—indeed to any mature person. By glorifying male sexuality, and in its verbal content, the speech was acutely insulting to teenage girl students. The speech could well be seriously damaging to its less mature audience, many of whom were only 14 years old and on the threshold of awareness of human sexuality. (*Bethel* 1986:678)

In addition to the fact that such a decision may be offensive to some teenage girl students who feel that they need no protection from lewd and lascivious descriptions of male sexuality, Burger's comments naturalized a specific form of male sexuality as normal.

The Court thus reinforced stereotypical notions of women as having no sexual agency, and reinforced sexuality as a male domain. Burger's condemnation of "glorified male sexuality" admits to little, if any, variation among men in how they choose to express themselves sexually.

Burger's statement reflects unexamined inequality based on gender. Male sexuality is almost always glorified. It is the standard by which we understand and define sex. As Catharine MacKinnon states, "the fact that male power has power means that the interests of male sexuality construct what sexuality as such means, including the standard way it is allowed and recognized to be felt and expressed and experienced, in a way that determines women's biographies, including sexual ones" (MacKinnon 1989). This is not to suggest that Burger is a radical feminist deconstructing male dominance. But his comments bring to light the ways in which male sexuality is continually glorified and relatively unchallenged, rarely taking into account "the consideration of the sensibilities of others," i.e., women and girls! Ironically, in an attempt to tame the repercussions of a society that confounds and recklessly promotes sex, Burger has inadvertently implicated and acknowledged the male standard by which we all, both woman and men, gauge and live out our sexuality.

SAME-SEX SEXUAL HARASSMENT

But what of men who do not conform to that stereotypic view of masculinity and male sexuality? Are they to be afforded constitutional protection? For some time, the answer from the bench was a resounding "no." Prior to the Supreme Court decision in the *Oncale* case, though, same-sex harassment as gender harassment received no judicial notice. The courts appeared divided and confused.

In the 1990s there were four different federal appeals courts that ruled on same-sex sexual harassment (SSSH) between 1992 and 1997. The Fourth Circuit ruled that SSSH was actionable only when the accused harasser was homosexual and therefore motivated by sexual desire (*McWilliams v. Fairfax County Board of Supervisors*, 72 F.3d 1191, 1195–96, 4th Cir. 1996). The Seventh Circuit, in *Doe v. City of Belleville*, ruled that many forms of SSSH were actionable because Title VII is sex-neutral and not intended to specifically protect women or men (*Doe v. Belleville*, 119 F.3d 563. 1997). The Eighth Circuit ruled that men could enact Title VII only if they proved that women were not subject to the same treatment as they had been (*Quick v. Donaldson Co.*, 90 F.3d 1372, 8th Cir. 1996). And finally, the Fifth Circuit ruled in *Garcia v. Elf Atochem* that SSSH did not fall under Title VII because it was intended to address "gender discrimi-nation," not harassment that is "sexual" (*Garcia v. Elf Atochem No. Am.*, 1994).

Just as women faced opposition when they entered "men's" fields, so too do men if they try to enter "real men's" fields. Men who are gender-nonconforming will face a hostile environment from other, gender-conforming men. And of course, when they file a claim of sexual harassment, it only amplifies the difference. "Real" men would never complain; they would fight their own battles and not seek state intervention.

Goluszek v. H.P. Smith and *Polly v. Houston Lighting and Power Company*

Let's first take the paradigmatic case of Anthony Goluszek. In 1988, Goluszek brought a sexual harassment suit against his employer, H.P. Smith, under Title VII of the Civil Rights Act of 1964. Goluszek worked as an electronic maintenance mechanic at H.P. Smith, a paper manufacturer in Illinois. He was a single male and lived with his mother. The court found that he was sexually very unsophisti-cated, with "little or no sexual experience," and was "abnormally sensitive to comments pertaining to sex." In his nearly all-male workplace, he was constantly harassed by fellow workers.

His night supervisor told him that he needed to "get married and get some of that soft pink smelly stuff that's between the legs of a woman." The following year, Goluszek reported a complaint to the same supervisor about a comment referring to a female coworker who "fucks." The supervisor's response was that if "Goluszek did not fix a machine, they would get Carla Drucker to fix Tony [Goluszek]." "Operators periodically asked Goluszek if he had gotten any 'pussy' or had oral sex. . . . [they] showed him pictures of nude women, told him they would get him 'fucked,' accused him of being gay or bisexual, and made other sex-related comments. The operators also poked him in the buttocks with a stick" (*Goluszek* 1988).

When Goluszek confronted his fellow employees and demanded that supervisors take some action, they dismissed their sexual comments as "mere 'shop talk.'" This undisputed hostile environment continued and went unabated for several years. During the same time period, Goluszek began to receive warnings, reprimands, and suspensions for tardiness and missed work, which eventually led to grounds for his release. He sued for sexual harassment, retaliatory discharge, and discrimination based on national origin.

Polly v. Houston Lighting and Power Company

In *Polly v. Houston Lighting and Power Company* (and *Houston Lighting v. International Brotherhood of Electrical Workers*), the plaintiff, Norman Polly, made similar allegations of same-sex sexual harassment and employer indifference. Polly was employed by Houston Lighting as a member of a traveling group of repairmen. Repeatedly harassed by fellow employees, he was berated with homophobic taunts, his genital grabbed and squeezed, and a broom handle forced against his rectum. Polly was fired for failing to report to work as ordered. He had already filed three charges of sexual harassment with the EEOC. He brought suit against Houston Lighting. The company, in turn, sued his union, which had demanded Polly's reinstatement at an arbitration hearing.

In both of these cases, the courts sided with the employers and threw out claims of same-sex sexual harassment. In *Goluszek*, the U.S. district court granted summary judgment to H.P. Smith on the sexual harassment and national origin claims (although they found some grounds for the retaliation claim). In *Polly v. Houston Lighting*, the district court dismissed claims of sexual harassment. In the *Goluszek* decision, the lower courts claimed that Title VII was designed to remedy discrimination "stemming from an imbalance of power and an abuse of that imbalance by the powerful which results in discrimination against a discrete and vulnerable group" (*Goluszek* 1988). Since men are not a vulnerable group, no sexual harassment could be said to have occurred. Had Goluszek been a woman, no doubt H. P. Smith would have taken action to alleviate the harassment. But as a man, he was not protected.

But when is a man not a man? When he's not a "real" man—is when other men challenge his masculinity. In *Goluszek*, the courts condoned the harassment because Goluszek was a male who was mistreated because he was insufficiently manly, and this identity is not constitutionally protected. Because he was a man biologically, he could not seek protection, despite the fact that he was not a "real" man.

To us, however, what is interesting is that, in so ruling, the court inscribed a certain vision of masculinity as the norm—physically aggressive, heterosexual, sexually crude and repulsive, predatory, nonrelational, vulgar, and violent. Any man who refuses to go along with this vision of sexuality has no remedy under law for what happens to him. "Goluszek may have been harassed 'because' he is a man," the district court opined, "but that harassment was not of a kind which created an anti-male environment in the workplace" (*Goluszek* 1988:1456).

Yet the harassment did create an "anti-male environment"—at least for males who did not conform to a stereotypic definition of masculinity and male sexuality. The court here normalized that stereotype so that any behavior that fell outside the stereotype's boundaries was no longer counted as "male."

In that sense, the case hinged on the court's unsociological myopia. The law protects someone who is targeted, and who "but for sex," would not have been targeted. In order to have an actionable claim, the plaintiffs must prove that they were harassed because of their sex—"whether," in the words of Title VII, "the harasser treats a member or members of one sex differently from members of the other sex." Thus, a harasser who treats members of both genders equally badly would not be liable for any action under Title VII (see, for example, Johnson 1994).

The anomaly of rejecting same-sex sexual harassment becomes clearer if we add one hypothetical fact to either *Polly* or *Goluszek*. Assume that a female employee had witnessed the events that occurred and filed a claim of sexual harassment based on the hostile work environment. If the same events had occurred and were simply witnessed by a woman, the woman probably would have a cognizable claim for a sexually hostile work environment. Thus, while the female bystander could recover for sexual harassment, the direct male victim would not have a remedy (Levit 1998:117).

By claiming that same-sex sexual harassment could occur if the person being harassed were gay, the courts further confused sexual desire with sexual harassment because of gender. It matters not at all whether the harassers were heterosexual or homosexual, and it is surely not the case that such harassment was motivated by lust—the two criteria the courts seem to have used in opposite-sex harassment cases (see Coombs 1999:125). But surely what underlies the harassment of Goluszek and Polly is not the sexual desires of the harassers or the targets (see, for example, Johnson 1994). Goluszek and Polly were gender nonconformists, acting in nonstereotypic ways that embody the very multiplicity of masculinities that social and behavioral sciences have been documenting. For example, in a qualitative study of workplace sexual harassment in the United Kingdom, Deborah Lee found that sexual harassment of men in the form of verbal sexual allegations feminizes those men who find such allegations distressing. The process of feminization is underpinned by the conceptualization of "appropriate" masculinity in play in the male victim's workplace (Lee 2000).

Thus, these two cases were cases of "gender harassment" in which the harassers acted as a form of gender police, punishing those who transgressed from the hegemonic stereotypes (Brake 1999). The courts reinforced those stereotypes by arguing that the targets of such harassment deserved what they got.

ONCALE V. SUNDOWNER OFFSHORE SERVICES

Yet there are signs that the Supreme Court, at least, has begun to acknowledge a multiplicity of masculinities, and that those who do not conform to stereotypic notions of gender may, themselves, be targets that are entitled to constitutional protection. The Supreme Court's decision in *Oncale v. Sundowner Offshore Services* provides a final case in point and suggests a hopeful direction in which such legal cases may proceed.

In August 1991, Joseph Oncale was employed by Sundowner Offshore Services as a roustabout on an offshore oil rig. Only men were employed on the rig. Crew members spent up to seven straight days on the rig, and then received seven days off. Early on in his employment, Oncale's supervisor and others began making sexual comments and threatened to rape him. Eventually, they assaulted him. One man placed his penis on the back of his neck; another shoved a bar of soap into his buttocks. After the company ignored his complaints, Oncale quit in fear of further sexual assault. The district court and circuit courts found no grounds for a same-sex sexual harassment case, stating that "Mr. Oncale, a male, has no cause of action under Title VII for harassment by male co-workers" (*Oncale v. Sundowner* 1996).

The Supreme Court reversed this decision in 1998 and, for the first time, found that sexual harassment may indeed occur to members of the same sex. In a short, unanimous opinion, Justice Scalia made clear that members of a group may, indeed, discriminate against members of that same group, and that sexual harassment need not be motivated by sexual desire to be understood as sexual harassment—that is, harassment on the basis of sex.

> We see no justification in the statutory language or our precedents
> for a categorical rule excluding same-sex harassment claims from the

coverage of Title VII. As some courts have observed, male-on-male sexual harassment in the workplace was assuredly not the principal evil Congress was concerned with when it enacted Title VII. But statutory prohibitions often go beyond the principal evil to cover reasonably comparable evils, and it is ultimately the provisions of our laws rather than the principal concerns of our legislators by which we are governed. Title VII prohibits "discriminat[ion] . . . because of . . . sex" in the "terms" or "conditions" of employment. Our holding that this includes sexual harassment must extend to sexual harassment of any kind that meets the statutory requirements. (*Oncale v. Sundowner* 1998)

Men—as men—may experience a hostile environment—even when it is created by other men. The *Oncale* decision is pivotal not only because it makes same-sex sexual harassment legally actionable, but also because it recognizes gender harassment as creating a hostile environment for men who do not conform to some stereotypic notions of masculinity. In that sense, the Court has opened a door for the recognition of masculinities and a disentangling of the hegemonic definition of masculinity as the standard against which all men are to be measured. Boys may continue to be boys, but other boys may now have a legal claim against them.

BEYOND ONCALE

It would be premature to suggest that the *Oncale* decision represents a full transformation of legal attitudes, auguring an era in which multiple masculinities may be acknowledged and gender nonconformity might be protected.[2] Although *Oncale* is a breakthrough in many respects, some legal scholars have critiqued its potential for effectively adjudicating same-sex sexual harassment cases (see, for example, Toker 1999). And, of course, it says nothing about sexual harassment that is, in fact, based on sexual orientation. But the decision throws into stark relief how prior court refusals to acknowledge multiple masculinities assumed and therefore reified a narrow, outdated, and indeed defamatory definition of masculinity.

A one-dimensional understanding of masculinity has deleterious consequences for not only men, but for women as well. "To the extent that 'male on male' horseplay or ritualistic, hazing-like behaviors are tolerated in the workplace, a hostile climate toward the female gender can exist, even if women are not present in the immediate environment" (Stockdale et al. 1999). In addition, this view assumes that women will—and should—continue to shoulder childcare responsibilities, while remaining ever vigilant against male sexual aggression.

It is by assuming that this stereotypic definition of masculinity—sexually omnivorous and predatory, violent and aggressive, risk taking and emotionally disconnected, disinterested in family life and in health—is the "normal" way for men to behave, that inequalities based on gender, both between women and men and among men, are reproduced. Until the courts can fully embrace multiple masculinities, they will remain an unsafe harbor for both women and "other" men.

NOTES

© 2004 by Tyson Smith and Michael S. Kimmel. This essay represents a preliminary working out of these issues. A substantially revised and expanded version is forthcoming in *Signs*. We are grateful to Jim Gruber and Phoebe Morgan for their comments on this essay.
1. In cases involving victims of both genders, the lower courts disagree. Courts have ruled that "equal opportunity sexual harassment is not actionable under Title VII" because the discrimination is not "because of sex." However, Mothershed (2002) argues that equal opportunity sexual harassment can and does result in members of one sex being exposed to disadvantageous conditions of employment to which members of the other sex are not. Mothershed has shown that through the lens of disparate impact courts will most likely find that equal opportunity harassment results in qualitatively different burdens on male and female victims. That is, equal opportunity harassment can harm men in ways that it does not harm women and women in ways that it does not harm men.

2. Debate continues on whether making same-sex sexual harassment actionable under Title VII benefits gays and lesbians. The "reasonable person" standard might discriminate against expressions of gay sexuality directly and indirectly, both inside and outside the workplace, by providing a financial incentive to employers to discriminate against gays and lesbians on the basis of their sexual orientation. "Proscription of same-sex sexual harassment should come only after Congress expressly prohibits employment discrimination on the basis of sexual orientation, removing an employer's financial incentive to discriminate on the basis of sexual orientation" (Spitko 1997).

REFERENCES

Adler, R. S., and E. R. Peirce. 1993. The legal, ethical, and social implications of the "Reasonable Woman" standard in sexual harassment cases. *Fordham Law Review* 61:773–827.

Bethel School District No. 403 v. Fraser. 478 S. Ct. 675 (1986).

Bingham, C., and L. Gansler. 2002. *Class action: The story of Lois Jenson and the landmark case that changed sexual harassment law.* New York: Doubleday.

Brake, D. 1999. The cruelest of the gender police: Student-to-student sexual harassment and anti-gay peer harassment under Title IX. *Georgetown Journal of Gender and the Law* 1:37–108.

Brannon, R., and D. David, eds. 1975. *The forty-nine per-cent majority.* Reading, Mass.: Addison Wesley.

Brod, H. 1994. Some thoughts on some histories of some masculinities: Jews and other others. In *Theorizing masculinities*, ed. H. Brod and M. M. Kauffman, 97–118. Thousand Oaks, Calif.: Sage.

Case, M. A. C. 1995. Disaggregating gender from sex and sexual orientation: The case of the effeminate man in the law and feminist jurisprudence. *Yale Law Journal* 105 (1): 17–39.

Connell, R. W. 1995. *Masculinities.* Cambridge: Polity.

Coombs, M. 1999. Title VII and homosexual harassment after Oncale: Was it a victory? *Duke Journal of Gender Law and Policy* 6:113–150.

Doyle, J. 1989. *The male experience.* Madison, Wisc.: Brown and Benchmark.

Ellison v. Brady. 924 F.2d 872, 9th Cir. (1991).

Franke, K. M. 1997. "What's wrong with sexual harassment?" *Stanford Law Review* 49:691–772.

Goluszek v. H. P. Smith. 86 C. 8412; US Dist. Ct. N.D. Illinois, E.D. (1988).

Gomez, J. 1986. Repeat after me: We are different. We are the same. *N.Y.U. Review of Law and Social Change* 14:935–953.

Hearn, J. 1996. Is masculinity dead? A critique of the concept of masculinity masculinities. In *Understanding masculinities,* ed. M. Mac an Ghaill, 202–217. Buckingham: Open University Press.

Jenson v. Eleveth Mines as cited in Bingham, C. and L. Gansler. 2002. *Class action: The story of Lois Jenson and the landmark case that changed sexual harassment law.* New York: Doubleday.

Johnson, K. 1994. Chiapuzio v. BLT Operating Corporation: What does it mean to be harassed "because of your sex"? Sexual stereotyping and the "bisexual" harasser revisited. *Iowa Law Review* 79:731–756.

Kimmel, M. 1994. Masculinity as homophobia: Fear, shame and silence in the construction of gender identity. In *Theorizing masculinities,* ed. H. Brod and K. Kauffman, 119–141. Thousand Oaks, Calif.: Sage.

———. 1995. *Manhood in America.* New York: Free Press.

Lee, D. 2000. Hegemonic masculinity and male feminization: The sexual harassment of men at work. *Journal of Gender Studies* 9 (2): 141–155.

Levit, N. 1998. *The gender line.* New York: New York University Press.

MacKinnon, C. A. 1989. *Toward a feminist theory of the state.* Cambridge: Harvard University Press.

Mothershed, K. F. 2002. How the "Equal Opportunity" sexual harassment discriminates on the basis of gender under Title VII. *Vanderbilt Law Review* 55:1205.

New York Times Magazine. 2002, October 27. Letters of response to Talbot's article entitled, "When Men Taunt Men, Is it Sexual Harassment?" Section 6, 8.

Oncale v. Sundowner Offshore Services, Inc. 83 F. 3d 118, 5th Cir. (1996).

Oncale v. Sundowner Offshore Services, Inc. 523 US S. Ct. 75 (1998).

O'Neil, J. M., G. Good, and S. Holmes. 1995. Fifteen years of theory and research on men's gender role conflict: New paradigms for empirical research. In *A new psychology of men,* ed. R. Levant and W. Pollack, 164–206. New York: Basic Books.

Polly v. Houston Lighting and Power Company. US District Court for Southern District of Texas, Houston division, 825 F. Supp. 135 (1993).

Schultz, V. 1998. Reconceptualizing sexual harassment. *Yale Law Journal* 107:1683–1805.

———. 2001. Talking about harassment. *Journal of Law and Policy* 9:417–440.

Smith, Tyson, and Michael Kimmel. 2004. The hidden discourse of masculinity in gender discrimination law. *Signs: Journal of Women in Culture and Society.* In press.

Spitko, E. G. 1997. He said, he said: Same-sex sexual harassment under Title VII and the "Reasonable Heterosexist" standard. *Berkeley Journal of Employment and Labor Law* 18:56.

Stockdale, M., M. Visio, and L. Batra. 1999. The sexual harassment of men: Evidence for a broader theory of sexual harassment and sex discrimination. *Psychology, Public Policy and Law* 5:630–664.

Talbot, M. 2002, October 13. When men taunt men, is it sexual harassment? *New York Times Magazine.* Section 6, 52.

Toker, R. L. 1999. Multiple masculinities: A new vision for same-sex harassment law. *Harvard Civil Rights–Civil Liberties Law Review* 34:603–628.

Woolf, V. [1938] 1966. *Three guineas.* New York: Harcourt, Brace.

Part II

Dominance, Harassment, and Women

Like the previous seven chapters, the readings in this part of the collection represent a broad range of approaches. But, unlike those preceding them, these six chapters focus more on women than on men. Specifically, they all attend to situations and experiences within *doubly* dominated settings.

Chapter 8 begins with a meta-analysis of European Union sexual harassment surveys. The first of its kind, Timmerman's critique of methodological shortcomings analyzes the reasons for the confusing array of sexual harassment prevalence rates found among eighty-four surveys. She then argues that the widespread use of a static or "one shot" measure of occupational or workplace sex ratios as a predictor of sexual

harassment is flawed because it does not take into account the dynamic nature of gender interactions as the sex ratio in an organization or workplace *changes* from being male dominant to more evenly balanced numerically.

Chapter 9 follows with the results of the first nationwide survey of policewomen's harassment in Finland. The analyses of Kauppinen and Patoluoto are groundbreaking in several ways: they compare the experiences and perceptions of policewomen to those of their male counterparts; they contrast the experiences of policewomen and men with those of hostile citizens (clients); and they compare the impacts of hostility from peers and the public on women and men's levels of job satisfaction and exhaustion. Their findings provide a springboard for future international comparisons of the link between male dominance and sexual harassment in policing institutions of differing nationalities.

Employing similar methodology, Embser-Herbert in Chapter 10 reports the results of a survey of women who have served in the U.S. military. Her study is the first to empirically demonstrate the significant roles that sexual orientation and homophobia play in women's experiences and perceptions of harassment. The author draws upon masculinity studies to conceptualize homophobia as an intervening link between male dominance and sexual harassment.

Chapter 11 retells the history of sexual harassment from the perspective of blue-collar pioneers in male-dominated occupations. By drawing on an extensive body of unpublished historical documents, Baker demonstrates that the complaints and activism of blue-collar women played a pivotal role in breaking the silence and raising awareness about sexual harassment. Over time, however, the perspectives of white-collar and academic feminists have dominated the discourse, and, as a result, the contributions that blue-collar women made have been marginalized. Baker's chapter reminds us that it was women working in male-dominated settings that pioneered the path to the public policies we enjoy today. Chapter 12 provides a counterbalance to Chapter 11, in that Corroto describes how sexual harassment is perpetrated and experienced among white-collar professionals. As a professor of architecture, she describes the ways in which her profession is doubly dominated and reports with great specificity how sexual harassment occurs among architects. Her study presents a challenge to policy advocates and activists by revealing the existence (and persistence) of pockets of resistance and male privilege in an otherwise progressive institution.

Finally, in the last chapter, Buchanan uses a multicultural standpoint to go beyond male domination. She begins by astutely describing the dominance of white women in sexual harassment theory and of white men in the study of masculinity. She then uses focus group data to empirically demonstrate the intertwining of racial and sexual harassment. Buchanan argues that for women of color, dominance is a much more complicated issue. Open coding of the resulting data revealed two notable types of harassment: racialized harassment by white women, and sexual harassment by white men. Both types are activated by stereotypes about black women that have a strong cultural basis in American society. Her chapter challenges researchers to account for the nexus of gender and race in future studies of either sexual harassment or male dominance.

Taken together, the following chapters further extend several themes discussed in Part I. As a problem that extends across international borders, sexual harassment has predictable causes and consequences, and it presents similar types of methodological challenges for researchers. Moreover, the thrust of theory development and policy implementation often ignores the unique situations and perspectives of minority groups, such as lesbians and blue-collar women. Finally, unique insights into the experiences of those who are routinely subjected to sexual harassment and the subsequent cumulative emotional and job-related costs are often found by using research techniques that are too often given short shrift by scholars, such as focus groups, intensive interviews, and participant observation.

8 / THE IMPACT OF MALE DOMINATION ON THE PREVALENCE OF SEXUAL HARASSMENT

An Analysis of European Union Surveys

Greetje Timmerman

This chapter addresses and evaluates male dominance and the prevalence of sexual harassment in studies of European workplaces from both methodological and theoretical points of view. First it discusses methodology as it has been applied in the European surveys (male dominated or not) and its relationship to the reliability of prevalence rates. I will show that high or low prevalence rates are, at least to some extent, due to the differences in measuring and sampling techniques. However, this is not the whole story. Differences in prevalence rates between countries in northwest and southern Europe are patterned in a fairly consistent manner that suggests that national or regional differences in gender-related behavior and attitudes supersede variations in methodology. I then shift the analysis to European studies that explore the prevalence of sexual harassment in male-dominated workplaces. Again, I will show how methodological problems affect the prevalence rates in this selection of studies. I argue that variations in measurement and the use of differing sampling strategies make it very difficult to compare prevalence rates between male-dominated and other types of work environments.

After dealing with the methodological aspects of sexual harassment research, I address the question of the prevalence of sexual harassment in male-dominated workplaces from another point of view, a theoretical one. As illustrated by a case study involving twelve different workplaces, an interesting relationship is shown between the levels of sexual harassment experiences reported by women and the degree of male domination in the workplace. In general, it can be seen that the ways in which women label their experiences, as well as their willingness to report them, are affected by the *degree* of male domination in the workplace. To explain this influence, women's reporting of sexual harassment is placed in the context of changing power balances between the sexes in the workplace (and in society in general). This theory of changing power balances, by the historical sociologist Norbert Elias, is presented as a useful approach for explaining both why reports of sexual harassment in non-male-dominated workplaces are lower than in male-dominated workplaces and why reports in highly male-dominated workplaces are lower than in moderately male-dominated workplaces.

DISTINCTIVE FEATURES OF EUROPEAN RESEARCH AND POLICY ON SEXUAL HARASSMENT

In order to fully understand the complex problems of comparing rates of prevalence, it is important to note the impact of a declining interest in sexual harassment, both *as a unique issue* of research and policy development and as one that is *distinctly gender based*. In Europe, most studies were conducted during the second half of the 1980s and throughout the 1990s (European Commission 1999, Timmerman & Bajema 1999b, 1999c). By the end of the 1990s, however, interest in sexual harassment as a topic of research waned. The research that is still being conducted on this issue concentrates on specific jobs, particularly on male-dominated occupations such as the police and the armed forces. This recent interest in sexual harassment as it occurs in male-dominated workplaces is certainly in line with a more general tendency in gender studies to observe masculinity in all its facets. However, the focus on male-dominated jobs could also be explained by the general assumption that sexual harassment is most likely to take place in those fields characterized by a male-dominated organizational culture. As such, a gender power analysis still seems to be the dominant theoretical perspective underlying the explanation of sexual harassment today.

Yet, at the same time, a tendency toward gender neutralization can be observed in a number of recent studies on harassment in male-dominated workplaces. During the 1990s consensus grew that sexual harassment would no longer be considered a problem concerning female workers exclusively. In many European countries an awareness arose that men could also be victims of sexual harassment. A similar shift in the victim-perpetrator model took place with respect to sexual violence: it became acceptable to recognize that boys as well as girls could be victims of child sexual abuse. Furthermore, other problems related to the workplace—e.g., violence at work, mobbing, aggression, and intimidation—drew the attention of researchers, politicians, and the general public, causing sexual harassment to become just one of a number of issues concerning violence at work. The same development can be traced in the field of education. Whereas the first studies exclusively focused on sexual harassment in schools, the problem is now being studied as part of the more general problem of school violence. This broadening of the problem has made the topic politically more acceptable. Harassment, even sexual harassment, is no longer perceived as an issue put forth only by a few orthodox feminists. Now any employee can become the victim of mobbing, intimidation, or harassment. This tendency to neutralize the gender-specific character of harassment, including sexual harassment, is also reflected in many national and local initiatives directed at preventing and combating sexual harassment in the workplace. Educational and labor organizations increasingly develop policies aimed at tackling the problem of violence in general. Sexual harassment is considered one of several manifestations of violence and aggression that people are confronted with in the workplace. This development is also apparent in recent research on sexual harassment where it is studied as part of the more general problem of "violence." Even though the concept of violence could be theorized either as a manifestation of specific definitions of masculinity or in terms of gender inequality, recent studies that examine violence at work include underdeveloped gender-specific power analyses.

From a historical point of view, the absence of gender-specific power analyses in recent harassment research is problematic, since sexual harassment of female workers is situated in the uneven power balance between the sexes in the workplace. For the first time in history, and in many countries all over the world, female employees are speaking out against the unwelcome sexual conduct of their male colleagues. In this chapter, increased reporting of sexual harassment is viewed in light of the historical process of changing power balances between the sexes in society, specifically in the workplace. Although male domination is a key factor in the prevalence of sexual harassment, our analysis of sexual harassment research in European workplaces shows that it is not male domination as such that explains the prevalence and nature of the problem. There appear to be significant differences between male-dominated and *very* male-dominated workplaces. The degree of male domination in the workplace affects several aspects, such as women's interpretation of the problem, their willingness to report it, and the types and frequency of harassment they experience.

A REVIEW OF RESEARCH ON SEXUAL HARASSMENT IN EUROPE

Is sexual harassment in Europe more prevalent in male-dominated workplaces than in workplaces with other sex ratios? The concept of "male dominance," as it is commonly used by researchers today, refers to environments where both *numerical* and *normative* dominance occur simultaneously. This means that in these workplaces a very high ratio of men is combined with an organizational or occupational culture that rewards traditional masculine values and behaviors, such as aggressiveness, denigration of women, sexual bravado, risk taking, emotional control, and technological prowess (Gruber 1998). In 1998 and 1999, a review study was conducted of the sexual harassment research projects that had been carried out in Europe (Timmerman & Bajema 1999b, Alemany 1999). There were approximately 84 research projects in the sixteen member states during the 1987–1997 period (Table 8.1). While a small number of studies (15) involved nationwide surveys of several branches of industry, most research was restricted to one branch, occupation, or profession (69 studies). Although some studies were qualitative in nature, most research was designed to determine the incidence or prevalence of sexual harassment through quantitative survey techniques. All of these studies surveyed the prevalence of sexual harassment reported by women; nearly a third of them also explored the sexual harassment of men.

It is clear that sexual harassment occurs in all types of European workplaces: in male dominated, female dominated, and less homogeneous workplaces. As Table 8.1 shows, the incidence or prevalence rates vary considerably, not only from one country to another but also within each country. With respect to *women*, the highest incidence rates (70–90 percent) are found in the national surveys carried out in Austria, Germany, and Luxembourg. The Austrian and Luxembourg surveys have a rate of around 80 percent, while German research shows that 72 percent of employees have been sexually harassed. Several branch studies also show high incidence rates. Among Austrians in public administration, the university, and the private sector, the incidence rate is 33 percent. A study of German local government found a rate of 80 percent. Research on U.K. police officers revealed that 50 percent of female employees had suffered sexual harassment of one kind or another. Other high percentages of sexual harassment were found in a U.K. study of health service workers (89 percent) and in a survey conducted by a Norwegian women's magazine (90 percent).

Another group of studies found intermediate incidence rates of 25 to 60 percent. For instance, the national Dutch, Finnish, Portu-

Table 8.1

Prevalence Studies of Sexual Harassment in Northwest and Southern Europe by Country and Gender (1987–1997)

	Sexual Harassment		Scope of Studies ($n =$)		
	Of women (%)	Of men (%)	National	Local	Total
Austria					
National study	81		1	4	5
Local government	73				
Occupational subgroups	33				
Training on the job	17				
Belgium					
Secretaries	29		2	2	4
Denmark					
National study	11		1	4	5
Finland					
11 occupational groups	34	26	2	5	7
National sex life study	27	30			
University staff[a]	11	11			
Finnish parliament	17				
Trade unions	9	3			
Union	17				
France					
National study	19		3	0	3
National study	9				
National study	8				
Germany					
National study	72		1	5	6
Local government	80				
Steelworkers	30				
Local government	50 +				
Greece					
Athens residents	60		0	1	1
Ireland					
Civil service	25	1	0	5	5
Electricity Supply Board	45				
Retail sector	14	5			
Italy					
Metallurgical sector	10		0	4	4
Rome, female jobs	35				
Postal sector	45				
Health, metallurgy, food	20				

Table 8.1 *(continued)*

Prevalence Studies of Sexual Harassment in Northwest and Southern Europe by Country and Gender (1987–1997)

	Sexual Harassment		Scope of Studies ($n =$)		
	Of women (%)	Of men (%)	National	Local	Total
Luxembourg					
Objective criteria (national)	78		1	0	1
Subjective criteria (national)	13				
Netherlands					
National study	32		1	10	11
Several case studies	58				
Local government[b]	54	27			
Police	56				
Secretaries	25				
Industrial office workers	13				
Norway					
Women magazine readers	90		0	8	8
Occupational subgroups	8				
Labor union	8				
Portugal					
National study	34	7	1	0	1
Spain			0	0	0
Sweden					
National study	17	1	1	13	14
Ambulance personnel	53	14			
Wood industry	23	4			
Social insurance office	9	4			
National study	2				
Health care workers	22				
University hospital	30	4			
Metro workers	27				
United Kingdom					
National study	54	9	1	8	9
Temp agency	47	14			
Health services[c]	89	51			
Police	50				
Total			15	69	84

[a] This is an overall rate for both women and men.

[b] These are mainly indirect experiences, for example, as a witness to the sexual harassment of female colleagues.

[c] This result is based on a small number of men ($N = 32$).

guese, and U.K. studies' prevalence rates of sexual harassment reported by female employees were 32, 27, 34.1, and 54 percent, respectively. Most occupational subgroup studies show results that fall within this intermediate range. For example, a Greek study in Athens found an incidence rate of 60 percent; an Irish report about the Electricity Supply Board found that 45 percent of their female employees had personally experienced sexual harassment; and several Italian surveys had rates of 35 percent (Rome) and 45 percent (postal sector). A Finnish study of eleven occupational groups and a Swedish survey of metro employees had sexual harassment incidence rates of 34 and 27 percent, respectively.

Finally, a third group of studies found relatively low rates (2–25 percent) among women respondents: three national studies in France (incidence rates of 19, 9, and 8 percent) and two in Sweden (2 and 17 percent). The Danish and Luxembourg surveys reported incident rates of 11 and 13 percent. Some of the occupational subgroup studies also show a low incidence rate: two Italian studies (9.9 percent in the metallurgical sector and 20.1 percent in different occupations); Norwegian research in several subgroups (8 percent); a Dutch labor union study of industrial office workers (13 percent); Irish subgroup studies of the retail sector (14 percent) and the civil service (25 percent); and Finnish studies of university staff (11 percent) and the parliament (17 percent).

All studies examining the sexual harassment experiences of *men* found prevalence rates of 1 to 30 percent. Among the national studies, the Swedish Statistical Office survey reported an incidence of 1 percent; a U.K. study, 9 percent; and a Finnish survey, 30 percent. The subgroup studies also reported incidence rates of 1 to 30 percent. For instance, an incidence rate of 1 to 14 percent was reported by the Irish case studies (civil service, 1 percent; retail trade, 5 percent) and the Swedish surveys (university, 4 percent; wood industry, 4 percent; social insurance office, 4 percent; ambulance personnel, 14 percent). Dutch local government employees (27 percent) and several Finnish subgroups (30 percent) reported somewhat higher rates.

Our review of European research reveals an enormous variation in prevalence rates. We do not want to suggest, however, that this broad variance of percentages reflects the actual occurrence of sexual harassment. On the contrary, our review of the various surveys finds substantial differences in terminology, definitions, questionnaire content, and the length of the time period that respondents were given to frame their harassment experiences (e.g., last six months). We will argue that, to some extent, the varying incidence and prevalence rates are a direct result of the methodology used in these studies (Timmerman & Bajema 1999a). In general, variations among the surveys indicate a relationship between incidence and prevalence on the one hand, and methodology on the other. Specifically, our analysis of all the surveys that estimate the prevalence of sexual harassment reveals that incidence rates can be linked to (a) variation in definitions, and (b) representativeness of the research sample.

VARIATION IN DEFINITIONS

The first issue, concerning the variation in definition, is related to the scope used to define the term, that is, how broad or narrow the definition of sexual harassment is, since this may influence the resulting estimates of sexual harassment (Fitzgerald & Shullman 1993). Generally speaking, asking just *one* question about experiences with unwanted sexual behavior produces a lower incidence rate than including a list of *ten or more* questions (Junger 1985, Van der Heiden 1986). The resulting lower incidence rates are reinforced by the fact that, in the perception of many respondents, the term *sexual harassment* refers to the more severe types of sexual harassment. Thus, simply asking respondents whether or not they have experienced "sexual harassment" produces lower incidence rates than inquiring after various forms of "unwanted sexual conduct." Examples of this problem include the relatively low incidence rates of 2, 11, and 13 percent in the Swedish survey (Statistika Centralbyran

1995), the Danish survey (Schultz 1991), and one of the Luxembourg national surveys (Margue 1995), respectively. In these studies *only one question* was asked about sexual harassment experiences. The restrictiveness of the questions is also the reason why the surveys in France show a lower level of harassment than in other countries. On the other hand, the high incidence rates reported in the national surveys carried out in Austria (81 percent), Germany (72 percent), and Luxembourg (78 percent) could be attributed to some degree to their *extended, comprehensive definitions* of sexual harassment (Holzbecher et al. 1991, Hopfgartner & Zeichen 1988, Margue 1995). The Luxembourg surveys are a good example of this problem. Respondents were queried about sexual harassment in two ways: by asking them if they had experienced one or more behaviors from an extensive list; and by asking them "Have you been sexually harassed at work?" The former method resulted in an incidence rate of 78 percent, while the latter tallied only a 13 percent rate! The Austrian and German national studies even included *sexist behavior or gender harassment* in their definition of sexual harassment (Holzbecher et al. 1991, Hopfgartner & Zeichen 1988), which further inflated their prevalence figures. Furthermore, variations in incidence rates may be related to *the reference to a particular period of time* a respondent is asked to use in recalling all of his or her experiences with sexual harassment. Most researchers do not refer to any particular period of time (e.g., "Have you had experiences in this job/company of sexual harassment?"). Only in a few studies were the respondents asked to answer questions about their experiences with reference to a specific time frame, for example, three months, one year, or two years. This explains, among other things, the extremely low incidence percentages found in the Swedish survey (Statistika Centralbyran 1995), since this study asked respondents to recall all incidents of sexual harassment that occurred during the last three months.

REPRESENTATIVENESS OF THE RESEARCH
The second cause of differences in incidence rates involves sampling procedures. In general, *random sampling* generally produces lower

percentages than nonrandom sampling. The problem of nonran-
domness is illustrated by the national surveys commissioned by the
German and Austrian labor union studies: between 72 and 81 percent
of the women who were questioned reported experiences of unwanted sexual behavior (Hopfgartner & Zeichen 1988, Holzbecher et
al. 1991). These samples consisted only of female labor union members, who were presumably more aware of sexual harassment than a
representative sample of all employees because of union-sponsored
material and training on the issue. Another example of high prevalence rates due to a lack of representativeness is the self-report samples (e.g., questionnaires in magazines or journals). It is generally
accepted that victims are more apt than nonvictims to respond to
these types of surveys. Extremely high percentages were found in a
U.K. study of health service workers (89 percent), and in a Norwegian women's magazine study (90 percent). Both samples were nonrepresentative because the questionnaires were published in a popular journal.

The European Commission, on whose initiative this review study
had been conducted, was especially interested in the differences
among the European countries. One of the most important questions was to what extent the prevalence of sexual harassment varied
across the sixteen member states. In our report we stated that, although the prevalence rates varied across the countries to a very
large extent, it is very difficult to answer this question because the
variations in methodology used in the studies limit any cross-cultural comparison. This is not to imply, however, that differences
among countries or cultural variations should be ignored with respect to the problem of sexual harassment. Our review study shows
several indications of an important cultural difference, that between
northwest and southern Europe.

National Cultures

Although the *number of studies* varies among countries all over Europe, considerably fewer studies have been conducted in southern

Europe compared to the northern and western countries. Between 1987 and 1997, only nine studies examined the incidence or prevalence rates of sexual harassment in the southern European countries (three studies in France, four in Italy, one in Greece, one in Portugal, and none in Spain).

Also, since the extent to which studies have been initiated by national governments reflects a certain degree of awareness or acknowledgment of the problem of sexual harassment, this may impact reporting levels by targets of harassment. In most northern and western countries the national government initiated one or more studies on the incidence or prevalence of sexual harassment (Belgium, Austria, Finland, Germany, Luxembourg, the Netherlands, Sweden, and the United Kingdom). In southern Europe, France is the exception in that all three of its studies were conducted on a national level. By contrast, Italy, Spain, and Greece had no nationwide studies. The research that was conducted in these latter countries was confined to a specific geographical region or a specific occupational category.

It seems, therefore, that differences in the number of surveys and the number of nationwide initiatives to study the problem reflect to some extent national and cultural differences between the northwest and the southern parts of Europe. Recent comparative research into gender equality at work in the European Union shows some revealing results in this regard. Plantinga and Hansen (2001) used several indicators of the relative opportunities for men and women (the "gender gap"), including differences in employment, wages, and the sharing of unpaid work, attitudes toward women's employment, and child-care facilities. These indicators were used to develop estimates for each of the sixteen member states. A few conclusions are inescapable, even though equal opportunity is a complex issue and comparative research in this field is very complicated. First of all, Sweden and Denmark had the highest scores on equal opportunity, and Italy, Greece, Spain, and the Netherlands showed the lowest. The employment regimes in the latter offer few positive incentives, and cultural attitudes, especially in Italy and Greece, seem to favor the employment of men over women. The position of the Netherlands could be ascribed to the large number of women working part-time, which is a unique situation in Europe. Ireland, Belgium, Germany, and France constitute a middle category. Though the employment regimes of Belgium and France are also fairly traditional in orientation, they invest in child care, and this results in a higher labor market participation of mothers with young children. Finally, the United Kingdom, Finland, Luxembourg, Austria, and Portugal form a "puzzling" cluster that needs further analysis. Portugal is an especially interesting case. According to the researchers, Portugal ranks "medium" with regard to the equal distribution of paid and unpaid work and scores well on the employment indicators compared to other southern European countries that have the lowest scores on equal opportunities. In Portugal, presumably, "informal care services (domestic servants, grandparents, and other relatives) are of particular importance" (Plantinga & Hansen 2001:300) in alleviating some of women's household and child-care responsibilities.

To summarize, comparative research into equal opportunities in paid and unpaid work generally shows that in most southern European member states gender equality at work is less realized than in other European countries. This is in line with the findings of our review study that a sharp division exists between northwest and southern Europe concerning sexual harassment research.

Prevalence of Sexual Harassment in Male–Dominated Workplaces

The incidence or prevalence rates of sexual harassment in numerically male-dominated workplaces (Table 8.1, *studies in italics*) do not present a different situation compared to the rates in other workplaces. Within the category of male-dominated workplaces, the incidence or prevalence of sexual harassment varies considerably (13–56 percent), and this is also the case in other workplaces (2–90 percent): 30 percent in the steel industry (Germany), 45 percent in the electricity sector (Ireland), 27 percent in the metro services

(Sweden), 23 percent in the wood industry (Sweden), and 13 percent in the industrial office environment (the Netherlands). The Finnish study conducted among women and men in eleven occupations indicates that the most harassment-prone occupations are those of waitress (or waiter), psychiatric nurse, female police officer, and construction worker. The former two are female dominated, and the latter two are highly male dominated. Furthermore, several studies in various countries (Sweden, France, Italy) suggest that it is particularly women working in the health care industry (e.g., female ambulance personnel) who suffer from a relatively high incidence of sexual harassment.

As stated before with respect to measuring sexual harassment in the European surveys, figures about incidence or prevalence do not give us a reliable picture of the extent of the problem. This methodology problem also affects the (lack of) validity in estimating the prevalence of sexual harassment in male-dominated workplaces.

So far, male domination has been addressed as a dichotomous variable. This is a common view in the European review, since most surveys distinguish between male-dominated and female-dominated workplaces. A few studies, however, distinguish between varying degrees of male domination, showing that women working in workplaces characterized by different degrees of male domination report different prevalence rates of sexual harassment. Thus, a more detailed analysis of male domination provides a better insight into the relationship between prevalence rates of sexual harassment and varying degrees of male domination at the workplace. In the next section, illustrated by one of the studies in the European review (Timmerman 1990), we will present arguments for such a detailed analysis.

PREVALENCE OF SEXUAL HARASSMENT AND DEGREE OF MALE DOMINATION: A CASE STUDY

In the Dutch study (Timmerman 1990), women's reports of unwanted sexual male conduct were explored within the numerical and hierarchical gender context of the workplace. The prevalence of unwanted sexual male conduct was examined in twelve different workplaces (seven workplaces in local governments, five workplaces in industrial firms). In each workplace a select sample was drawn (N = 128; 90 female and 38 male respondents). All twelve workplaces were categorized in terms of sex ratio and vertical division of labor by sex (the distribution of women and men throughout the hierarchical structure of the workplace). Based on these two criteria, the workplaces were divided into three groups: workplaces that were very male dominated, somewhat male dominated, and relatively non male dominated. The results of the study (Table 8.2) show a relation between the degree of male domination and the reported frequency of sexual harassment by women (N = 86, with 4 missing cases), though this relation is not linear.

Not surprisingly, the lowest rate of sexual harassment was found in workplaces with relative equality between the sexes (48 percent). In these workplaces a considerable number of female employees were working in all levels of the hierarchical structure. On the other hand, it could be expected that female respondents working in very male-dominated workplaces would report most incidences of sexual harassment. This was, however, not the case. On the contrary, women in workplaces with a very uneven power balance between

Table 8.2

Reports of Sexual Harassment by Degree of Male Dominance (N = 86)

	Unwanted Sexual Behavior, % (n)		
	Yes	No	Total
Degree of Male Domination			
Very male dominated	57% (12)	43% (15)	100% (27)
Somewhat male dominated	81% (29)	19% (7)	100% (36)
Non male dominated	48% (14)	52% (9)	100% (23)
Total	(55)	(31)	(86)

Chi square = 7.63, $p < .05$.

the sexes did not tend to report most cases of sexual harassment (57 percent). Most incidences were reported in somewhat male-dominated workplaces (81 percent). In these workplaces the power balance between male and female employees was changing, not yet to equality but toward a *less uneven balance*. Thus it seems that harassment is most likely to take place where the entrance of a significant number of women goes hand-in-hand with a change in traditional power relations in the workplace. Gruber and Bjorn (1982) found that women autoworkers were most apt to be harassed in workplaces not where they were solo pioneers or a distinct minority but where their numbers made them a "threatening minority"—a visible presence that was nonetheless considerably short of numerical equality.

To explain these findings, the Dutch study elaborated on a theoretical perspective that conceptualizes the definition and reporting of sexual harassment as a *process* situated in a changing social and organizational context (Elias 1939). In this perspective, it is unlikely that sexual harassment will be reported in very male-dominated workplaces and that most sexual harassment will be reported in workplaces that are in a process of shifting power balances between the sexes. Based on Elias's theory of changing power relationships between social groups, it is possible to address the developmental character of the definition of sexual harassment within the context of changes in the power balance in the workplace (Elias & Scotson 1965). In the following section we will first address the main line of reasoning in Elias's changing power model and then show how the model was applied in our case study.

A Changing Power Model

Relations between men and women in organizations can be regarded as typical for relations between *members of an established group and outsiders* (Elias & Scotson 1965). In many traditionally male-dominated organizations, men form the established group and women are considered to be outsiders. A typical characteristic of members of the most powerful group in a community is that they consider themselves to be "superior" in comparison to others and that they manage to impose this belief in their own superiority on members of other, less powerful groups, namely outsiders. Outsiders tend to base their self-image on the image that the established group has of them. In other words, there is a link between the image people have of themselves and others and the social power structure of which they are a part. When power relations start to change, images of "us" and "them" as well as the way people relate to each other begin to change as well.

The established group has various methods of maintaining a belief in its own superiority. There is usually a high degree of social cohesion within the group. Group boundaries are closely guarded, and there is pressure on group members to think in a uniform way. Social control often prohibits contact with members of the other group, who are regarded as outsiders. One of the most decisive factors influencing the degree of internal cohesion is *the duration of the ties*, which is, of course, much longer within the established group than in the group of outsiders. These enduring ties are found notably in traditionally male-dominated professions and organizations.

When the power balance starts to shift toward the outsiders, the established group (and especially those members in the lower ranks) feel the change as a threat to their self-esteem. Tension between the two groups increases, as can often be seen in the increased number of open conflicts and acts of resistance. During such a process of change it is usually possible to distinguish an *assimilation* phase and an *emancipation* phase. Throughout the assimilation phase the outsiders make gains, but their "us" image is still clearly based on how the established group regards them. Their initial reaction is to follow the behavioral codes of the established group, and in most cases they adapt their behavior to the norms and values shared by that group. This is usually the case when the outsiders are pioneers or tokens and they feel a huge amount of pressure to conform. Acts of opposition against and resistance to these single individuals are often less open and less extreme than when the outsider group consists of a larger number of people. The reaction need not always be negative: the single individual could be cherished or presented as evidence that the established group is in fact open to accepting outsiders such as women or ethnic minorities.

However, as the number of outsiders increases, so do their sense of justice and their indignation at their treatment. During this emancipation phase a tense, competitive relationship usually evolves between the two groups. The established group feels more and more pressured to restrain itself, and the differences between the two groups become more manifest. This phase, during which old standards of behavior are criticized but new models of behavior have not yet been developed, can be regarded as a *transition* phase.

The establishment of new standards of social behavior is often preceded by a period of considerable insecurity. A typical example is the insecurity teachers feel because they no longer dare to pat a child's head after the recent stream of publications in which cases of sexual child abuse by teachers were brought into the open. The benefit of this insecure transition period is that people become aware of a variety of aspects regarding their behavior that former generations had often taken completely for granted. This process of increasing awareness seems to be an indispensable step in the process of attaining greater equality between the established group and the outsiders. The theory of change in the established-outsider relationship is summarized in Table 8.3.

This model was applied in the Dutch case study. To examine the (changing) power balances between the sexes in the workplaces, all twelve workplaces were first analyzed in terms of the indicators of changing established-outsider relationships: social cohesion ("duration of ties"), social control, and tensions and conflicts between and within the sexes. Second, these immaterial aspects of the relationships between the sexes were related to the material aspects (sex ratio and hierarchical structure) of the twelve workplaces.

The results of this analysis indicate that some workplaces could be distinguished as examples of first-phase figurations, while other

Table 8.3

Changing Power Relationships Between Established Group and Outsiders in Work Organizations

	Very Male Dominated	Male Dominated (Transition Phase)	Non Male Dominated
Sex ratio	Nearly all men, women small minority	Increasing numbers of women	Equal numbers of men and women
Balance of power	Very unequal	Unequal	Equal
Cohesion among males	Very strong	Strong	Weak
Conflict			
Within group	Weak	Increasing	Weak
Between the sexes	Weak	Strong	Weak
Sexual harassment	Ignored	Increased reporting	Fewer incidents

workplaces show many characteristics of second- or third-phase figurations (Table 8.3). In first-phase figurations, the very uneven material balance of power between the sexes is expressed in the superior status and we-image of the group of established men. Only men historically occupy some of these workplaces. The strong cohesion and informal ties within the men's group are closely linked to the segregation of work according to gender. There is a sharp dividing line between men's work and women's work, which is maintained and reinforced by the mechanism of gender stereotyping. The social and functional contacts between men and women are very much restricted. Although some women have experiences with unwanted sexual advances by male colleagues that make them feel very uncomfortable, these forms of behavior are rarely expressed as being problematic. Many women ignore the sexual advances and avoid direct confrontations with their male colleagues. The threshold of women's tolerance for male sexual advances is rather high, which corresponds to the cultural and material conditions of these workplaces. For both women and men, an open expression of their unwanted sexual experiences is made difficult by the strong consensus and the uniformity in beliefs of the group of established men, especially concerning the issue of responsibility for sexual harassment. Most men and women are of the opinion that women should (for their own benefit) adapt to the customs of a male-dominated workplace and that women who are harassed have asked for it because of the way they dress or behave at work. The milder, verbal forms (such as sexual remarks and jokes) are viewed as an inherent aspect of these working environments: women who do not approve of these "innocent" sexual advances are said to lack a sense of humor. Women who disapprove of these practices and who publicly express their disapproval experience social punishments like exclusion from the group or stigmatization. The fact that the minority of women who experience unwanted sexual advances do not raise the issue or complain about it relates strongly to the configurational context of the workplace. They would have little to gain and a great deal to lose.

In second-phase figurations, the issue of sexual harassment is brought into the open by a substantial number of women. Sexual harassment is, however, not the only subject of discussion in these workplaces. Tensions and conflicts about the inequality in the positions of men and women, the gender division of work, and standards of conduct are more or less an integral part of these figurations. Although the material power structure between the sexes is still uneven, the social power of women gradually increases. A few women have gained access to higher-status jobs, and the division of work according to gender is less rigid compared to first-phase figurations. On the level of social and informal contacts, more sexual heterogeneity exists. Differences in attitude toward matters of sexual inequality are also found among women and, to a lesser extent, among men. According to these women, most men respond in a defensive, ridiculing, or hostile way to the issue of sexual harassment during regular discussions. Although some of the men disapprove of sexual harassment, they feel reluctant to publicly challenge the language and behavior of their male colleagues. Women who have experienced sexual harassment talk to each other about how to deal with the issue, and this increases solidarity among them. According to some of the women, discussions in the mixed workplace about sexual harassment are part of the process of changing traditional social and sexual codes. In general, the lack of consensus and the multiformity of opinions and attitudes that goes hand-in-hand with a changing balance of power between the sexes create more opportunities for women to raise the issue of sexual harassment.

In third-phase figurations, where the balance of power between the sexes is relatively equal, the reported frequency of sexual harassment is found to be rather low. This does not mean that sexual harassment is not considered to be a serious problem, or that women are reluctant to speak openly about the issue. Although some women in our sample gave examples of unwanted sexual advances by men, many women and men referred to their working environment when explaining why sexual harassment is not a daily or structural problem at their workplace. The distribution of women and men throughout the hierarchical structure of the workplace is less unequal in these companies, jobs are less segregated by gender, and the informal contacts are mixed. According to the workers, such a situation creates a climate in which serious sexual harassment is not very likely to occur. When incidents of sexual harassment do take place, they are discussed publicly and women feel they have the support of many of their male and female colleagues when confronting the harasser. Compared to men in second-phase figurations, more men in these third-phase figuration workplaces take the issue of sexual harassment seriously.

CONCLUDING REMARKS

The European review of sexual harassment research indicates that during the 1990s many research projects were conducted in the various member states. Our analysis of incidence and prevalence rates shows that one cannot conclude that sexual harassment is more prevalent in male-dominated workplaces. Apart from the method-ological flaws in the research, which make it very difficult to draw reliable conclusions about incidence, the European review study does not indicate that women in male-dominated occupations have more experiences with sexual harassment than women in other oc-cupations. Specifically, the numerical definition of "male domi-nance" does not appear to be a discriminating variable explaining differences in the incidence of sexual harassment. Variety in defini-tions has also contributed to the differences in incidence rates. One of the main problems has been the use of the term *sexual harassment*, which has caused confusion in many studies. When women were asked whether they had ever been harassed, those who said they had referred typically to the worst types of harassment. In other words, they tended to interpret this concept in a restrictive way, whereas if women were presented with a list of unwelcome types of male be-havior, the percentage of women who could be considered to be victims of some form of sexual harassment increased significantly.

Furthermore, the analysis of 84 studies reviewed by this European survey also shows that national and cultural differences are related to the awareness and definition of the problem of sexual harassment. First, in the southern countries the degree of awareness of the prob-lem of sexual harassment is relatively low, as is indicated by the fact that far fewer studies and surveys have been conducted, with the exception of France, than in the northwestern member states. In the 1980s and 1990s many women in the southern countries tended to consider sexual harassment as an experience they had to endure be-cause it was part of being a woman. Second, comparative research on equal opportunities in the member states displays the overall view that southern countries have the lowest scores on gender equal-ity in paid and unpaid work.

In summary, the European review of sexual harassment surveys shows that it is very difficult to answer the simple question "Is sexual harassment more prevalent in male-dominated workplaces than in those that are not male dominated?" Variation in measurement, sampling strategies, and, to some extent, differences in national cultures are all reasons why the prevalence rates found in the surveys are not necessarily a reflection of "real" incidence. By taking greater care in measuring and sampling, future researchers can improve the validity and reliability of their surveys.

Considering this book's mission, the analysis of European surveys also points out the need for more sophisticated measurement of male domination. Illustrated by a detailed analysis of twelve workplaces, one of the Dutch studies in the European review reveals how the reporting of sexual harassment by women is related to a process of changing power relations between the sexes in the workplace. Reports of sexual harassment are low in very male dominated workplaces and relatively high in workplaces that are still somewhat male dominated. Instead of treating male domination as a dichotomous variable, it seems more fruitful to study the *degree* of male domination as an important variable affecting sexual harassment prevalence. To explain this variation, the study draws on existing sociological theory. Elias's historical sociological perspective is used to explore the prevalence and definitions of sexual harassment in workplaces, both male dominated and not, within the context of changing power balances between the sexes in the workforce. According to Elias, changing manners and standards of human behavior must be considered an expression of changes in the power balance and interdependence between social groups. Women raising the issue of sexual harassment could be interpreted as an expression of change in the balance of power at work between the sexes. In most European countries one of the most far-reaching social changes of the last few decades has been the enormous rise in the number of women, particularly married women, entering the labor market. Although women are still by no means sufficiently represented in middle and higher positions, or in occupations and sectors that have traditionally been male dominated, the massive influx of women into the labor market does imply that the power balance between the sexes in organizations is changing and that women are much more visible in many organizations than they were before. One of the most important consequences of this development is that an ever increasing number of men are confronted with women in their workplace as their coworkers. It is particularly in male-dominated workplaces that men need to learn how to work with women; they are being asked to adapt their ingrained social habits and behavior to meet women's wishes. Women are less and less prepared to accept behavior that, as recently as thirty years ago, was more or less taken for granted. In this context, speaking out against unwanted male sexual behavior, whether or not this behavior is labeled as sexual harassment, is a manifestation of this phase. The attention paid to sexual harassment during the past decades, and even the very fact that it has been discussed at all, can be regarded as a manifestation of the changing relations between men and women in the workplace (Timmerman 1990).

NOTE

Special thanks to Lomeke Schuringa for her inspiring comments on this paper.

REFERENCES

Alemany, C. 1999. Sexual harassment at work in five southern European countries. In *Sexual harassment at the workplace in the European Union*. Luxembourg: European Commission.

Elias, N. 1939. *The civilizing process*. Oxford: Basil Blackwell.

Elias, N., and J. Scotson. 1965. *The established order and the outsiders: A sociological inquiry into community problems*. London: Frank Cass and Co.

European Commission. 1999. *Sexual harassment at the workplace in the European Union*. Luxembourg: Office for Official Publications of the European Communities.

Fitzgerald, L. F., and S. L. Shullman. 1993. Sexual harassment: A research analysis and agenda for the 1990's. *Journal of Vocational Behavior* 42:5–27.

Gruber, J. 1997. An epidemiology of sexual harassment: Evidence from

North America and Europe. In *Sexual harassment: Theory, research, and treatment*, ed. W. O. Donohue. Needham Heights, Mass.: Allyn and Bacon.

Gruber, J. 1998. The impact of male work environment and organizational policies on women's experiences of sexual harassment. *Gender and Society* 12 (3): 301–320.

Gruber, J., and L. Bjorn. 1982. Blue collar blues: The sexual harassment of women autoworkers. *Work and Occupations* 9:271–298.

Holzbecher, M., A. Braszeit, U. Muller, and S. Plogstedt. 1991. *Sexuelle Belästigung am Arbeitsplatz*. Stuttgart, Berlin, Köln: Schriftenreihe des Bundesministers für Jugend, Familie, Frauen und Gesundheit, Verlag W. Kohlhammer.

Hopfgartner, A., and M. M. Zeichen. 1988. *Sexuelle Belästigung am Arbeitsplatz*. Wien: Frauenreferat, Schriftenreihe No. 20.

Junger, M. 1985. *The measurement of sexual harassment*. The Hague: Ministry of Justice.

Margue, C. 1995. *Sexual harassment: A day-to-day reality at the workplace in Luxembourg*. Luxembourg: ILReS S.A.

Plantinga, J., and J. Hansen. 2001. Assessing equal opportunities in the European Union. In *Women, gender and work*, ed. M. F. Loutfi, 273–305. Geneva: International Labor Office.

Schultz, A. 1991. *Sexual harassment in Danish workplaces*. Kopenhagen, Denmark: Danish Gallop Institute.

Statistika Centralbyran, Arbetarskyddsstyrelsen. 1995. *Hotad, mobbad eller sexualt trakasserad pad jobbet*. Stockholm: Author.

Timmerman, M. C. 1990. *Werkrelaties tussen vrouwen en mannen. Een onderzoek naar ongewenste intimiteiten in arbeidssituaties*. Amsterdam: Sua.

Timmerman, M. C., and C. Bajema. 1999a. Incidence and methodology in sexual harassment in Northwest Europe. *Women's Studies International Forum* 22 (6): 673–668.

———. 1999b. Sexual harassment in European workplaces. A review of research in 11 Member States (1987–1997). In *Sexual harassment at the workplace in the European Union*. Luxembourg: European Commission.

———. 1999c. Sexual harassment in Northwest Europe. *European Journal of Women's Studies* 6 (4): 419–441.

Van der Heiden, A. W. M. 1986. *Questions and answers about sexual harassment*. The Hague: Ministry of Justice.

9 / SEXUAL HARASSMENT AND VIOLENCE TOWARD POLICEWOMEN IN FINLAND

Kaisa Kauppinen and Saara Patoluoto

Gender segregation of work life is common in all European Union countries, but especially so in Finland (Melkas & Anker 1998). In 2000 only 16 percent of Finnish employees worked in occupations where the division of sexes was between 40 and 60 percent (Kauppinen et al. 2000). Gender segregation is especially strong in the Finnish police force, a masculinized, male-dominated occupation. This chapter reports the results from the first empirical study to be done of policewomen in Finland (Nuutinen, Kauppinen, & Kandolin 1999).

Our chapter breaks ground in three ways. First, we frame our study by comparing harassment rates across Europe and the United States. Second, we examine the impact of one unique aspect of police work—the frequent and routine contact with citizens (or "clients")—on experiences of sexual harassment and the consequent impacts of these experiences on women and men's job dissatisfaction and burnout. Third, we look at how rank affects officers' perception of the problem and their sense of support from other officers. The results of our study show that because they are highly visible members of a male-dominated occupation, women police officers experience higher levels of harassment and violence than other working women. We argue that interactions with men (co-workers, superiors, and citizens/clients) and traditional attitudes about women's roles are the determinate factors that shape their experiences.

WOMEN IN POLICE WORK

In 2001 only 8 percent of all Finnish police officers were women, up just one percentage point from 1998. An international comparison finds this figure to be particularly low. In Sweden, for example, 16 percent of all police were women in 1997 (Polisforbundet 1998); in England and Wales, the corresponding figure was 14 percent (Her Majesty's Chief Inspector of Constabulary 1996, quoted in Brown 1998). Women constitute 12 percent of police officers in the United States (Bureau of Labor Statistics 2001). The Netherlands reports a greater disparity. There, less than 5 percent of patrol officers are women (Ott 1989).

Since 1973, Finnish women have had access to police schools and police organizations. Until 1987 there were quotas on the number of women taken, and those who were accepted were held to the same physical ability requirements as the men. The 1987 Act on Gender Equality removed the quota and changed the requirements to match those of women's physical ability. These changes have increased the number of women seeking police careers. For example, today women make up about 20 percent of the student population in police school. Also, there are recruitment campaigns targeting women and encouraging them to apply to the police school. Despite these changes, the number of women serving in the Finnish police force remains low.

There is only a modest amount of European research on police-women. Most has been conducted in Great Britain (e.g., Brown 1993, 1998, 2000, Holdaway & Parker 1998), the Netherlands (Ott 1989), and Sweden (Polisforbundet 1998, Polishogskolan 1992). In a study of female police officers in England and Wales (1998), Brown found that women were under-represented in the police force and that they continued to experience problems of discrimination and sexual harassment. In a comparative study of women police officers in Great Britain and Ireland (2000), Brown found that the level of sexual harassment in England and Wales was 86 percent, in Scotland 70 percent, in Northern Ireland 81 percent, and in the Republic of Ireland 63 percent. She argues that higher levels of feminist awareness in England, Scotland, and Wales might account for higher reporting rates of discrimination and sexual harassment, whereas the opposite could be true for Irish policewomen. She quotes Porter (1998), who claims that the strong influence of the Church encourages Irish women to cling to traditional values and thus resist feminist awareness. Holdaway and Parker (1998), argue that structural, engendered inequalities and occupational cultures must also be taken into account when examining women and men in police officers' work. They suggest that men's views of women's roles, as a mother or wife, for example, can constrain and engender the way policemen view and treat women in their professional roles. This well-researched phenomenon, termed *sex-role spillover* by Gutek and Morasch (1982), has been observed in other studies of women in policing (Pope & Pope 1986, Brown 2000, Martin 1996). The sex-role spillover model predicts that cultural attitudes and gender-based behaviors are far more likely to pervade workplaces that are composed predominately of one sex than in those that are gender balanced numerically. Larwood and Wood (1979) argue that, because of sex stereotypes and traditional role expectations in gender-imbalanced occupations, women are often caught in a low-expectations trap. This often leads women to try twice as hard to prove that they are as competent as men at their jobs.

Ott's (1989) study of women police officers in the Netherlands found a high incidence of sexual harassment among the Dutch police: 90 percent of the female respondents reported being victims of coarse sexual language. Their explanation supports the *social power theory* of gender inequality—that when women are in a minority position, men try to preserve their domain for themselves and react to women aggressively. Ott refutes Kanter's (1977) claim that group dynamics are almost always unfavorable for a numerical minority, and argues instead that interactions are to a large extent determined by the relative social status of the groups involved. She claims that women in policing are viewed as lower-status intruders who diminish the group's prestige and are therefore sexually harassed. She found that this was especially true in units where they were solo female officers.

In Sweden women police officers' work experiences have received attention only recently. The Police Officers' Association's [Polisforbundet] (1998) study presents statistics on violence and sexual harassment in the police force. In 1997, 11 percent of both women and men had been subject to psychological violence from colleagues; 65 percent of women and 64 percent of men had been subjected to physical violence or threats by citizens during the past twelve months. Eight percent of female police officers had experienced sexual harassment at the workplace, and 22 percent from clients. In the Police College's [Polishogskolan] (1992) study, 31 female and 6 male police officers were asked about their perceptions of both positive and negative characteristics of police work and women's and men's suitability for various tasks in the police force. Women's positive characteristics were said to be flexibility, empathy, and social communication. Men were said to have more physical power and prestige. The interviewees thought that women were more suitable for handling tasks like incest, family violence, and violence victims. Tasks requiring considerable physical strength were thought to suit men better.

WORKPLACE VIOLENCE

When addressing violence, it is important to remember that it can occur within an organization or be perpetrated by clients or customers (Leather 2002). The European Commission defines workplace violence as incidents in which persons are abused, threatened, or assaulted in circumstances related to their work that involved an explicit or implicit challenge to their safety, well-being, or health (Wynne et al. 1997). Psychological violence refers to situations in which a person is subject to long-term bullying, mocking, or repressive behavior from colleagues or supervisors (Vartia & Hyyti 2002). Physical violence pertains to instances in which a person is subject to threats or acts of physical or sexual violence (Piispa & Saarela 2000).

Psychological violence and harassment occur mostly in workplaces where the pace of work has increased, where there is little socializing with coworkers because of increased amounts of work, conflict, or poor workplace atmosphere, or where pay and performance bonuses are a common practice (Sutela 1998). Also, an organization's financial hardship and threats of retrenchment are factors that increase psychological violence and harassment. Psychological violence often occurs repeatedly over a long period of time, and in some cases a single incident can spark repeated harassment that results in serious consequences for the victim (Di Martino 2002). In 2000, 5 percent of Finnish women and 3 percent of men were subjected to psychological violence at work, and 1 percent had experienced physical violence. Women were targets of physical violence at work (2 percent) more frequently than men (1 percent) (Piirainen et al. 2000).

SEXUAL HARASSMENT

The European Commission divides sexual harassment into three categories: (1) verbal—sexual remarks, jokes, comments about appearance; (2) nonverbal—staring, suggestive looks; and (3) physical—unwanted physical contact and sexual assault or rape (European Commission 1999). The new European Union (EU) directive on equal opportunities defines sexual harassment as a situation "where any form of unwanted verbal, non-verbal or physical conduct of a sexual nature occurs, with the purpose or effect of violating the dignity of a person, in particular when creating an intimidating, hostile, degrading, humiliating or offensive environment" (Council Directive 2002/73/EC). Sexual harassment has been found to be a means by which the more powerful control, manipulate, or humiliate those with less power (Kauppinen 1999). According to the 2001 Finnish Gender Barometer (Melkas 2001), 18 percent of women and 5 percent of men indicated that they had been sexually harassed, either verbally or physically, at their workplaces.

FINNISH SURVEY

Data for this study were collected during the summer of 1998 in Finland by using a questionnaire-based survey of all women police officers ($N = 495$). There were 392 responses from female police officers (79 percent response rate). The sample base of male police officers consisted of their whole population, a total of about 7,000 persons. Because female police officers' average age and years in service were significantly lower than the men's, and since female police officers were not equally divided among police stations, a stratified sample in which age and service station were standardized was used to select male police officers. A total of 353 men completed the surveys (71 percent response rate).

Results

The Police Organization. The Finnish police organization is divided into three ranks: (1) junior constables (lowest), (2) police officers and senior constables, and (3) commissioners and department heads (highest). Women were largely concentrated in the lowest ranks of the police hierarchy: 88 percent worked as junior police constables, 11 percent belonged to the middle rank, and only 1 percent had reached the highest ranks. Men generally held higher ranks than women did: 60 percent belonged to the lowest ranks, 31 percent to the middle, and 9 percent to the highest ranks of the police organization.

Thirty-two percent of the women respondents were "pioneers" who started in police work before 1987. There was a significant age difference between the two groups of women: the average age of the older or pioneer women was 44 years, and that of the younger generation was 32. Over three-quarters of the men (76 percent) had entered the police force before 1987.

Older and younger women differed significantly in terms of career development: 28 percent of the older women belonged to the middle ranks and 3 percent to the highest ranks. Among the younger women, only 3 percent had advanced to middle ranks. When compared to their female colleagues, men's career advancement was faster and resulted in higher positions: 52 percent of older men had reached the middle ranks. Younger men had made less progress in their careers than older men but still more than younger women had.

Job Satisfaction, Well-being, and Exhaustion with Client Work. There was a high degree of job satisfaction among both of the sexes: approximately three-quarters of women and men felt very satisfied with their work. Sixty-five percent of female and 54 percent of male police officers felt that the workplace atmosphere was free of conflict and competition. One-third of women and men rated the atmosphere as supportive. However, there were sharp differences of opinion between younger and older women officers: 71 percent of the younger women but only 51 percent of the pioneers felt that the atmosphere was free of conflict and competition. Older women were also more critical of their superior's behavior and organizational skills, and did not rate him as highly as the younger women did. Age differences were not found among men on these survey items.

Exhaustion with client work was examined by three questions: (1) whether client work is straining, (2) whether one treats clients as faceless objects, and (3) whether one becomes insensitive to clients. Ten percent of both women and men responded that client work was straining; 8 percent of female and 12 percent of male police officers said they treated clients as faceless objects; and 15 percent of women and 24 percent of men had become insensitive to clients.

Overall, exhaustion with client work correlated significantly with incidents of sexual harassment and violence at work.

Tasks of Women and Men. Nearly all policewomen and about 60 percent of policemen thought that women and men are equally suitable to work as a police officer. There were many tasks that both women and men believed to be more suitable for women, such as investigation of crimes committed by women, and crimes and violence against women and children, particularly sexual assault and rape. Men, on the other hand, were seen as more suitable for handling tasks involving physical strength, such as in special emergency and dog-handling units. The responses reflect traditional attitudes toward gender roles: men are seen to handle better tasks involving physical power, whereas women are seen as more competent in tasks requiring verbal and emotional skills.

Similar attitudes were found when the respondents were asked whether they would prefer to work with a female or male police officer: 72 percent of female and 81 percent of male police officers preferred to face a dangerous situation with a male police officer. Only 19 percent of female and 14 percent of male police officers preferred to go to a house call with a woman officer. This reflects the dangerous nature of police work.

Attitudes Toward Policewomen. We examined whether the respondents believed that attitudes among officers in the low and middle ranks differed significantly from those with high ranks. Specifically, they were asked if they thought that attitudes toward policewomen were protective, flirtatious, or demeaning, that women's opinions were neglected, or that women officers received special privileges because of their minority status. Table 9.1 shows that both female and male police officers think that attitudes toward women differ considerably between officers in lowest and middle ranks versus those in the highest rank. Generally, they believed that officers in the lowest and middle ranks had more negative attitudes than their superiors did.

Table 9.1

Women's and Men's Perceptions of Officers' Reactions to Women by Rank

	Women's Responses (%)		Men's Responses (%)	
Attitudes Toward Women	Lowest/Middle	Highest	Lowest/Middle	Highest
Overprotective	49	28[a]	58	41[a]
Flirtatious	48[a]	19	28	18
Demeaning	24	17	12	11
Women's opinions are neglected	22[a]	21[a]	9	12
Women criticized for even minor mistakes	17[a]	8[b]	1	2
Women get special privileges	4[a]	4[a]	16	22
Men are overpolite or formal	2[a]	11	9	14

[a] Statistically very significant differences between older and younger officers ($p < .001$).

[b] Statistically significant differences between older and younger officers ($p < .01$).

About half (49 percent) of female and male (58 percent) officers thought that the lowest- and middle-rank men's attitudes toward women were more overprotective than those of their superiors. There was a highly significant difference between younger and older women's opinion: a larger number of younger women believed that officers' attitudes toward them were overprotective (56 vs. 36 percent, respectively). Women were more apt than men to think that lowest- and middle-rank officers' attitudes toward them were flirtatious (48 vs. 28 percent). However, both female and male officers thought that the attitudes of their superiors were considerably less flirtatious than those of their peers. Twice as many women as men (24 vs. 12 percent) described lowest- and middle-rank officers' attitudes toward them as demeaning and degrading.

About one-fifth of the women thought that male police officers neglected their opinions. Only about 10 percent of male police officers considered this to be the case. Almost no men thought that women were criticized for minor mistakes. In contrast, nearly one-fifth of female officers thought that lowest- and middle-rank officers criticized women even for minor mistakes, and 8 percent believed that their superiors did so as well. Considerably more men than women thought that women got special privileges, for example, easier tasks or better equipment, because of their gender. Highest-rank officers' attitudes toward women were described by both male and female respondents as more overpolite or formal than those of their peers.

Sexual Harassment. Sexual harassment was studied from two perspectives: (1) whether one had been exposed to abusive or sexist language from clients or members of the workplace, and (2) whether one had been exposed to unwanted sexual advances during the past twenty-four months. The questions were directed to both women and men (Table 9.2). Women were targets of abusive sexist language in the past twenty-four months much more often than men were. There was no difference in younger and older women's exposure to such language. Women were offended verbally more often by clients (44 percent) than by members of their workplace (34 percent). Name-calling was the most frequent problem women experienced from clients (33 percent); dirty jokes and rude language were the most frequent forms of verbal abuse mentioned by men. Offensive comments about men's appearance and sexuality came mostly from clients (8 percent) and less frequently from colleagues (1 percent).

Unwanted sexual advances were measured by asking whether the respondent had been, in the past twenty-four months, a target of unpleasant looks, leering, and gestures reflecting unwanted sexual messages; physical touching and pawing or unwanted kissing; propositions of sex in an offensive way; inappropriate and sexually colored telephone calls and other messages; or threats or pressure in case of noncompliance with suggestions (Table 9.2).

Men were very seldom targets of unwanted sexual advances from members of the workplace; only a token few had experienced it. For women, being a target of unwanted sexual advances from members of the workplace was more common. However, both women and

Table 9.2

Exposure to Sexual Harassment by Clients and Coworkers in Past 24 Months

	Women (N = 392)		Men (N = 362)	
	Clients (%)	Workplace (%)	Clients (%)	Workplace (%)
Sexist Language				
Dirty jokes and rude language	21	32	15[a]	14[a]
Comments on appearance/sexuality	25	13	8[a]	1[a]
Name-calling, e.g., bitch, whore	33	2	4[a]	0
One or more forms	44	34	19[a]	14[a]
Sexual Advances				
Elevator looks, leering, gestures	15	6	6[a]	0
Touching, pawing, or kissing	8	10	9	0
Offensive sexual propositions	9	4	9	0
Sexual or suggestive calls/messages	4	4	4	0
Threats/pressures for noncompliance	1	1	0	0
One or more forms	23	15	16	0
Violence[b]				
Threats by telephone or letter	21		32[a]	
Threatened face-to-face	42		58[a]	
Attacked physically	24		37[a]	
Injured by a physical attack	22		26	

[a] Indicates a statistically significant difference between older and younger officers.
[b] Violence is from clients only. There were no incidents from fellow officers.

men were targets of unwanted advances from clients (23 percent and 16 percent, respectively). There was a highly significant difference between younger and older male police officers in terms of being a target of elevator looks, leering, and gestures reflecting unpleasant and unwanted sexual messages from clients. For women, age did not make a significant difference in this regard.

The most typical forms of unwanted sexual advances from clients toward women were elevator looks, leering, and gestures reflecting unpleasant and unwanted sexual messages (15 percent). Touching, pawing, and unwanted kissing were the most common forms of sexual advances from members of the workplace (10 percent). Propositions of sex in a direct and offensive way by clients were somewhat frequent (9 percent), but threats and pressures in case of noncompliance with sexually colored suggestions were rare (1 percent), as were inappropriate telephone calls and other sexually colored messages (4 percent).

Psychological and Physical Violence. The amount of psychological violence or mobbing was examined by asking (1) Does psychological violence occur at your workplace? and (2) Have you been the object of psychological violence at work or at work-related situations? Leymann's (1996) definition of psychological violence was given: "Psychological violence in working life involves hostile or unethical communication, which is directed in a systematic way by one or few individuals mainly towards one individual who is pushed into a helpless and defenseless position. These actions occur on a frequent basis or over a long period of time."

A separate analysis of officers' experiences with and attitudes toward physical and psychological violence (analysis not shown) found that 23 percent of female and 19 percent of male officers had experienced psychological violence at work. Fourteen percent of women had been subject to psychological violence at the workplace, compared to 8 percent of men ($p < .01$). Among the women who had been subject to psychological violence at work, most thought that attitudes toward women were less positive than toward men. A growing problem in police work is physical violence and intimidation by clients. Seventy-seven percent of policemen and 68 percent of women thought that the threat of physical violence had increased in the last five years. Nineteen percent of men and 14 percent of women were worried about being victims of violence at work.

The occurrence of physical violence at work was examined by asking whether one had been (1) threatened on the telephone or by letter, (2) threatened face-to-face, (3) attacked physically, and (4) injured in a violent attack. Men had encountered physical violence at work during the past twenty-four months significantly more often than women had. Younger men's experiences with physical violence were significantly greater than those of older male officers. The most typical form of physical violence experienced by both sexes was being threatened face-to-face (58 percent of men and 42 percent of women). About a third of men and a quarter of women had been physically attacked by clients, and 26 percent of men and 22 percent of women had been injured as a result (Table 9.2).

Well-being, Sexual Harassment, and Violence at Work. For both women and men, verbal harassment and unwanted sexual advances as well as psychological and physical violence at work were related to job dissatisfaction and exhaustion with client work. Table 9.3 presents a summary of correlations between forms of sexual harassment and violence and job-related and psychological outcomes. Psychological and physical violence were related to job dissatisfaction and exhaustion with client work for women and men. Perceived psychological violence had a strongly negative effect on job satisfaction for both sexes. Perceived psychological violence at the workplace had a

Table 9.3

Health Consequences of Sexual Harassment and Violence by Gender

	Job Satisfaction		Exhaustion with Client Work	
	Women	Men	Women	Men
Job characteristic				
Perceived psychological violence at work	—	—		+
Victim of psychological violence at work	—	—		
Threatened by letter or telephone by clients			+	+ +
Injured by physical attack from clients		—		+
Threat of violence at work has increased			+	+
Sexist language by clients			+	+
Sexual advances at work			+	

$+ / + +$ Increasing/strongly increasing effect, significant correlation ($r > .13 / > .30$).

—Decreasing/strongly decreasing effect, significant correlation ($r > .13 / > .30$).

stronger negative correlation with job satisfaction than having been a victim of psychological violence. This was true for women and men. Male police officers who had been injured in an attack expressed low job satisfaction along with high levels of exhaustion. Threats by telephone or letter increased women's and men's exhaustion with client work. Also, the perception that the threat of violence had increased in recent years was correlated with exhaustion with client work for women as well as men.

Female police officers were bothered by the occurrence of sexual harassment. Sexist language and unwanted sexual advances at work made women police feel exhausted with client work. The sexist language of clients increased exhaustion among male officers as well.

Summary and Discussion

The number of women in the Finnish police force has remained relatively low. Women are mostly situated in the lowest rank of the police organization and concentrate on tasks seen as stereotypically suitable for women. As in the Swedish police force (Polishogskolan 1992), both female and male police officers in Finland believed that women are better suited to handle tasks that involve crimes by or against women or that require social skills and empathy. Most female and male Finnish police officers preferred to face a dangerous situation with a male colleague. Although these results reflect traditional attitudes toward gender roles, they do not necessarily indicate ingrained sexist attitudes, since 60 percent of Finnish police officers thought that both sexes are equally suitable for police work, and most Swedish officers thought that the ability to work as a police officer depends more on one's capabilities than on one's sex.

Based on this study, attitudes toward women differed on the basis of rank. Women thought that lowest- and middle-rank officers' attitudes were in general more protective and flirtatious than highest-rank officers' attitudes. Highest-rank officers' attitudes toward women were believed to be less negative than those of lowest- and middle-rank officers. Younger women thought that male officers' attitudes toward them were more protective than older women did. This "generation gap" is evident in other opinions too, and may reflect the fact that older women are treated with more respect than their younger sisters because of the former's higher position in the police organization or their greater tolerance of the workplace culture.

Forty-four percent of Finnish policewomen stated that they had experienced verbal sexual harassment during the past twenty-four months. This is low compared to the high 90 percent of the Dutch female police officers who reported being a target of coarse verbal remarks (Ott 1989). Twenty-three percent of Finnish female police officers were victims of unwanted sexual advances from clients, and 15 percent from members of the work collective. These figures are higher than for Swedish policewomen, of whom 8 percent had been sexually harassed by a colleague and 22 percent by a client (Polisforbundet 1998), but significantly lower than in Great Britain and the Republic of Ireland, where levels of harassment exceeded 60 percent (Brown 2000). However, levels of verbal sexual harassment and unwanted advances among Finnish policewomen are higher than the general level of sexual harassment in Finnish workplaces (18 percent) as measured by the Finnish Gender Barometer. Gruber, Husu, and Kauppinen (forthcoming) suggest that the low level of reported sexual harassment in Finland may be partly explained by the relatively low level of awareness of what exactly sexual harassment is.

It is interesting to note that reported levels of verbal sexual harassment and unwanted sexual advances among policewomen in both Finland and Sweden are considerably lower than in other European countries. Also, the fact that sexual harassment among policewomen is much higher than the general level of sexual harassment in Finnish workplaces is notable. Several factors may account for this. Attitudes toward sexual harassment are twofold among police officers. On one hand it is seen as degrading and disagreeable; and, on the other hand, it is seen as part of a job in a male-dominated work culture where group loyalty and solidarity are highly valued.

This is reflected in women's strong desires to assimilate into the police force. Since policewomen do not want to be singled out as troublemakers, some close their eyes to sexual harassment. It is apparent that many of these women use *internally focused strategies*—ignoring the behavior, redefining their treatment as something other than harassment, reassessing their harassers' motives (Fitzgerald, Swan, & Fischer 1995)—as means of coping with the discriminatory and sexually based behavior of their colleagues and clients.

Compared with national rates, the high level of sexual harassment among the policewomen is partly due to their token status in a male-dominated occupation (Gutek & Morasch 1982). Based on a study of women in male-dominated occupations in Finland, Kauppinen-Toropainen (1991) found that women in male-dominated occupations suffered more sexual harassment than other working women did. This is especially true for policing, as women are in a distinct minority position in the organization.

Also, psychological violence or mobbing among policewomen was high (14 percent) compared to the level of violence experienced by women in Finnish workplaces in general (5 percent). Psychological violence against women was significantly higher than that against men (8 percent). The victimized women did not believe that men and women were treated equally in police organizations. The high level of psychological violence against women may be due to their token position in the police force. Psychological violence at work was related to job dissatisfaction for both female and male police officers.

Physical violence rates against police officers were high, reflecting the dangerous nature of the police work—24 percent of women and 37 percent of men had been attacked on the job. This is substantially higher than the general level of violence in Finnish working life—2 percent for women and 1 percent for men. Physical violence and its threat in police organizations were more prevalent among men than among women. Perpetrators of physical violence in police work were mostly clients. Physical violence and its threat by clients were related to exhaustion with client work, burnout, and for some, physical injuries. The current personnel strategy of the Finnish police speaks directly to the issue of work stressors and allows for the provision of a personal training program for everyone to maintain physical and psychological work ability, and in this way to reduce stress and anxiety.

Our results found that sexual harassment and violence are serious problems for Finnish policewomen, and act as stressors and reasons for job dissatisfaction. Currently, sexual harassment and violence are receiving increased attention both as academic research subjects and issues in the media. New EU-wide and national legislation have also been developed to answer the growing need to provide protection and support for employees. It is likely that increased attention to and knowledge of matters of sexual harassment and violence will reduce their occurrence by enabling employees to tackle the issues and to get help when needed. The future holds promise for women in policing. Increasing the number of women in policing will make women's position easier. Also, the Finnish police force's strategy on the provision of equal opportunities emphasizes professional behavior and civility. It specifically addresses the issue of sexual harassment and provides a clear mandate for zero tolerance.

REFERENCES

Brown, Jennifer. 1993. Qualitative differences in men and women police officers' experience of occupational stress. *Work and Stress* 7 (4): 327–340.

———. 1998. Aspects of discriminatory treatment of women police officers serving in forces in England and Wales. *British Journal of Criminology* 38 (2): 265–282.

———. 2000. Discriminatory experiences of women police: A comparison of officers serving in England and Wales, Scotland, Northern Ireland and the Republic of Ireland. *International Journal of the Sociology of Law* 28:91–111.

Bureau of Labor Statistics. 2001. *Occupational Employment and Wages, 2001.* USDL 02-619. Table 1. Washington, D.C.: Government Printing Office.

Council Directive 2002/73/EC of the European Parliament and Council of 23 September 2002 amending Council Directive 76/207/EEC on the implementation of the principle of equal treatment for men and women as regards access to employment, vocational training and promotion, and working conditions [online]. http://europa.eu.int/smartapi/cgi/sga_doc?smartapi!celexapi!prod!CELEXn umdoc&lg = en&numdoc = 32002 L0073&model = guichett (Accessed May 12, 2002).

Di Martino, Vittorio. 2002. Violence at the workplace: The global response. *Asian-Pacific Newsletter on Occupational Health and Safety* 9 (1): 4–7.

European Commission. 1999. *Sexual harassment at the workplace in the European Union*. Luxembourg: Office for Official Publications of the European Communities.

Fitzgerald, L., S. Swan, and K. Fischer. 1995. "Why didn't she report him?" The psychological and legal implications of women's responses to sexual harassment. *Journal of Social Issues* 51 (1): 117–138.

Gruber, J., L. Husu, and K. Kauppinen. Forthcoming. Finland: The problematic march towards gender equality. In *Sexual harassment: A cross-cultural perspective*, ed. E. DeSouza and J. Pryor. Silver Spring, Md.: Greenwood Publishing Group.

Gutek, Barbara A., and Bruce Morasch. 1982. Sex-ratios, sex-role spillover, and sexual harassment of women at work. *Journal of Social Issues* 38:55–74.

Holdaway, Simon, and Sharon K. Parker. 1998. Policing women police: Uniform patrol, promotion and representation in the CID. *British Journal of Criminology* 38 (1): 40–60.

Kanter, Rosabeth Moss. 1977. *Men and women of the corporation*. New York: Basic Books.

Kauppinen, Kaisa. 1999. Sexual harassment in the workplace. In *Women and occupational health*, ed. P. Kane. Geneva: World Health Organization.

Kauppinen, T., P. Heikkila, S. Lehtinen, K. Lindstrom, S. Nayha, A. Seppala, J. Toikkanen, and A. Tossavainen, eds. 2000. *Tyo ja Terveys Suomessa v. 2000* (Work and health in Finland in 2000). Helsinki: Tyoterveyslaitos.

Kauppinen-Toropainen, Kaisa. 1991. Miehet naisvaltaisissa ja naiset miesvaltaisissa ammateissa: Ainokaisaseman analyysi (Men in female-dominated and women in male-dominated occupations: An analysis of token status). *Tyo ja Ihminen* 3:218–238.

Larwood, Laurie, and Marion Wood. 1979. *Women in management*. London: Lexington Books.

Leather, Paul. 2002. *Managing work-related violence: Current knowledge and future directions*. Paper presented at the European Week for Safety and Health at Work: Preventing Psychosocial Risks at Work: European Perspectives. Bilbao, November 2002. www.osha.eu.int.

Leymann, Heinz, and Annelie Gustafsson. 1996. Mobbing at work and the development of post-traumatic stress disorder. *European Journal of Work and Organizational Psychology* 5 (2): 251–275.

Martin, Carol. 1996. The impact of equal opportunities policies on the day-to-day experiences of women police constables. *British Journal of Criminology* 36 (4): 510–528.

Melkas, Helena, and Richard Anker. 1998. *Gender equality and occupational segregation in Nordic labor markets*. Geneva: International Labour Office.

Melkas, Tuula. 2001. *The gender barometer 2001*. Living conditions 2002:2, Gender Statistics. Statistics Finland.

Nuutinen, Iira, Kaisa Kauppinen, and Irja Kandolin. 1999. Tasa-arvo poliisi-toimessa: Tyoyhteisojen ja henkiloston hyvinvointi (Equality in the police force: Well-being of personnel and work organizations). Helsinki: Tyoterveyslaitos, Sisaasiainministerio.

Ott, E. Marlies. 1989. Effects of the male-female ratio at work: Policewomen and male nurses. *Psychology of Women Quarterly* 13:41–47.

Piirainen, H., A-L. Elo, M. Hirvonen, K. Kauppinen, R. Ketola, H. Laitinen, K. Lindstrom, K. Reijula, R. Riala, M. Viluksela, and S. Virtanen. 2000. *Tyo ja terveys: Haastattelututkimus v. 2000. Taulukkoraportti* (Work and health: An interview study in 2000. Table report). Helsinki: Tyoterveyslaitos.

Piispa, Minna, and Kaija Leena Saarela. 2000. Tyovakivalta. In *Tyon Vaarat 1999: Koetut tyoperaiset sairaudet, tyotapaturmat ja tyovakivaltatapaukset* (Dangers of work 1999: Work-related illnesses, accidents and violence at work), ed. Seppo Paananen. Tyomarkkinat 2000:15. Helsinki: Tilastokeskus.

Polisforbundet. 1998. *Sa har vi det pa jobbet: En rapport om polisens arbetsmiljo* (This is how we have it at work: A report about the police's work environment). Stockholm: Polisforbundet.

Polishogskolan i samarbete med Statshalsan Kungsholmen. 1992. *Kvinnor i polisyrket: En pilotstudie av svenska kvinnor i poliskarriaren* (Women in police: A pilot study of Swedish women in police). Stockholm: Polishogskolan i samarbete med Statshalsan Kungholmen.

Pope, K. E., and D. W. Pope. 1986. Attitudes of male police officers towards their female counterparts. *Police Journal* 59 (3): 242–250.

Sutela, Hanna. 1998. Tasa-arvo, oikeudenmukaisuus, tyopaikan sosiaaliset suhteet. In *Tehokas, tehokkaampi, uupunut: Tyoolotutkimuksien tuloksia, 1977–1997* (Efficient, more efficient, exhausted: Results of work condition surveys, 1977–1997), ed. Anna-Maija Lehto and Hanna Sutela. Tilastokeskus: Tyomarkkinat 1998:12.

Vartia, Maarit, and Jari Hyyti. 2002. Gender differences in workplace bullying among prison officers. *European Journal of Work and Organizational Psychology* 11 (1): 113–126.

Wynne, R., N. Clarkin, T. Cox, and A. Griffiths. 1997. *Guidance on the prevention of violence at work.* Luxembourg: European Commission, DG V.

10 A MISSING LINK
Institutional Homophobia and Sexual Harassment in the U. S. Military

Melissa Sheridan Embser-Herbert

While sexual harassment occurs throughout the labor force, it is even more widespread in male-dominated occupations (Gruber 1998, Schneider 1982, Whaley & Tucker 1998). With women constituting no more than 15 percent of military personnel, the United States military remains a male-dominated occupation (Women's Research and Education Institute 2002). In addition, sexual harassment is endemic to the U.S. armed forces, and rates remain well above the national average (Firestone & Harris 1994, Nelson 2002). At the same time that the military was confronted with an unprecedented number of sexual harassment scandals, it was also forced to grapple with the issue of sexual orientation more publicly than ever before. In fact, it was not long after the military instituted a policy of zero tolerance regarding sexual harassment that the United States Congress passed the "Don't Ask, Don't Tell" policy banning gay and lesbian service members. Yet, except when complaints of same-sex harassment are made by heterosexuals, the issues of sexual harassment and sexual orientation are treated as unrelated. Doing so fails to account for the lived experience of many military women. Homophobic forms of sexual harassment—allegations of lesbianism and pressures for sexual favors as a test of heterosexuality—are common, and the ban on gays and lesbians complicates the reporting of sexual harassment.

This chapter draws upon survey results to examine how military women conceptualize and experience sexual harassment. It draws upon qualitative and quantitative analyses to highlight the link between sexual harassment and homophobia. Specifically, it describes how homophobia affects experiences and perceptions, and it explores how being a lesbian or bisexual impacts both of them. The results suggest that 69 percent of military women are sexually harassed. Sixty-four percent of them feel that sexual harassment is a problem, and 76 percent feel that the U.S. armed forces have not done enough to eliminate the problem. The fear of being labeled "lesbian" is a significant factor affecting how women experience and respond to harassment. The findings also point to diversity among women. In some cases, lesbians and bisexuals experience and perceive sexual harassment differently than their heterosexual counterparts do. These outcomes indicate that progress on the sexual harassment problem may be tied to the reform of sexual orientation policies. For example, lifting the ban on homosexuality would eliminate the threat of being labeled a lesbian and therefore encourage more proactive responses.

THE U.S. ARMED FORCES AS DOUBLY DOMINATED

Unlike in civilian occupations, the domination of military work by men is legally sanctioned. Although women have always performed services for and with the military, it was not until World War I that women were recognized as military personnel in any official capacity. During World War II, women were recruited in significant numbers, but in 1948 federal law capped their participation at 2 percent of total service personnel. This restriction was lifted in 1967; however, women continued to experience limits on their participation in terms of occupation and duty assignment. With the end of the draft in the early 1970s, opportunities for women expanded. Since the early 1990s, even more restrictions on women, particularly some of those concerning combat assignments, have been lifted. As these changes have taken place, the number of women serving in the U.S. military has continued to grow (Titunik 2000). But, despite fairly aggressive integration policies, military women remain significantly outnumbered by their male counterparts.

Male domination of the U.S. military is supported both structurally and culturally. Prior to the elimination of the draft, the military served as the primary socialization agent for the masculine identity of late adolescent American males. Both formal policy and informal practice reproduce hierarchical relations between men and solidarity among them in ways that encourage the subordination of all women and some men (Cockburn 1991). Sociologist Erving Goffman (1977) noted, "A considerable amount of what persons who are men do in affirmation of their sense of identity requires their doing something that can be seen as what a woman by her nature could not do, or at least could not do well" (p. 326). At least in Western societies like the United States, war and the preparation for war have been defined as something women either should not do or cannot do well. Thus, even in the absence of a draft,[1] the military, with its mission of preparing for war, remains a socially sanctioned mechanism for the achievement of a masculine identity (Connell 2000).

But, even more importantly, in the military, achieving masculinity takes this process one step further and demands the denigration of the feminine and the subordination of women. As Beck (1991) explains:

> A man has an easier time reaffirming his masculinity when he can measure it against femininity represented by a woman who has accepted the subordinate societal role. However, he may feel his manly self-image threatened—especially at a time he needs it to be reaffirmed—when he finds himself in competition with a woman who could win something he needs for himself, or who could gain dominance of the immediate environment. (p. 33)

Thus, when military men—either as a group or as individuals—feel as though women have "invaded their turf," they harass women, hoping that, ultimately, they will leave. Such tactics have been well documented by women who made early inroads into "male" occupations, from the trades to the professions (Collison & Collison 1996, Gruber & Bjorn 1982, Rosenberg, Perlstadt, & Phillips 1993).

SEXUAL HARASSMENT IN THE UNITED STATES ARMED FORCES

In the military, a common way to accomplish masculinity and preserve the patriarchy is to engage in activities that highlight the various ways in which women are not like men—ways in which they are "the other." As in civilian institutions, gender discrimination occurs throughout the armed forces with regularity. However, in military institutions, sexualized forms of discrimination are especially pernicious. In addressing the sexual harassment scandals at Aberdeen Proving Ground, Regina Titunik (2000) writes, "What was remarkable . . . was the fundamental consensus on all sides that these incidents of sexual misconduct were not isolated or anomalous, but reflected a deeper, systemic problem in the military" (p. 231). More recently, revelations concerning the United States Air Force Academy, the degree to which the chain of command was complicit in the cover-up, and the disregard of reports of sexual assaults have provided unfortunate evidence of the degree to which the denigration of women remains at the core of the military as an institution.[2]

Sexual harassment in the military is an issue for service members, the chain of command, members of Congress, and those who advocate on behalf of women in the military. During the twelve years it was published, *Minerva's Bulletin Board: The News Magazine on Women and the Military*, routinely provided accounts of the harassment that plagued the United States military. During the mid-1990s, the *Bulletin Board* carried continual "updates" of the different outcomes of the infamous 1991 Tailhook convention (e.g., "Tailhook tidbits," "Tailhook—It's not over yet").[3] Published accounts of other incidents ranged from service members whose careers have ended or have been seriously compromised because of their harassing behavior or alleged harassment ("Gulf war sexual assault case ends with bad conduct discharge," "Navy Captain cleared of harassment loses promotion") *or* because they were victims of harassment ("Family of harassment victim sues after soldier's suicide"), to accounts of those who seem to move forward unscathed, regardless of their involvement in harassing behavior ("Admiral's career advances despite harassment controversy"). In response to repeated high-profile incidents of sexual harassment in the military, then Secretary of Defense William J. Perry (1996) stated:

> Our policy on sexual harassment is crystal clear. We believe that sexual harassment is wrong, ethically and morally. We believe it is wrong from the point of view of military discipline. And we believe it is wrong from the point of view of maintaining proper respect in the chain of command. And for all of these reasons therefore, we have a zero tolerance for sexual harassment.

In addition to adopting a zero tolerance policy, the Department of Defense mandated sexual harassment training for all personnel. Yet, in one instance, after undergoing a daylong sexual harassment seminar, "two sailors . . . demonstrated their grasp of the basic principles by grabbing the nineteen year old woman, holding her down while they simulated sex acts and then threw her over the side of the craft into frigid waters" ("Sexual harassment training not yet perfected"). While many reported incidents also include civilians, government employees and not, as both perpetrators and victims ("Report on a decade of sexual harassment in VA results in major changes"), the findings presented here focus strictly on women service members' harassment by other service members. It is my contention that harassment is a serious problem for all women in the military. Even if a woman is herself not a victim, harassment limits the full participation of women as a group.

HOMOPHOBIA AND SEXUAL HARASSMENT

A hallmark of hegemonic masculinity is homophobia (Connell 1995). Few, if any, institutions are more openly antigay than the U.S. military. In fact, evidence of the *propensity* for homosexuality is a ground for discharge. Federal law concerning "gays in the military" is alleged to permit gays, lesbians, and bisexuals to serve in the military provided they "don't tell." Yet, it is common knowledge that even a rumor of homosexuality is enough to ruin a service member's career.[4]

Sexual harassment that is specifically homophobic is a tactic commonly employed by military men. In fact, it is so common that the label *dyke baiting* has emerged to describe the behavior. Accusations of lesbianism affect *all* women, regardless of their sexual orientation (Pharr 1988). When allegations of lesbianism can be used to end a woman's career, it matters little if the allegations are true (Service-members Legal Defense Network 2002, Shilts 1993). The threat of being labeled a lesbian may keep women apart, may encourage them to form unwanted relations with men, and may keep them from performing to the level at which they are capable (Herbert 1998).

Some women may be asked to "prove" that they are heterosexual, while others may be harassed for assumptions of "hyperheterosexuality," or the perception that a woman is not just heterosexual, but sexually available. One respondent in my research noted that a woman in her unit "was subjected to sexual taunts, come-ons, etc., because she was very pretty and wore make-up" while another said that "women who are too feminine are perceived . . . as playthings, as 'fresh meat'" (Herbert 1998:67). Those same data, however, showed that emphasizing one's femininity and highlighting features deemed attractive to heterosexual men is an effective strategy to avoid being labeled a lesbian. Thus, women are caught in a double bind. To avoid being labeled a lesbian, one must prove one is sexually attractive to men. To avoid unwanted sexual advances, one must prove one is not sexually available.

In considering the unique role that homophobia plays in the sexual harassment of women in a male-dominated institution like the military, I decided to compare the experiences and perceptions of lesbian and bisexual women with those of heterosexual women. I was particularly interested in the degree to which both groups experienced sexual harassment that was homophobic in character. Finally, I tested the degree to which other factors—type of service, rank, and years of service—might differentiate between women.

THE SURVEY

This analysis is based on forced-choice questionnaires administered to 326 women who were either veterans of or currently serving in the United States military. The final sample involved 241 heterosexual women and 85 lesbian or bisexual women. Lesbian and bisexual women were oversampled in order to obtain a sufficient number for analysis. The women served in the Army (46 percent), Air Force (30 percent), Navy (20 percent), and Marine Corps (4 percent). While 216 (66 percent) were enlisted personnel, 110 (34 percent) were officers. Their ranks ranged from E2, the equivalent of an Army private, to O6, the equivalent of an Army colonel. The sample contained 185 (57 percent) junior persons (i.e., E1–E4 enlisted pay grades and officers in O1–O3 pay grades) and 141 (43 percent) senior persons (i.e., noncommissioned officers E5 and above and field officers O4 and above). To ensure that respondents had spent time in the day-to-day world of the military, participation required at least one year of active duty in the United States military at some time since 1976.[5]

Because it is virtually impossible to locate a random sample of women veterans or women in the military,[6] I recruited respondents by posting notices at women's bookstores and in gay and lesbian community centers, on computer bulletin boards, in publications such as *Minerva's Bulletin Board* and *The Register* (the newsletter of the Women in Military Service for America), and at college and university veterans program offices around the nation.

The questionnaire contained almost two hundred questions, including demographic data. The substantive questions were divided into the topical areas labeled: military service, education, personal assessment, personal resources, gender, and sexuality. "Personal assessment" included the items addressing harassment as well as agree/disagree responses to statements such as "I feel that my time in the military made me a better person." "Personal resources" included questions about outside activities (e.g., "I participated in informal team sports on base") as well as items on subjects such as counseling, smoking, drug and alcohol use, and appearance. A number of open-ended items were included to allow respondents to provide, in their own words, descriptive accounts of the experiences that were being measured in the closed-ended items as well as information about which I might not have thought to ask. These items, reflected throughout this chapter, provided some of the richest data I received.[7]

Several items from these surveys were analyzed using frequency distributions and cross-tabulations with the chi-square statistic to determine significance. I also utilized logistic regression analyses to examine the relationships between several independent variables (e.g., age, rank, sexual orientation, branch of service) and the dichotomous dependent variables of (1) whether respondents thought sexual harassment was a problem in the military and (2) whether they had experienced harassment.

Is Sexual Harassment a Problem for Women in the Military?

Respondents were asked to answer yes or no to the following statement regarding their perceptions of harassment: "I think that sexual harassment is a problem for most women in the military." Sixty-four percent of the sample indicated that, yes, sexual harassment was a problem. Respondents were then asked to indicate whether they felt that the following statement regarding their own experience was definitely not true, probably not true, uncertain, probably true, or definitely true: "I believe that I was sexually harassed while in the military." Sixty-nine percent indicated that this was probably true (20.6 percent) or definitely true (48.8 percent). There was a significant relationship (chi square $= 97.98$, $p = .000$) between experiencing sexual harassment and perceiving that it is a problem in the military. Fifty-seven percent of respondents indicated that they believed both that sexual harassment is a problem *and* that they were sexually harassed. Slightly less than one-quarter (23 percent) said they had not been harassed, nor did they believe harassment was a problem. Eight percent felt that it was a problem, but that they had not been harassed. Interestingly, 13 percent felt that they had been harassed but that this was not a problem for most women in the military.

Those respondents who indicated that they had been sexually harassed were asked to "describe the type of incident to which you are referring." The question asked only for an example and not an exhaustive list. Nonetheless, various themes were represented frequently enough that they are likely representative of the quality of harassment, albeit not the quantity. In analyzing these responses the following themes or categories emerged: (1) "jokes" and other remarks, (2) inappropriate references to body parts, (3) requests for sexual favors, (4) sexual assault, and (5) harassment related to sexual orientation. I first offer some of the responses that characterize the sheer number of incidents that they viewed as harassment. I then provide some examples from the open-ended items to illustrate the different themes listed above.

When prompted to describe an incident, one Navy enlisted woman responded, "I am not referring to a type of incident here— there were too many." An Army enlisted woman wrote, "Where do I begin?" while another wrote, "I could write a book." An Army officer responded similarly when she stated, "You've got to be kidding! It was a day by day thing, most of us could write the proverbial book." Another, an enlisted woman in the Air Force, wrote, "Which incident? There were so many." Thus, while many women experience harassment, it is clear that, for at least some women, the harassment is not a matter of an isolated incident but, as one woman wrote, "an overall climate in which sexual harassment is the norm rather than the exception."

A Marine noncommissioned officer wrote, "A male sergeant . . . took it upon himself to try to humiliate or anger me with name calling, lewd joke telling, started rumors about my sexuality." An Air Force noncommissioned officer wrote, "Asking me what I 'named' my other breast as I wore a nametag over one." One Navy enlisted woman responded that "supervisors called me names such as 'sweetie-pie,' 'cutie.'" This type of harassment is on the boundary of harassment that is sexual in nature and harassment focused on gender. It is included here because the respondent considered it sexual harassment, but more importantly because it is, arguably, harassment focused on the woman as a sexual being rather than merely on her status as a woman (e.g., You can't handle a rig that heavy"). This respondent continued with "Several supervisors made repeated passes at me though I tried to make it clear that I wasn't interested. They called us women 'WAVES' [an official military term for Navy women] and liked to make 'jokes' about 'riding the waves.'"

Harassment was not limited to the barracks, the office, or field environments. The physical training required of most military personnel was also a site for harassment. In temperate weather women typically wear running shorts and a T-shirt and are engaged in sweaty, tough, physical endeavors. An Army captain was told that while doing push-ups she had to touch her breasts to the ground in order to pass. Doing so is not a requirement for doing a proper push-up. An Army enlisted woman was told, while doing physical training, that she was "drawing attention" to herself by her nipples being hard, although it was 45 degrees outside. These responses demonstrate the pervasiveness of harassment across the work environment and illustrate the degree to which women simply cannot escape being targets for harassment.

A number of respondents identified situations in which sexual favors were requested, sometimes in exchange for something else a superior could do for, or against, the woman being harassed. An enlisted woman in the Army wrote, "[I] worked for a Lieutenant Colonel who told me if I sat on his lap and asked nicely I could get a day off." Others wrote about the fact that to not submit to sexual advances implied that one must surely be a lesbian, a point to which I will return shortly. Sometimes the incidents didn't explicitly indicate requests, but were "displays" of sexuality by male service members. One Army noncommissioned officer wrote, "I remember my First Sergeant coming in my barracks room while I was sleeping to show me his 'hard on.'" The latter example illustrates one of the ways in which harassment in the military can be even more threatening and more pervasive than in civilian settings. Women who live in the barracks sleep, shower, dress, and seek to relax in this environment; it is their home. But, with a chain of command that has access to one's "home" 24/7, a woman is never completely safe from the intrusion of men who wish to make her the target of their remarks. One response that appeared with unexpected frequency was that of rape. The survey did not include an item asking about rape explicitly. Thus, the five women who volunteered this information in the open-ended item should be viewed as a minimum estimate of the degree to which military women experience violent sexual assault. The DoD 1995 Sexual Harassment Survey reported that 4 percent of respondents, about 1,890 women, had experienced rape or sexual assault in the military (Bastian, Lancaster & Reyst 1996). One Army enlisted woman wrote: "I was proud to serve in the U.S. Army, but it was hard for us women. The sexual harassment was terrible. I was raped by men in my unit. To this day I have problems with it and am very angry. I had planned on being in the service a long time." A naval officer wrote: "From my recruiter to my immediate supervisor at my last command I was sexually harassed by men of various ranks above and below mine and was even raped by a senior officer following a 'Hail and Farewell.'" An Air Force noncommissioned officer indicated that she had been "raped by a co-worker while on TDY [temporary duty]." She added, "When I reported it to my supervisor, he said I had probably asked for it."

Again, there is no escape in a setting in which women live, eat, and sleep among their harassers. This also means that potential harassers are privy to far more of a woman's personal life than is typically the case in the civilian world. In a world in which men both dominate *and*, I would argue, can easily [choose to] misread a woman's actions, the potential for abuse and assault increases exponentially. Place this within an institutional culture in which men are taught that the degree to which they are "real men" is correlated with the degree to which they "conquer" femininity—be it metaphorically or via real women—and one has a potentially explosive mix.

In considering the various ways in which women might experience harassment, I was curious as to whether lesbian or bisexual women and heterosexual women differed in their perceptions and experiences of harassment. I was also interested in the degree to which sexual harassment was homophobic in character. The qualitative responses to open-ended prompts for details illustrate how homophobic sexual harassment affects both lesbian or bisexual and heterosexual women. An Air Force enlisted woman wrote: "Another airman (female) and I moved to an off-base apartment and our male co-workers insinuated constantly that we were lesbians. They'd say things like, 'Does Judy ever ask if she can be Frank with you?' And, 'Are you Frank with each other?'" An Army enlisted woman described the "Dykebusters" as "an organization of enlisted guys designed to make women, especially lesbians, feel uncomfortable. My best friend was straight and on my door was written *Mr.* and Mrs. (her first name) because we were close and hung out, etc." An Army noncommissioned officer wrote: "An E-7 whom I worked for actually made a comment that I really should start sleeping with men again if I were going to get anywhere in the military. In a room full of people." Another respondent wrote, "As a woman you were either a slut or gay. . . . Co-workers were constantly on the make, trying to decide [in] which category to place women." Yet another woman who was raped in her room by an upperclassman while attending the Naval Academy wrote: "There had been rumors about my sexuality and he was hoping to 'set me straight.' Upon reporting the incident to my company officer, I was told that it was my own fault—being there was temptation—besides he had a promising career, while I would likely end up in supply."

How Well the U.S. Armed Forces Handles Sexual Harassment

Questions were asked to probe how respondents felt about the military's efforts to deal with the sexual harassment problem. Respondents were asked to indicate yes or no to the following statement: "I think that the military has done as much as they can to eliminate sexual harassment among service members." It should be remembered that, of the 326 respondents, some had left active duty prior to the institutionalization of sexual harassment training into military education. Although accounts of these efforts have been widely publicized in the civilian press, it is impossible to say whether a respondent was thinking specifically of what had been done during her time in service or since that time. Nonetheless, 76 percent felt that the military had not done as much as it could to eliminate these problems among service members.

Not all comments were negative. Some women, for example, described incidents in which men tried to help them avoid harassment. An Air Force major wrote, "My commander was constantly trying to touch the female staff members and making lewd suggestions. My male staff tried to protect me with furniture placement and their own body placement and it worked on occasion." Another described the way she had been harassed by women, "I was harassed by two female nurses who lowered my evaluations when I would not go out with them." Thus, while the focus of this research is the harassment of women by men, it should be recognized that not *all* men are harassers and not *all* harassers are men (see Chapter 6 of this volume).

In short, whether one has experienced sexual harassment personally or not, and a majority have, the majority do believe it to be a problem. Lesbian and bisexual women were far more likely to perceive sexual harassment as a problem for most women in the military. Eighty-six percent of lesbian and bisexual women believed this was the case, compared to only 57 percent of heterosexual women. Regarding the views of junior women versus senior women,[8] 69 percent of junior women felt that harassment was a problem, compared to 59 percent of senior women. The relationships between enlisted or officer status and military branch were not significant. Thus, of the four independent variables—sexual orientation, seniority status, rank, and branch of service—sexual orientation appears to be the most predictive of whether or not one believes sexual harassment is a problem (Table 10.1).

Logistic regression is a useful tool for identifying risk factors for becoming a member of a particular group. In this case, I wanted to further examine what types of variables might increase the likelihood that a woman would perceive sexual harassment to be a serious

Table 10.1

Who Believes Sexual Harassment Is a Problem? (N = 326)

Status	% Yes	Chi Square Probability	Logistic Regression Analysis Probability > Chi Square
Sexual Orientation			
Lesbian/bisexual	86	.000	.0001
Heterosexual	57		
Seniority			
Junior	69	.068	.0472
Senior	59		
Rank			
Enlisted	67	.152	.4173
Officer	59		
Branch			
Army	69	.270	.9097
Navy	66		
Marine	54		
Air Force	58		

problem. I recoded the responses so that the respondents were organized into two groups: those who thought sexual harassment was a problem and those who did not. The factors tested were sexual orientation, junior or senior status, enlisted or officer status, and military branch. The finding that lesbian and bisexual women were more likely to perceive sexual harassment to be a problem remained strong ($p = .0001$). Additionally, junior personnel were more likely to perceive harassment to be a problem ($p = .047$). Again, enlisted or officer status and branch were not significant (Table 10.1).

To further examine the issue of who perceived sexual harassment to be a problem, I separated the sample by sexual orientation to determine whether or not the variables of junior or senior status or enlisted or officer status were significant for one group or another. For lesbian and bisexual women there was the possibility of a marginally significant relationship. Eighty-nine percent of lesbian and bisexual enlisted women believed harassment was a problem, compared to 74 percent of officers (Table 10.2). Yet, because of the small sample size, the chi-square statistic (3.003) with a probability of .083 is unreliable. None of the other relationships neared significance.

Table 10.2

Experiences and Perceptions of Sexual Harassment: Lesbians and Bisexuals *(N = 85)*

Status[a]	Who Believes It Is a Problem?		Who Experiences Sexual Harassment?	
	% Yes	Probability	% Yes	Probability
Seniority				
Junior	89	.341	83	.576
Senior	81		78	
Rank				
Enlisted	89	.083	88	.003
Officer	74		58	

[a] The sample size within each branch is too small to generate meaningful statistics. Statistics for branch are not shown.

Thus, there is the possibility that enlisted women who identify as lesbian/bisexual are more likely to believe harassment is a problem for most women, though this finding remains questionable (Table 10.2).

Femininity and Heterosexuality

Recent scholarship on male domination suggests that the perception of a woman's masculinity and femininity affects her status in a male-dominated institution (Connell 2000). Specifically, in a patriarchal institution, masculine women are more likely to be accepted as "brothers" but damned as defective women. Conversely, highly feminine women are likely to be excluded from the brotherhood but accepted as potential sex partners. I was curious as to whether there was a sense among the respondents of whether perceptions of gender might be a factor in who is likely to be subject to harassment. I asked: "Who do you think is more likely to experience sexual harassment in the military?" The possible responses were as follows:

1. Women who are more feminine in appearance.
2. Women who are more masculine in appearance.
3. Regarding "feminine" or "masculine" appearance, women do not experience any more or less harassment than others.
4. I don't think any women really experience sexual harassment anymore.

Fifty-eight percent of respondents felt that it made no difference whether one was perceived to be "feminine" or "masculine" (Table 10.3). But 38 percent indicated that they believed that women who were more feminine were more likely to be the target of harassment. In contrast, only 3 percent felt that women who were more masculine would be the focus of harassment. One percent indicated that they felt harassment was no longer a problem.

Not all the women who perceived sexual harassment experienced behaviors that legally constitute it and only a small number of those who had experienced such behavior perceived it to be a problem.

Table 10.3

Who Is More Likely to Experience Sexual Harassment in the Military?
(N = 326)

Response	%
Women who are more feminine in appearance.	38
Women who are more masculine in appearance.	3
I don't think that women experience any more or less harassment than others on the basis of their "feminine" or "masculine" appearance.	58
I don't think any women really experience sexual harassment anymore.	1

Thus, upon examining perception, I turned my attention to the question of who experienced harassment, as opposed to those who perceived it to be a problem. The analysis revealed similar differences between lesbians/bisexuals and heterosexual women as found in the analysis of their perceptions. Eighty-one percent of lesbian and bisexual women indicated that they had experienced harassment, compared to 65 percent of heterosexual women (Table 10.4). Unlike the case regarding perception, junior or senior status was not significant in its relationship to experiencing harassment. However, in this instance enlisted or officer status was significant, with enlisted personnel more likely to experience harassment. Again, branch was not a statistically significant factor.

To determine what factors might increase the risk of being sexually harassed, I again used a logistic regression model with "having experienced sexual harassment" as the dependent variable. The risk factors were sexual orientation, junior or senior status, enlisted or officer status, and military branch. The finding that lesbian and bisexual women were more likely to have experienced sexual harassment remained strong. Junior or senior status, enlisted or officer status, and branch were statistically insignificant. Thus, when controlling for these four variables, the significant relationship between enlisted or officer status and having experienced harassment that was observed in the cross-tabulation dropped out. Thus, when con-

Table 10.4

Who Experiences Sexual Harassment? (N = 326)

Status	% Yes	Chi Square Probability	Logistic Regression Analysis Probability > Chi Square
Sexual Orientation			
Lesbian/bisexual	81	.006	.0014
Heterosexual	65		
Seniority			
Junior	72	.250	.1688
Senior	66		
Rank			
Enlisted	73	.036	.1544
Officer	62		
Branch			
Army	72	.514	.8664
Navy	69		
Marine	54		
Air Force	67		

sidering all women, the demographic characteristics of junior or senior status, enlisted or officer status, and branch can be viewed as only marginally important in predicting who experiences harassment (Table 10.4).

As in the analysis of perception, I again separated the sample by sexual orientation to determine whether the variables of junior or senior status or enlisted or officer status were statistically more significant for one group than the other. The relationship between junior or senior status and experiences of harassment was not significant for either lesbian/bisexual or heterosexual women. The relationship between enlisted or officer status and experiences of harassment was statistically insignificant for heterosexual women. However, for lesbian and bisexual women, enlisted/officer status appears to be significant with regard to one's likelihood of experiencing harassment. Again, the chi-square statistic is not reliable because of the small sample size. However, the fact that 88 percent of lesbian and bisexual enlisted women experienced harassment, compared to 58 percent of lesbian/bisexual officers, suggests that being an enlisted lesbian/bisexual woman may make one more vulnerable to harassment. Thus, as with the issue of perceiving harassment to be a problem, it appears that not only are lesbian/bisexual women more likely to perceive and experience harassment, but this may, not surprisingly, increase when they are enlisted personnel rather than officers. (see Table 10.2, column 2, Who experiences sexual harassment?)

DISCUSSION

Given the armed forces' history as a highly patriarchal institution, we should not be surprised that military women continue to experience harassment, nor that many believe that harassment is pervasive within the military setting. What may be surprising is the way that perceptions and experiences appear to vary by the sexual orientation of the respondent. In fact, the analysis shows sexual orientation to be a consistently robust factor. These findings suggest that, at least within the U.S. armed forces, the oppression of women and homophobia are linked.

Although these data cannot provide empirical support for all of the possible answers to the above questions, it is possible to speculate as to why such differences might exist.[9] The first possibility, I believe, is that lesbian and bisexual women, because of their further marginalized status, may be more aware of, or sensitive to, issues of gender and sexuality, such as harassment, and may be more attuned to identifying situations of harassment. These issues may simply have more salience for lesbian and bisexual women. This possibility may be supported by the data if we consider some of the comments made regarding what constitutes harassment.

A heterosexual, enlisted woman in the Air Force wrote, "Nothing was ever out and out harassment—just *lots* of innuendo/dirty jokes sort of things. 'Nice' harassment as opposed to 'sleep with me or else' sort of things." In this instance a distinction is made between "nice," or "acceptable" harassment and "real" harassment. A heterosexual, noncommissioned officer in the Navy wrote, "From what I've heard about sexual harassment, lewd jokes would be considered harassment. These were quite common in training and on the job, but personally I never took them as such." Another heterosexual, enlisted woman, also in the Air Force, wrote, "To me there is a fine line between harassment and a man coming on to a woman. In my experiences, I had men come on to me strongly, including my boss. I did not and still don't view that as harassment." None of the lesbian or bisexual respondents offered these types of comments. While these remarks provide anecdotal evidence at best, the responses do suggest that, for some heterosexual women, incidents that might be considered to be harassment by lesbian and bisexual women are not perceived as harassment by them. The latter response also speaks to the question of perception and salience. If a woman is a lesbian, she may be far more likely to view any "come on" as harassment or as unacceptable behavior. Heterosexual women, however, may be in the position of having to gauge whether the behavior is "acceptable mating behavior" as opposed to harassment. Thus, one explanation for differences in perceptions and in whether or not an incident is experienced as harassment may be awareness of gender or sexuality issues and/or whether the woman is *ever* receptive to such behaviors.

Another possible explanation for why the data suggest that lesbian/bisexual women experience more harassment is that they may truly be the targets of more, and potentially more vicious, harassment. If this were true, then certainly they would perceive harassment to be a greater problem. But, why might a lesbian or bisexual woman be more likely to be the target of harassment?

Recall the woman who indicated that an upperclassman at the Naval Academy had thought he might "set her straight." Other women indicated that they were often pressured for dates or sex and that if they did not consent they would hear comments like "If you won't go out with me you must be a lesbian." If a woman is not identified as "paired" with a man, she is considered "fair game." If she rejects the advances of a man she "must" be a lesbian. If not, after all, perhaps there is something "wrong" with him. My research beyond the specific issue of sexual harassment is rife with examples in which women were coerced for sex as a means of "proving" that they were not lesbian. Lesbians, and bisexual women not identified as having male partners, may be more subject to such harassment simply because they are identified as "available" or vulnerable. It is not far-fetched to suggest that their male peers know full well the institutional pressure they feel to prove that they are not lesbians. This is not to say that heterosexual women who are identified as "available" do not face similar experiences, but that when compared to a woman who may never be identified as paired with a man, those experiences may be significantly fewer.

What might these findings teach us about male dominance? We know that sexuality is one mechanism for oppressing women. Does it matter that lesbian and bisexual women and heterosexual women might experience and perceive harassment differently? I think that it provides us with some insight into the fact that men will attempt to exert control via sexuality, regardless of one's sexual orientation. But it also, I believe, provides a compelling illustration of the degree to which a policy that explicitly targets only *some* women, in fact, allows men, both individually and collectively, to retain a degree of power and control over all women, whether as individuals or collectively. Ultimately, I believe that the similarity of their experiences is more important than the differences. Additionally, as I said at the outset, one result of the threat of being labeled a lesbian may be that women are kept apart from one another. "Don't Ask, Don't Tell" provides the perfect mechanism for the strategy of "divide and conquer." By addressing the problem of sexual harassment—and specifically by eliminating the opportunity for harassment situated in homophobia—all women would benefit, as well as a large number of men.

There exists a small, yet rich, body of literature addressing the issue of sexual harassment in the military and, in particular, the role of sexual orientation in this relationship.[10] For example, citing

DePauw (1988), Thomas and Thomas note that "anecdotal evidence suggests that threatening to denounce a woman as homosexual is *the* most prevalent form of sexual harassment in the military" (1996: 73). However, this literature is based on little to no quantitative data. The anecdotes are compelling and the theory sound, but I am as yet unaware of another data set that examines the perceptions and experiences of sexual harassment by respondents' sexual orientation. The primary contribution of the work presented here is that we are able to examine the perceptions and experiences of military women by sexual orientation.

The 1995 data set compiled for the Department of Defense does offer important findings, especially with regard to the importance of military branch and rank. For example, as with the research presented here, more junior personnel are at somewhat greater risk of experiencing sexual harassment. And, because of the magnitude of the survey—90,000 respondents—the data regarding branch are much more informative. For example, their study found that a larger percentage of women in the Marine Corps reported incidents of unwanted, uninvited sexual attention. In the research presented here, the number of Marine Corps respondents is too small to draw such conclusions. Yet, the DOD study offers nothing about the relationship between sexual orientation and sexual harassment. Understandably, a study conducted by an organization, the United States government, that condemns people for being gay, lesbian, or bisexual can hardly be expected to collect any data—let alone accurate data—regarding the sexual orientation of respondents.

Thus, the findings presented here provide empirical support for the work that provides a solid theoretical framework for understanding the relationship between sexual orientation and sexual harassment in the military (e.g., Benecke & Dodge 1990). These findings also contribute to the more general research on sexual harassment in the military, scholarship that is largely devoid of any examination of sexual orientation. As such, though smaller in scope, these findings offer, I believe, insight that is critical to any thorough understanding of the way that sexual harassment functions *with* the ban on gays and lesbians to limit the full participation of all women in the United States military. The question, however, remains: what can we do about it?

CONCLUSION

What might I offer as a solution to the problem of sexual harassment in the military? Clearly, there is no "magic bullet." Years of training sessions, stand-downs, special programs, and claims of zero tolerance have had some impact, but certainly not the impact they should have had. This is partly a reflection of the status of women throughout society. As mentioned earlier, the harassment of women may actually increase as gender integration increases. But, to the degree that a significant amount of the harassment has to do with proving one's heterosexuality, one logical solution would be to lift the ban on lesbians (and gay men) in the military. In doing so, one's sexual orientation would become largely irrelevant. Threats that one "must" be a lesbian would become hollow. Not only would this improve the lives of the lesbian and bisexual women who do choose to serve in the military, but it would also improve the lives of the heterosexual women who also receive pressure to prove that they are, in fact, heterosexual. Sexual orientation would become one more characteristic, like race or gender, that while not problem-free, could no longer be used as effectively as a weapon in the domination and control of women's lives and careers.

Across society—be it the household, educational institution, or workplace—harassment on the basis of sexuality exists. And, in each setting, while unique from one another, the harassment of women by men functions to maintain the domination of men over women, at both the individual and collective levels. In each setting, when we dismantle the mechanisms through which such domination is maintained, we take one step further toward achieving gender equality. In the military, removing the ban on lesbians and gay men would be a huge step toward such a goal.

Because the ban on lesbians and gay men compels military personnel to constantly prove their heterosexuality, the military is, in fact, a highly sexualized workplace. Gender remains salient because of its relationship to expectations surrounding sexuality. In our culture, the way in which gender and sexuality are embedded within one another means that as long as sexuality is at the core of what it means to participate in the military, so, too, will masculinity—and, indirectly, femininity—remain at that core. Remove the importance of sexuality, specifically heterosexuality, and the centrality of masculinity is also challenged. That is, the military could remain numerically and ideologically male without having masculinity at its center. And, if a majority of service members engaged in professional socialization without that socialization being about what it means to be masculine, we might envision a sea change in the impact of militarization more broadly. The role that the military plays in the maintenance of patriarchy would be greatly diminished because the military would no longer be defined by the assertion of power and control by men. The military would no longer have as one of its implicit goals the maintenance of traditional conceptions of masculinity. And, I believe, once we achieve this, we could diminish the role of the military in the power elite. With that, the patriarchal hegemony of our culture would begin to lose some of its vitality. Women, whether lesbian, bisexual, or heterosexual, might then begin to participate as full and equal members of society, free of male dominance and the sexual harassment that currently exists to facilitate that domination.

NOTES

1. The United States continues to mandate draft registration for men upon their 18th birthday, but there has been no actual draft since the early 1970s.
2. For thirty-nine years the words "Bring me men" welcomed those arriving at the Air Force Academy in Colorado Springs. In March 2003, these words, each two feet tall, were removed as part of an effort to change

the culture in which women have always been second-class citizens. It is worth noting the critical response of alumni, one of whom said, "[I don't] understand how they [the words] have anything to do with correcting problems in the way sexual assaults are reported."

3. In 1991 at their annual convention, male aviators were accused of assaulting close to one hundred women, both military and civilian. For an in-depth account of the investigation, see *The Tailhook report: The official inquiry into the events of Tailhook '91.* (New York: St. Martin's Press, 1991).

4. See, for example, *Conduct unbecoming: The eighth annual report on "Don't Ask, Don't Tell, Don't Pursue, Don't Harass,"* published by the Servicemembers Legal Defense Network.

5. The requirements ("one year of active duty" and "since 1976") were formulated for specific reasons. I wanted to ensure that respondents had spent at least a minimum amount of time in the environment of the military, both in training and in permanent-duty station assignments. My goal was to ensure that respondents had spent time in the day-to-day world of the "real" military. Additionally, the 1970s were full of changes for the U.S. military, but particularly for women. In 1972 women were first permitted to participate in the Reserve Officers Training Corps, the training mechanism for military officers that operates in conjunction with colleges and universities around the nation. In 1973 the draft was abolished, resulting in an increased need for the enlistment of women. The end of the Vietnam War led to the need to adapt to peacetime operations. In 1976 the first women were permitted to enter the service academies (e.g., West Point). Nontraditional career fields, previously closed to women, were becoming more available to military women. And in 1978 the Women's Army Corps was permanently disbanded. "WAC" battalions began to train men, and women entered units that were largely male. These changes occurred at different times across branches, but regardless of branch, the 1970s were a time of radical change throughout the military of the United States. Given that the focus of this research is on the experience of women in the male-dominated world of the military, I wanted to hear from those women who served in the military when women and men served together. To that end, I chose 1976 as a pivotal year. Any woman who has served since

1976 has served in an environment that is much more sex-integrated than at any time in the past. It was these experiences that I wished to examine.

6. For example, in 1985 the Veterans Administration sought to obtain a random sample of women veterans. To gather a sample of 3,003 women veterans, they made 526,367 telephone calls to households in the United States (Veterans Administration, *Survey of female veterans: A study of the needs, attitudes, and experiences of women veterans* [Washington, D.C.: Office of Information Management and Statistics, IM & S 70-85-7, 1985]). There are no sampling frames of women veterans from which to draw a sample.

7. To view the complete survey, see the Methodological Appendix in M. Herbert, *Camouflage isn't only for combat: Gender, sexuality, and women in the military* (New York: New York University Press, 1998).

8. Junior women included enlisted women (E1–E4) and officers (O1–O3); senior women included enlisted women (E5–E9) and officers (O4–O6).

9. For earlier work that addresses the same question, see Beth E. Schneider (1982), Consciousness about sexual harassment among heterosexual and lesbian women workers, *Journal of Social Issues* 38 (4): 75–98. In brief, Schneider found that lesbians were more likely than heterosexual women to apply the term *sexual harassment* to their experiences. She provides several possible explanations for this finding, ranging from heightened levels of hostility when examining experiences retroactively to lesbians having less need to minimize and control negative feelings about their work experiences.

10. See Sharon R. Bird (1996), Welcome to the men's club: Homosociality and the maintenance of hegemonic masculinity, *Gender and Society* 10 (2): 120–132.

REFERENCES

Admiral's career advances despite harassment controversy. 1996, Spring. *Minerva's Bulletin Board: The News Magazine on Women and the Military*, p. 4.

Bastian, L., A. Lancaster, and H. Reyst. 1996. *Department of Defense 1995 sexual harassment survey.* Rep. No. 96-014. Arlington, Va.: Defense Manpower Data Center.

Beck, Lois M. 1991. Sexual harassment in the Army: Roots examined. *Minerva: Quarterly Report on Women and the Military* 9 (1): 29–40.

Benecke, Michele M., and Kirsten S. Dodge. 1990. Military women in non-traditional job fields: Casualties of the armed forces war on homosexuals. *Harvard Women's Law Journal* 13: 215–250.

Cockburn, Cynthia. 1991. *In the way of women: Men's resistance to sex equality in organizations.* London: Macmillan.

Collison, Margaret, and David L. Collison. 1996. It's only "Dick": The sexual harassment of women managers in insurance. *Work, Employment, and Society* 10 (1): 29–56.

Connell, R. W. 1995. *Masculinities.* Berkeley: University of California Press.

———. 2000. *The men and the boys.* Berkeley: University of California Press.

DePauw, Linda Grant. 1988. Gender as stigma: Probing some sensitive issues. *Minerva: Quarterly Report on Women and the Military* 6 (1): 29–43.

Family of harassment victim sues after soldier's suicide. 1993, Winter. *Minerva's Bulletin Board: The News Magazine on Women and the Military,* p. 9.

Firestone, Juanita M., and Richard J. Harris. 1994. Sexual harassment in the U.S. military: Individualized and environmental contexts. *Armed Forces and Society* 21 (1): 25–43.

Goffman, Erving. 1977. The arrangement between the sexes. *Theory and Society* 4:301–331.

Gruber, James. 1998. The impact of male work environments and organizational policies on women's experiences of sexual harassment. *Gender and Society* 12 (3): 301–320.

Gruber, James, and Lars Bjorn. 1982. Blue collar blues: The sexual harassment of women autoworkers. *Work and Occupations* 9 (3): 271–198.

Gulf war sexual assault case ends with bad conduct discharge. 1993, Winter. *Minerva's Bulletin Board: The News Magazine on Women and the Military,* p. 8.

Herbert, Melissa S. 1998. *Camouflage isn't only for combat: Gender, sexuality, and women in the military.* New York: New York University Press.

Navy Captain cleared of harassment loses promotion. 1996, Spring. *Minerva's Bulletin Board: The News Magazine on Women and the Military,* p. 4.

Perry, W. J. 1996. Department of Defense News Briefing, November 13. http://www.defenselink.mil.

Pharr, Suzanne. 1988. *Homophobia: A weapon of sexism*. Inverness, Calif.: Chardon Press.

Report on a decade of sexual harassment in VA results in major changes. 1993, Spring. *Minerva's Bulletin Board: The News Magazine on Women and the Military*, p. 7.

Rosenberg, Janet, Harry Perlstadt, and William R. F. Phillips. 1993. Now that we are here: Discrimination, disparagement, and harassment at work and the experience of women lawyers. *Gender and Society* 7 (3): 415–433.

Schneider, Beth E. 1982. Consciousness about sexual harassment among heterosexual and lesbian women workers. *Journal of Social Issues* 38 (4): 75–98.

Servicemembers Legal Defense Network. 2002. *Conduct unbecoming: The eighth annual report on "Don't Ask, Don't Tell, Don't Pursue, Don't Harass."* Washington, D.C.

Sexual harassment training not yet perfected. 1993, Summer. *Minerva's Bulletin Board: The News Magazine on Women and the Military*, p. 1.

Shilts, Randy. 1993. *Conduct unbecoming: Gays and lesbians in the U.S. military*. New York: St. Martin's Press.

Tailhook—It's not over yet. 1994, Fall/Winter. *Minerva's Bulletin Board: The News Magazine on Women and the Military*, p. 5.

Tailhook tidbits. 1994, Summer. *Minerva's Bulletin Board: The News Magazine on Women and the Military*, pp. 3–4.

Thomas, Patricia J., and Marie D. Thomas. 1996. Integration of women in the military: Parallels to the progress of homosexuals? In *Out in force: Sexual orientation and the military*, ed. G. Herek, J. Jobe, and R. Carney, 65–85. Chicago: University of Chicago Press.

Titunik, Regina. 2000. The first wave: Gender integration and military culture. *Armed Forces and Society* 26 (2): 229–257.

United States Department of Defense. 1995. Sexual harassment study. http://www.defenselink.mil/news/fact_sheets/sxhas95.html.

Whaley, Gary L., and Shirley H. Tucker. 1998. A theoretical integration of sexual harassment models. *Equal Opportunities International* 17 (1): 21–29.

Women's Research and Education Institute. 2002, March 31. Table WM-1, Active Duty Service Personnel by Branch of Service, Officer/Enlisted Status, and Sex. http://www.wrei.org/projects/wiu/wim/index.htm.

11 BLUE-COLLAR FEMINISM
The Link Between Male Domination and Sexual Harassment

Carrie N. Baker

This chapter provides a historical context for analyzing the link between sexual harassment and male domination. It highlights the central role that blue-collar women working in male-dominated fields played in the movement against sexual harassment. The history of sexual harassment has been told many times, but these accounts have not adequately acknowledged the contributions of blue-collar women to the development of the legal definition of sexual harassment in the United States. Sexual harassment policy generally has been credited to the activism of middle-class feminists. Catharine MacKinnon, for example, is considered to be the "prime architect of sexual harassment jurisprudence" (Stoltenberg 2002, Gitlin 1998, Arriola 1990:29). The history told in this chapter concentrates on the contributions of women working in male-dominated blue-collar occupations, who played an instrumental role in furthering an understanding of sexual harassment as discrimination rooted in male domination.

In the 1970s, middle-class feminists developed the idea that sexual harassment was a form of male domination (Wehrli 1976, AASC 1977, Farley 1978, MacKinnon 1979). They believed that sexual harassment was not just an individualized act of abuse, but a means by which men in power controlled and excluded weaker members of the workplace, including not only women, but also minorities and less economically advantaged men. Therefore, they contended that sexual harassment would disappear only by eliminating the unequal relations of power sustained by male dominance. Despite this broad conceptual understanding, the activism of middle-class feminists focused on one form of sexual harassment—a male supervisor sexually propositioning a subordinate employee and punishing her if she refused, later known as quid pro quo sexual harassment. By the end of the decade, courts generally accepted the feminist argument that quid quo pro sexual harassment was sex discrimination in violation of Title VII of the Civil Rights Act of 1964. This definition of sexual harassment, however, was limited.

In contrast to white-collar feminists, women working in traditionally male-dominated blue-collar occupations focused on broadening the legal definition of sexual harassment to include behavior that created a hostile environment. These women spoke up about male supervisors as well as coworkers who verbally and physically harassed them in the workplace, driving many women out of male-dominated fields. This form of harassment, which included violent acts, often sexual but sometimes not, most clearly exemplified the feminist argument that sexual harassment was really about male domination. As a result of these experiences, blue-collar women fought to expand the legal definition of sexual harassment to include behavior creating a hostile environment. The activism of blue-collar feminists led to an expansion of the legal definition to include hostile environment harassment (29 C.F.R. § 1604.11, 1981).

The following pages retell the story of how the problem of sexual harassment was first articulated and the early campaign to eradicate it. In so doing, it places the words and actions of activists, particularly blue-collar women, at center stage. The analysis is based on the archives of early feminist organizations that fought sexual harassment, including correspondence, publications, and brochures, as well as court records, congressional hearings, media coverage of the issue, and interviews with early activists. The time period covered is from the mid-1970s to the early 1980s. The link that second-wave feminists, especially blue-collar women, drew between male domination and sexual harassment can make an important contribution to contemporary analyses of this issue. A reconsideration of the blue-collar experience elucidates this link and will suggest how to move beyond the current narrow legalistic focus of public policy, which has proved inadequate to address the problem of sexual harassment.

EARLY FEMINIST UNDERSTANDINGS OF SEXUAL HARASSMENT

In April of 1975, feminist activists in Ithaca, New York, coined the term *sexual harassment* for a media blitz to promote a speak-out on sexual harassment, which was sponsored by Working Women United (WWU), a newly formed organization of women dedicated to fighting for equality in the workplace. The next year in Boston, Massachusetts, a collective called the Alliance Against Sexual Coercion (AASC) formed specifically to combat sexual harassment. From the start, these feminists developed theories about the causes, meanings, and solutions to sexual harassment and agitated for legal remedies. Male domination was a central paradigm that feminist activists used to understand sexual harassment (Wehrli 1976, AASC 1977, Farley 1978, MacKinnon 1979).

Members of the Alliance Against Sexual Coercion attributed sexual harassment to multiple systems of dominance institutionalized in American society, including sexism, capitalism, and racism. The first extended analysis of the links between male domination and sexual harassment appeared in a master's thesis written by AASC member Lynn Wehrli in 1976 (Wehrli 1976). In conjunction with several other AASC members, Wehrli developed what she called a "dominance" theory of sexual harassment.[1] Wehrli argued that sexual harassment in the workplace was both an expression and a means of perpetuating the unequal power relationships between men and women and between employers and employees. Wehrli explained that the extent to which dominance was exercised through sexual harassment depended on social conditions, personal choice, and threats to dominance. Threats to dominance included an active feminist movement and the entrance of women into traditionally male-dominated fields like construction. In the face of these threats, men reasserted their dominance by sexually harassing women. Dominance took a sexual form because of the predominant view of women as sexual objects and the strong cultural associations between dominance, masculinity, and sexual prowess (Wehrli 1976). Subsequent AASC literature emphasized the role of "structures of power" such as capitalism, sexism, racism, heterosexism, and ageism in perpetuating sexual harassment. AASC members Martha Hooven and Nancy McDonald (1978) contended that the conditions of work under capitalism, which gave women little autonomy or control, were important factors in women's vulnerability to sexual harassment.

One important way that AASC linked systems of dominance and sexual harassment was by characterizing sexual harassment as a form of violence against women. Drawing on the "violence, not sex" view of rape developed in the antirape movement, feminists argued that sexual harassment was more a form of violence and abuse than an expression of sexual interest. They often analogized sexual harassment to rape, calling it "economic rape." AASC members believed that sexual harassment must be understood within the broader climate of violence in American culture, especially against women, including rape, wife abuse, forced sterilization, abusive advertising and pornography, and the institutionalization of women. A 1977 AASC brochure explained: "men are socialized to dominate women through the use and threat of violent behavior" (AASC 1977:5). In the workplace and in society generally, men marginalize women through the threat of violence (AASC 1981b:18). Another AASC publication contended that harassers, rapists, and batterers were not "psychologically aberrant misfits," but were "responding 'logically' to cultural forces which encouraged their violence," like the media and male peer groups (AASC 1980:52). AASC member Mary Bularzik saw sexual harassment as an issue of violence against women because it was "consistent, systemic, and pervasive, not a set of random isolated acts" (Bularzik 1978:26). Bularzik described violence against women as a "mechanism of social control" central to male oppression of women and as a social phenomenon, not an individual interaction (Bularzik 1978:26).

While the AASC identified multiple systems of dominance as the cause of sexual harassment, other feminists focused on patriarchy as the main cause (Farley 1978, MacKinnon 1979). WWU member Lin Farley argued that sexual harassment originated with patriarchal relations, not capitalism, and that "sexual harassment of women at work arose out of man's need to maintain his control of female labor" (Farley 1978:261). Freada Klein of AASC criticized Farley for focusing exclusively on patriarchy as the cause of sexual harassment to the exclusion of class and race. According to Klein, Farley ignored the "complexities of sexual harassment" by identifying patriarchy as the "ultimate source of sexual harassment" and failing to "sort out under what conditions sex, race or class each become the most conspicuous form of oppression" (Klein 1978:34). Klein believed that patriarchy and capitalism reinforced each other in the phenomena of workplace harassment and that racism had a major role in the origins of working women's problems. In response, Farley defended the centrality of patriarchal relations in sexual harassment theory by noting that "the idea that capitalism itself somehow came up with the idea of sexual harassment is absurd" (Farley 1979:25). She contended that capitalism had in fact threatened male control of women by creating a free labor market in which women competed with men. In response, male trade unions gained control of the majority of occupations by systematically denying training to women and isolating them into a few occupations. Men then used sexual harassment to maintain job segregation. According to Farley, this "periodic push-pull between capitalism and the Patriarchy" had frequently happened and was happening in 1978 (Farley 1979:25). Despite these differences, both Farley and Klein believed that male dominance was one of the fundamental causes of sexual harassment.

Catharine MacKinnon also conceptualized male dominance as the root cause of sexual harassment. Her path-breaking book provided the first in-depth legal analysis of sexual harassment (*Sexual Harassment of Working Women* 1979). MacKinnon argued that sexual harassment was not merely an individual injury, but group-based discrimination that harmed all women by reinforcing women's subordinate status in the workplace. Sex segregation in the workplace and male control of hiring, firing, supervising, and promoting women made them systematically vulnerable to sexual harassment. According to MacKinnon, sexual harassment was sex discrimination because it expressed and reinforced women's social inequality to men (MacKinnon 1979).

Along the same lines, the Working Women's Institute (the successor to WWU) argued that inequality between women and men in the workplace and in society was the basic cause of sexual harassment. The institute maintained that sexual harassment grew out of the social subordination of women to men, as manifest in sex segregation in the labor force, unequal pay, and limited opportunities for advancement for women. Furthermore, men harass women because cultural stereotypes about proper sex roles lead men to treat women workers as "sexual beings first and as breadwinners second" (Crull 1982:4–5). Peggy Crull expanded on this analysis by suggesting that men harass not only because they have the power and can, but also because they do not have power or they fear losing it. Crull explained higher rates of sexual harassment in male-dominated jobs as resulting from the fact that men in these jobs feel that their power at work is threatened. They use sexual harassment as a way of "subduing women" or driving them out altogether. As opposed to an "overflow" of power, this is an "attempt to regain waning power" and "restore women to traditional roles through the use of sexual intimidation" (Crull 1982:6).

While most early feminists saw patriarchy as the primary cause, a few others included capitalism and racism as well. At the core of feminist theory on sexual harassment was male dominance—particularly the idea that sexual harassment was not a personal sexual problem, but a social problem rooted in male abuse of power over women. Despite their broad conceptualization of sexual harassment, activists associated with the Working Women's Institute and the Alliance Against Sexual Coercion at first focused primarily on one particular form of sexual harassment—a male supervisor sexually propositioning a subordinate employee and firing her when she refused (Baker 2001). Blue-collar women working in male-dominated occupations, however, soon began to speak out about other forms of sexual harassment.

BLUE-COLLAR ACTIVISM AGAINST SEXUAL HARASSMENT

In the late 1970s, antidiscrimination laws and the resulting affirmative action programs encouraged the gender integration of male-dominated workplaces and occupations. While women have successfully integrated professions like law, medicine, and higher education, male-dominated blue-collar occupations like construction and coal mining have been nearly impervious to integration. As women pioneered these masculine domains, many experienced especially pernicious forms of sexual harassment. The harassment blue-collar women experienced went beyond sexual propositioning to include severe verbal abuse and physical violence (Gruber & Bjorn 1982, Messerschmidt 1993). Many blue-collar women understood the harassment to be acts of resistance—attempts to discourage them from infiltrating higher-paying male-dominated fields. One study from the early 1980s revealed that blue-collar women tended to view sexual harassment as an attempt by men to preserve dominance over women in the workplace (Maypole & Skaine 1982).

In response, women from across the country working in construction, coal mining, firefighting, law enforcement, and other nontraditional occupations organized against sexual harassment. As with the African American women who brought many of the first sexual harassment cases (Baker 2004), the working environments, backgrounds, and identities of blue-collar women in male-dominated fields shaped their experiences of sexual harassment and their strategies and resources for addressing the problem. Through unions and employee associations, these women urged courts and policy makers to broaden their definitions of sexual harassment to include not just sexual demands by a supervisor of a subordinate employee, but also hostile environment harassment—when coworkers create a hostile working environment through sexual or nonsexual behavior aimed at creating an intimidating or offensive environment for women.

Blue-collar women working in male-dominated fields influenced the development of public policy in many ways. The activism of blue-collar women led to the first federal regulations on sexual harassment (41 C.F.R. § 60-4, 1978). Representatives of blue-collar women's organizations testified at several of the early federal hearings on sexual harassment (U.S. Congress 1979, U.S. Congress 1981, Women in construction 1978, Dullea 1977). Most significantly, blue-collar women won several precedent-setting hostile environment sexual harassment lawsuits, thereby establishing legal prohibitions against this conduct (*Brown v. City of Guthrie*, 22 Fed. Empl. Prac. Cas. BNA 1627, W.D. Okla. 1980; *Minnesota v. Continental Can Company*, 297 N.W.2d 241, Minn. 1981; *Bundy v. Jackson*, 641 F.2d 934, D.C. Cir. 1981; *Henson v. City of Dundee*, 682 F.2d 897, 11th Cir. 1982). By telling stories that clearly demonstrated the fundamentally abusive nature of sexual harassment, blue-collar women made a significant contribution to increasing public awareness about sexual harassment—that it was motivated not by sexual desire, but by men's desire to keep women subordinate in the workplace and that it was a serious problem that harmed women in the workplace. Their stories provided strong evidence to support the feminist theory linking sexual harassment and male domination.

Women in Construction

The activism of women in construction led to the first federal regulations against sexual harassment (41 C.F.R. § 60-4, 1978). In the spring of 1975, female construction workers from all around the country met to discuss the hurdles they faced entering this male-dominated field. A year later, they brought two lawsuits under Executive Orders 11246 and 11375, which prohibited federal contractors from discriminating on the basis of sex (*Advocates for Women et al. v. Usery*, Civil Action No. 76-0862, D.D.C., filed May 14, 1976; *Women Working in Construction et al. v. Usery*, Civil Action No. 76-527, D.D.C., filed April 13, 1976). The lawsuits protested sex discrimination in hiring practices and harassment of women in the construction industry and requested that the U.S. Department of Labor set hiring goals and timetables for women in the construction industry. The plaintiffs included Advocates for Women in San Francisco; Women in Trades in Seattle; United Trade Workers Association in Tacoma, Washington; and Women Working in Construction and Wider Opportunities for Women in Washington, D.C., all of which helped women obtain employment in the construction industry. In addition to the plaintiffs, women from several other organizations participated in the lawsuit, including Skilled Jobs for Women in Madison, Wisconsin; the Tucson Women's Commission; the Chicana Service Action Center in Los Angeles; Women in Apprenticeship Program in San Francisco; and the Chicana Rights Project of the Mexican American Legal Defense and Education Fund in San Antonio, Texas.

These litigants and their supporters testified before Department of Labor officials about their experiences of sexual harassment. According to their testimony, their male coworkers ostracized them and scrutinized them on the job. They described experiencing verbal harassment by hostile male coworkers, including sexist jokes and sexual allusions, that made them feel alienated and isolated from their coworkers. One woman, Libby Howard, told of the obscene graffiti campaign waged against her for more than five years while she worked as one of just a few women on a work crew of two thousand. Women testified about their experiences of physical violence, threats, and sexual abuse. A representative from Women Working in Construction testified that she was badly hurt when working as an apprentice because her foreman forced her to ascend a rickety scaffold, in spite of her protests, and the scaffold collapsed. Anna Ramos of the Chicana Service Action Center in Los Angeles told Department of Labor officials of three cases involving violence against female construction workers in California, including one woman whose thumbs were smashed after she refused to quit a job. Women also testified that male coworkers made crude remarks, gestures, and pranks and used pornography to drive women from the workplace (Women in construction 1978, Dullea 1977).

To settle these lawsuits, the Department of Labor adopted the first federal regulations against workplace harassment based on sex in April of 1978 (41 C.F.R. § 60-4, 1978). In addition to setting hiring goals and timetables for women in construction and in apprenticeship programs, the regulations required federal construction contractors to ensure and maintain a working environment free of harassment, intimidation, and coercion and required contractors to assign two or more women to each construction project if possible. The guidelines also required contractors to ensure that all foremen, superintendents, and other on-site supervisory personnel were aware of and carried out the contractor's obligation to maintain a harassment-free working environment, with specific attention to minority or female individuals (41 C.F.R. § 60-4, 1978). Furthermore, the Department of Labor agreed to conduct outreach programs for women, to establish a monitoring committee to measure the implementations and effectiveness of the regulations, and to maintain records of compliance reviews and complaints against federal construction contractors.

Despite these promises, the Department of Labor did a poor job of enforcing the regulations, and women continued to experience pervasive sexual harassment. Nevertheless, Joan Graff of the Equal Rights Advocates has said that the regulations had a significant impact because they were "the first in a long series of steps that legitimized [nontraditional] jobs for women." The regulations were an "important public pronouncement" that women could do the work; they "shifted public opinion and expectation about who could and should be able to do [nontraditional] jobs" (Graff 2001). These regulations were also a step toward official recognition of the harms of sexual harassment.

Coal-Mining Women

In addition to scrutinizing the construction industry, the Department of Labor also investigated the coal-mining industry. Like female construction workers, women entering coal mining in the late 1970s faced discrimination and sexual harassment. Battling the long-held superstition that women were "bad luck" in the mines, female coal miners formed the Tennessee-based Coal Employment Project (CEP) in 1977 to help women break into coal mining and to support them on the job. In May of 1978, CEP filed a complaint with the Department of Labor against Consolidation Coal Company of Pittsburgh (CONSOL), the largest coal company in the United States. The plaintiffs, employed at the Shoemaker coal mine in Benwood, West Virginia, alleged that they suffered sex discrimination in the coal mines. A settlement of the case provided for hiring quotas, back pay, and affirmative action programs to protect female miners from discrimination.

As women broke into mining, however, they experienced pervasive sexual harassment. The Coal Employment Project began hearing isolated stories about sexual harassment in 1978. At the First National Conference of Women Coal Miners in June of 1979, sexual harassment was only mentioned "in whispers, in corners here and there" (Prieto 1983:17). Women were too embarrassed, ashamed, and isolated to report sexual harassment, feeling that they had somehow provoked the behavior. Shortly after the conference, however, a woman wrote an anonymous story about sexual harassment that appeared in the newsletters of the United Mine Workers of America and the Coal Employment Project. More women began to contact CEP with their stories of harassment, expressing relief that the subject was out in the open. At a November 1979 conference of female miners sponsored by the United Mine Workers of America in Charleston, West Virginia, female miners for the first time spoke out about sexual harassment (Prieto 1983:17).

The Second National Conference of Women Coal Miners in May of 1980 was a major turning point. Sexual harassment emerged as a major theme of the conference. CEP offered a sexual harassment workshop, which ran twice, packed to capacity both times. In the workshop, women broke the silence about the common practice of sexual harassment inside coal mines. One woman exclaimed, "At last! Somebody else has been going through all this! I thought it was just me!" (Coal Employment Project 1980). The female miners passed several resolutions on sexual harassment. They asked CEP to conduct a study of sexual harassment in coal mines and to produce a brochure about women's legal rights. They resolved to demand that unions and employers adopt policies against sexual harassment and incorporate information about the issue into training sessions. They also asked CEP to produce information about the issue to be sent to new miners, to be posted on bulletin boards, and to be distributed through newsletters (Coal Employment Project 1980).

Through these efforts, activists gained an understanding of the scope and effects of sexual harassment. The CEP survey showed rampant and violent sexual harassment against female coal miners in ten states. More than half (54 percent) of all female miners were propositioned by their bosses at least once, 76 percent were propositioned by coworkers, and 17 percent had been attacked physically (White, Angle, & Moore 1981). The findings reported three forms of harassment unique to female coal miners. When women began to enter the mines, male miners revived a traditional initiation rite that had more or less been discontinued by the 1970s in which miners would strip and grease a new miner. In a 1977 case before the Kentucky Commission on Human Rights, miner Frieda Myers won a $2,000 conciliation agreement from Peabody Coal Company because she was stripped and greased by her male coworkers. In the conciliation agreement, Peabody agreed to issue a policy statement to "adopt safe working conditions for all employees and particularly to insure that female employees shall not be subjected to abuse, insult or injury related to their sex" (Prieto 1983). A second form of harassment female miners experienced involved what were usually routine searches of workers entering the mines for cigarettes or other smoking materials. Women complained that they were searched in sexually suggestive ways. A third form of harassment involved men drilling holes in women's bathhouses and peering at women showering and dressing. In 1981, female miners at CONSOL sued for invasion of privacy and sexual harassment, alleging that CONSOL permitted the operation of a peephole into the women's shower at the Shoemaker mine for thirteen months. During the trial of the case, the parties settled for an undisclosed amount. This case sparked additional sexual harassment complaints (Hoffman 1983:250, Lane 1981:17).

In response to their findings about sexual harassment, CEP developed services for female coal miners and worked to advance public policy on sexual harassment. To assist women in the mines, CEP provided counseling and support, including writing letters to employers on behalf of sexually harassed women. CEP published a brochure and a booklet on sexual harassment in coal mining. It also addressed sexual harassment and assault of women in rural and mountain communities by working to establish support services for these women. CEP formed a "buddy system" to connect female miners with women in nearby communities who were considering a career in mining. This program later became known as the Coal Mining Women's Support Team. CEP also participated in the development of public policy on sexual harassment. For example, in June of 1980, Pat Baldwin, a miner and head of the Western Kentucky

Women's Support Team, testified before the Kentucky Commission on Human Rights at a hearing on sexual harassment. In April 1981, Baldwin and CEP's director, Betty Jean Hall, who was an attorney, testified at hearings on sexual harassment before the Senate Committee on Labor and Human Resources in Washington D.C. (U.S. Congress 1981). The Coal Employment Project later filed a brief in *Meritor Savings Bank v. Vinson* (477 U.S. 57, 1986), the first Supreme Court case on sexual harassment. The activism of female coal miners, which was often covered in the press (Baker 2001:297, 473–474), increased public awareness of the seriousness of sexual harassment and advanced public policy on the issue.

Unions

Female labor union members also began to organize on the issue of sexual harassment during this time period. In 1979, women's activism within the United Mine Workers of America led President Arnold Miller to make a public commitment to eradicating sexual harassment in the mines (Women miners reassured 1979). Also in 1979, the United Auto Workers (UAW) won specific clauses on sexual harassment in contracts with Ford and Chrysler. The Ford contract confirmed that sexual harassment charges were subject to grievance procedures and committed the union and the company to investigate sexual harassment through the Fair Employment Practices Committees. Chrysler agreed to issue a policy statement to its management informing them that sexual harassment would not be tolerated. In 1981, the UAW issued a strong and clear policy statement against sexual harassment, deploring harassment as "a serious obstacle to the achievement of full employment opportunity for workers of both sexes" (Fraser 1981).

Female union members raised awareness of sexual harassment by discussing the issue at union meetings, conducting surveys, and writing articles and pamphlets. For example, a 1978 issue of *Hammer House*, the newspaper of the International Association of Machinists in Wichita, Kansas, contained an article calling on all workers to fight sexual harassment and pointing out the class interest of employers in women's oppression (International Association of Machinists 1979). Three members of the United Auto Workers, Elissa Clarke, Jane Slaughter, and Enid Eckstein, contributed to a handbook on sexual harassment for the Labor Education and Research Project in Detroit, Michigan, published in June of 1980 (Clarke et al. 1980). The pamphlet was cowritten with Connye Harper, a black female attorney and founder of the Women's Justice Center in Michigan, and Rita Drapkin, who was a member of the Teamsters and founder of the Cleveland, Ohio–based Hard Hatted Women, which supported women in skilled trades and nontraditional jobs. The handbook gave practical advice on how to combat sexual harassment on the job, within unions, and at educational institutions.

Organizations representing blue-collar women also influenced public policy by testifying at government hearings on sexual harassment and filing amicus curiae briefs in significant sexual harassment lawsuits. In 1979, union representatives of the United Auto Workers, the Industrial Union of Electrical, Radio and Machine Workers, and the Coalition of Labor Union Women testified on sexual harassment at federal hearings (U.S. Congress 1979). In addition to Betty Jean Hall of the Coal Employment Project and Pat Baldwin of the Western Kentucky Coalmining Women's Support Team, who spoke at 1981 federal hearings on sexual harassment, other blue-collar women's groups supported the testimony of Eleanor Holmes Norton at these hearings, including the Association of Illinois Women Coal Miners, the Coalition of Labor Union Women, the East Tennessee Coalmining Women's Support Team, the Lady Miners of Utah, Wider Opportunities for Women, and Women Miners of Wyoming. Several other blue-collar women's groups submitted statements to the congressional committee, including the Phoenix Institute in Salt Lake City, Utah, a community-based employment and training contractor focused on placing low-income women in blue-collar jobs (U.S. Congress 1981). In *Meritor Savings Bank v. Vinson* (477 U.S. 57, 1986), the first Supreme Court case on sexual harassment, several organizations representing blue-collar women participated as amici, including Non-Traditional Employment for Women, Wider Opportunities for Women, the Workers Defense League, the American Federation of Labor and Congress of Industrial Organizations, the Coalition of Labor Union Women, and the Coal Employment Project. Through these activities, blue-collar women contributed significantly to the development of public policy on sexual harassment.

Litigation

In the late 1970s and early 1980s, women were challenging sex discrimination and harassment in a variety of male-dominated occupations, including public utilities, law enforcement, road construction, air traffic control, janitorial work, manufacturing, and the military (Baker 2001:501–502). By this time, courts were uniformly ruling that a supervisor's sexual demands of a subordinate employee, known as quid pro quo sexual harassment, were prohibited by Title VII of the Civil Rights Act of 1964, which prohibited employment discrimination. This prohibition, however, did little to help women working in male-dominated occupations who experienced hostile environment sexual harassment not only from supervisors, but also from coworkers. Several women initiated lawsuits to convince courts to expand Title VII to cover hostile environment harassment. These lawsuits had a significant impact on the development of sexual harassment law. Phyllis Brown, a civilian police dispatcher, won the first successful hostile environment claim in federal court in May of 1980 (*Brown v. City of Guthrie*, 22 Fed. Empl. Prac. Cas. BNA 1627, W.D. Okla. 1980). Factory worker Willie Ruth Hawkins won one of the first successful coworker harassment cases in July of 1980 (*Minnesota v. Continental Can Company*, 297 N.W.2d 241, Minn. 1981). In the early 1980s, Sandra Bundy, who worked in the D.C. Department of Corrections, and Barbara Henson, a police dispatcher, also won precedent-setting hostile environment sexual harassment cases (*Bundy v. Jackson*, 641 F.2d 934, D.C. Cir. 1981; *Henson v. City of Dundee*, 682 F.2d 897, 11th Cir. 1982). The cases of Hawkins and Bundy, in particular, illustrated the feminist point that sexual harassment was about male domination.

Willie Ruth Hawkins was one of two women working at the Eagan, Minnesota, plant of Continental Can Company. Starting in December of 1974, three of Hawkins's white male coworkers repeatedly made explicit sexually derogatory remarks and verbal sexual advances to Hawkins and touched her sexually. One of her coworkers, Cliff Warling, said to Hawkins that he "wished slavery days would return so that he could sexually train her and she would be his bitch," making reference to the movie *Mandingo*. Warling and other male coworkers told her that "a female has no business in a factory" and "if a female would work [in] a factory, she has to be a tramp." Hawkins repeatedly complained to her supervisor, but Continental did nothing. One supervisor told Hawkins that there was nothing he could do and that she had to expect that kind of behavior when working with men. In October 1975, the harassment of Hawkins escalated to physical violence. Warling approached Hawkins from behind while she was bending over and grabbed her between the legs. Hawkins complained immediately, but again Continental did nothing. A few days later, Hawkins's husband came to the plant and confronted Warling, who denied the incident. When Mr. Hawkins returned later that evening to escort his wife home, they discovered that her car headlights were broken. Relations between the Hawkinses and her coworkers deteriorated further, culminating in a coworker threatening Willie Ruth Hawkins with a gun in front of her children. At that point, the Hawkinses solicited the support of New Way Community Center and the Urban League, who threatened boycotts and adverse publicity if Continental did not respond. Continental then suspended two of the harassers and held a plant meeting to inform all employees that Continental would not tolerate verbal or physical sexual harassment and discrimination. Fearing for her safety, Hawkins did not return to work and was later fired.

Hawkins filed a sex discrimination lawsuit under the Minnesota

Human Rights Act against Continental for failing to act sooner on her complaints. When the lawsuit was finally resolved in 1981, the Minnesota Supreme Court found in favor of Hawkins, ruling that Continental was liable for sex discrimination because it failed to stop coworker sexual harassment (*Minnesota v. Continental Can Company*, 297 N.W.2d 241, Minn. 1981). The National Organization for Women and the Working Women's Institute filed an amicus curiae brief in this case in support of Hawkins. This case was one of the first to hold an employer liable for coworker sexual harassment. As with many of the cases involving blue-collar women, the facts of Hawkins's case clearly demonstrate how men harassed women in order to maintain their dominance in the workplace. Using sexual language and physical assaults, Hawkins's coworkers sought to push her out of her job because they did not want women working in the factory.

Another precedent-setting Title VII sexual harassment case was the case of Sandra Bundy. A young black woman, Bundy was a vocational rehabilitation specialist with the District of Columbia Department of Corrections, responsible for finding jobs for former criminal offenders. Four of Bundy's supervisors routinely and graphically demanded sexual favors in calls to her home, as well as in office confrontations. They did not fire or refuse her a promotion for rejecting their advances, but they made her working environment unbearable. The situation was so severe that the trial judge in the case noted that "improper sexual advances to female employees [was] standard operating procedure, a fact of life, a normal condition of employment" at the Department of Corrections. Bundy complained repeatedly to her supervisors, but they merely harassed her further. One supervisor to whom she reported harassment responded, "I want to take you to bed myself" and "any man in his right mind would want to rape you." In dismissing her claim, the trial judge argued that Bundy's supervisors "did not consider plaintiff's rejection of their improper sexual advances as a reason or justification for harassing the plaintiff or of otherwise taking adverse action against her. It was a game played by the male superiors—you won some and you lost some. It was not a matter to be taken seriously" (*Bundy v. Jackson*, 19 Fair Empl. Prac. Case BNA 828, D.D.C. 1979). The judge's description of sexual harassment as "standard operating procedure, a fact of life, a normal condition of employment," as well as "a game played by male superiors" reflects how men controlled the working environment to the detriment of women.

Bundy appealed, and the appellate court reversed the ruling in a precedent-setting decision. The D.C. Circuit Court ruled that Title VII prohibited sexual harassment even in the absence of tangible job consequences if the hostile work environment caused psychological or emotional harm to the plaintiff. Noting that "the nuances and subtleties of discriminatory employment practices are no longer confined to 'bread and butter issues,'" the court argued that hostile environment sexual harassment "injects the most demeaning sexual stereotypes into the general work environment and always represents an intentional assault on an individual's innermost privacy." The court noted that to deny Bundy's claims would be to allow employers to sexually harass women with impunity simply by "carefully stopping short of firing the employee or taking any other tangible actions against her." Employers could thereby make sexual intimidation a "condition" of employment. Perhaps most significantly, the court explicitly acknowledged the gendered power dynamics underlying sexual harassment when it stated that "so long as women remain inferiors in the employment hierarchy, they may have little recourse against harassment beyond the legal recourse Bundy seeks in this case" (*Bundy v. Jackson*, 641 F.2d 934, D.C. Cir. 1981).

The case of *Bundy v. Jackson* was significant in at least two respects. First, the case set an important legal precedent by allowing a claim of hostile environment sexual harassment under Title VII. This legal precedent from the D.C. Circuit Court of Appeals was very influential on other courts. Second, the case was a focal point for public discussion of sexual harassment and a rallying point for feminists in the early 1980s. Donna Lenhoff, who testified at congressional sexual harassment hearings in 1979, discussed the egregious facts of *Bundy* to support her argument that Title VII should prohibit hostile environment harassment (U.S. Congress 1979). Sandra Bundy herself submitted written testimony at congressional hearings in 1980, describing her experiences of sexual harassment and her extended legal battle to gain relief. Bundy's case was discussed widely in law reviews and was covered extensively in the press, generating sympathy for victims of sexual harassment (Baker 2001:418). The case left no doubt as to the harm caused by sexual harassment. Hawkins, Bundy, and other blue-collar women made a significant contribution to the development of public policy on sexual harassment by winning precedent-setting hostile environment sexual harassment cases in state and federal courts.

Litigation initiated by blue-collar women influenced not only the development of the law, but also the views of middle-class feminists who were organizing on the issue. Working Women's Institute, for example, broadened its understanding of sexual harassment as it worked with blue-collar women, including firefighters, coal miners, and construction workers. It came to appreciate that sexual harassment was not only sexual conduct, but also hostile conduct aimed to drive women out of male-dominated workplaces. Karen Sauvigné, the institute's program director, remembers one institute volunteer in particular who helped broaden the institute's conception of sexual harassment in this way—Brenda Berkman, who sued the New York City Fire Department because they refused to hire her on the basis of her gender. Working with Berkman, Betty Jean Hall and Pat Baldwin of the Western Kentucky Coalmining Women's Support Team, Joyce Miller of the United Auto Workers, the Coalition of Labor Union Women, and other blue-collar women made the staff at the institute realize that sexual conduct was one of many tools that men use to create a hostile working environment when they want to keep women out. The institute's research director, Peggy Crull, remembers that Sandra Bundy's case led her to gain new understanding about sexual harassment (Crull 2001). In this way, the activism of blue-collar women working in male-dominated fields influenced not only the law, but also feminist organizations working on sexual harassment by calling attention to hostile environment sexual harassment.

CONCLUSION: FEMINIST THEORY AND FUTURE DIRECTIONS

A history of the development of sexual harassment policy in the United States that focuses on the role of blue-collar women provides new insights into how policy makers came to define sexual harassment and highlights the central role played by blue-collar women in the movement against sexual harassment. Their vivid stories of abuse left no doubt about the role that sexual harassment played in maintaining male domination, and their activism was instrumental in winning legal prohibitions of hostile environment sexual harassment. However, despite the development of legal prohibitions, many women still lose hostile environment sexual harassment cases because courts have been slow to understand the role that sexual harassment plays in maintaining male domination. Courts have often excluded evidence of non-sexual harassing behavior and have been resistant to acknowledge the significance of patterns of behavior that create a hostile environment for women (*Rabidue v. Osceola Refining Co.*, 805 F.2d 611, 6th Cir. 1986, Schultz 1998). Women continue to experience high rates of hostile environment sexual harassment, especially in male-dominated occupations (Eisenberg 1998, Martin 1997, Messerschmidt 1993). Laws against sexual harassment have changed those rates very little.

Contemporary feminist jurisprudence has offered many explanations and suggested solutions for the failures of sexual harassment law. However, unlike early feminist theory, only rarely has it focused on the role of male domination. In a 1998 review of the "new jurisprudence of sexual harassment," Kathryn Abrams criticized feminist legal theorists for failing to "conceptualize the wrong as the institutionalization of women's subordination" (Abrams 1998:1171). When sexual harassment has been characterized in terms of male dominance, the issue has been cast in narrowly sexual terms. Vicki Schultz (1998:1689) has argued that contemporary discussions of sexual harassment are based on a "sexual desire-dominance paradigm" that obscures much gender-based hostility directed at women in the workplace. Public discourse on sexual harassment assumes sexual desire to be the central dynamic, rather than gender-based hostility rooted in male attempts to assert power over females. Schultz attributes this tendency to focus on sexual misconduct rather than nonsexual forms of misconduct to radical feminist thought, which drew parallels between sexual harassment and rape and which "highlighted the centrality of sexual exploitation in creating women's inequality" (Schultz 1998:1689).

A look back at the early activists against sexual harassment reveals a more complex understanding of sexual harassment and suggests other reasons for the narrow focus of contemporary sexual harassment jurisprudence. From the beginning, feminists expressed skepticism about the potential of legal remedies to sexual harassment. AASC, in particular, emphasized that women should not rely exclusively on grievance procedures and legal remedies developed by employers and governments, but should act collectively to combat sexual harassment. AASC argued that government solutions did not serve women well because they were bureaucratic and legalistic. Employer concern with sexual harassment, they suggested, did not stem from a desire to help women, but rather was an attempt to avoid lawsuits, lowered productivity, and unionization of workers. Mary Ann Largen of the Washington-based advocacy organization New Responses, Inc., also expressed skepticism about the ability of laws and courts alone to eradicate sexual harassment or the "imbalance of power which fosters the behavior." Largen testified before Congress in 1979 that "it is a cultural phenomenon and will be eliminated only through re-socialization and re-education . . . a change in attitudes as well as behaviors" (Largen 1979:41). At bottom, activists were concerned that government and employer initiatives against sexual harassment might co-opt women's collective efforts to challenge the "root cause of sexual harassment—sexism" (Backhouse 1981:91). Feminists feared that government and employer control of remedies for sexual harassment would have the effect of reinforcing the status quo rather than challenging it.

AASC did not completely reject legal strategies to combat sexual harassment, but argued that these strategies should "exist alongside other strategies that focus on education and organization of women to take power in their homes and their jobs" (AASC 1981a:31–33). It emphasized the importance that women become "*active* participants" by "learning to join together and speak out against the exploitative aspects of their lives" (Backhouse et al. 1981:85–87, 91). AASC encouraged women to take the situation into their own hands and make choices about their tactics, not give up control of the situation to an outside investigator or agency or rely on employers to solve the problem (Dubrow 1980:25). It suggested tactics such as talking to other women in the workplace, placing leaflets in bathrooms, publicizing the name of the harasser, surveying the workplace, forming a workplace safety committee, sending a warning letter to the harasser or the employer, or conducting an educational picket in front of a workplace.

But as the 1980s progressed, collective action against sexual harassment became rarer and rarer and the issue became firmly entrenched in an individualistic legal framework. Resistance to sexual harassment became centered around legal challenges, and law came to dominate discussions of the issue. Comparing the sexual harassment workshops at the National Conference of Women Coal Miners during the 1980s shows how approaches to the issue evolved. The 1980 workshop was very much like a speak-out, with women telling their stories of sexual harassment and abuse. The workshop produced nine resolutions that focused on understanding sexual harassment, educating miners about the issue, generating discussion about it, and organizing against it in the workplace and in unions (Coal Employment Project 1980). By 1989, the sexual harassment workshop was almost entirely about the law. The workshop had a panel of speakers that consisted of two lawyers, one male and one female, and a male union administrator. The discussion primarily addressed legal remedies under Title VII sex discrimination law. When one workshop participant suggested that sexual harassment was a safety issue and that women might approach union safety committees about the issue, the female attorney said, "I've never thought of it that way. But then that wouldn't be the lawyer doing the case." The male attorney on the panel, who seemed equally surprised by the suggestion, was hesitant and discouraging, saying:

> You can do what you can do. You can do anything you can get away
> with. If your objective is to stop the harassment, that's a clever way
> of doing it. But that's a *bold* way of doing it. I bet not too many
> people would have the wherewithal to get that done. I think that's a
> major step. And I tip my hat to that person. I'm not going to say it
> can't be done. (Coal Employment Project 1989)

Outside of this interchange, there was little discussion of nonlegal solutions to sexual harassment. Firmly conceptualized in narrow legalistic terms, resistance to sexual harassment no longer had revolutionary potential.

While activists succeeded in achieving laws prohibiting sexual harassment, they did not succeed in eliminating what feminists understood to be the basis of sexual harassment—systems of dominance, particularly male domination. Within a narrow legal framework controlled by bureaucrats, lawyers, and employers, sexual harassment has become a personnel problem to be handled through employer grievance procedures, EEOC complaints, and Title VII lawsuits. Individualistic legal action took the place of collective resistance. Largely absent from current discourse on sexual harassment is the feminist insight that drove the development of public policy in the 1970s and early 1980s: that sexual harassment is a form of male dominance to be addressed collectively. This history suggests that more attention should be paid to contemporary feminist scholarship that conceptualizes sexual harassment as a problem of male domination (Cockburn 1991, Yount 1991, Abrams 1998, Schultz 1998, Morgan 2001) and that this understanding is best achieved by placing the experiences of blue-collar women at the center of the analysis.

NOTE

1. This theory is commonly attributed to Catharine MacKinnon (MacKinnon 1979), but it first appeared in print in Wehrli's thesis and in the publications of AASC and WWU member Lin Farley (AASC 1977, Farley 1978).

REFERENCES

Abrams, Kathryn. 1998. The new jurisprudence of sexual harassment. *Cornell Law Review* 83:1169–1230.

Alliance Against Sexual Coercion (AASC). 1977. *Sexual harassment at the workplace.* Boston: Author.

———. 1980. Three male views on harassment. *Aegis* (Winter/Spring): 52.

———. 1981a. Organizing against sexual harassment. *Radical America* (July/August): 17–34.

———. 1981b. Sexual harassment and coercion: Violence against women. *Aegis* (Winter/Spring): 18.

Arriola, Elvia R. 1990. "What's the big deal?" Women in the New York City construction industry and sexual harassment law, 1970–1985. *Columbia Human Rights Law Review* 22:21–71.

Backhouse, Connie, et al. 1981. *Fighting sexual harassment.* Boston, Mass.: Alyson Publications, Inc. and the Alliance Against Sexual Coercion.

Baker, Carrie N. 2001. *Sex, power, and politics: The origins of sexual harassment policy in the United States.* Ph.D. dissertation, Emory University.

———. 2004. Race, class, and sexual harassment in the 1970s. *Feminist Studies* (forthcoming).

Bularzik, Mary. 1978, June. Sexual harassment at the workplace: Historical notes. *Radical America* 12:25–43.

Clarke, Elissa, et al. 1980. *Stopping sexual harassment: A handbook.* Detroit: Labor and Education Research Project.

Coal Employment Project. 1980, May. *Sexual harassment in the mines work-*

shop. Second National Conference of Women Coal Miners, Beckley, West Virginia. Videocassette. In Coal Employment Project, Archives of Appalachia, Sherrod Library, East Tennessee State University, Johnson City, Tennessee. Accession 355, Tape 59.

————. 1989, June. *Sexual harassment/discrimination and CEP legal referral network*. Eleventh National Conference of Women Coal Miners, Illinois. Audiocassette. In Coal Employment Project, Archives of Appalachia, Sherrod Library, East Tennessee State University, Johnson City, Tennessee. Accession 355, Tape 14, Series XII A.

Cockburn, Cynthia. 1991. *In the way of women*. Ithaca, N.Y.: ILR Press.

Crull, Peggy. 1982. Sexual harassment and male control of women's work. *Women: A Journal of Liberation* 8:3–7.

————. 2001. Interview by author, February 27, New York City. Tape recording. On file with author.

Dubrow, Laurie. 1980. *Sexual harassment and the law*. Cambridge: Alliance Against Sexual Coercion.

Dullea, Georgia. 1977, August 23. Women win fight for more construction jobs, less harassment. *Washington Post*, L-30.

Eisenberg, Susan. 1998. *We'll call you if we need you: Experiences of women working in construction*. Ithaca, N.Y.: Cornell University Press.

Farley, Lin. 1978. *Sexual shakedown: The sexual harassment of women on the job*. New York: McGraw-Hill.

————. 1979. Response to sexual shakedown review. *Aegis* (January/February): 25.

Fraser, Douglas A. 1981, January 15. Letter from Douglas A. Fraser, President, International Union, UAW to UAW Administration, January 15, 1981. Policy on the elimination of sexual harassment at the workplace.

Gitlin, Todd. 1998, April 5. A clarifying moment in politics of gender. *Washington Post*, C-4.

Graff, Joan. 2001. Interview by author, February 14, San Francisco. Tape recording. On file with author.

Gruber, James E., and Lars Bjorn. 1982, August. Blue-collar blues: The sexual harassment of women autoworkers. *Work and Occupations* 9:271–298.

Hoffman, Jan. 1983. Digging in hell: The story of women coal miners. *Mademoiselle* (May): 16.

Hooven, Martha, and Freada Klein. 1978. Is sexual harassment legal? *Aegis* (September/October): 28.

International Association of Machinists. 1979. Combat sexual harassment on the job. *Aegis* (May/June): 24–28.

Lane, Raymond M. 1981. A man's world: An update on sexual harassment. *Village Voice* (December 15–22): 1.

Largen, Mary Ann. 1979. *Sexual harassment in the federal government: Testimony before the Subcommittee on Investigations of the Committee on Post Office and Civil Service*, 96th Congress, 1st Session; October 23, November 13; 38–53.

MacKinnon, Catharine. 1979. *Sexual harassment of working women.* New Haven, Conn.: Yale University Press.

Martin, Molly, ed. 1997. *Hard hatted women: Life on the job*, 2nd ed. Seattle, Wash.: Seal.

Maypole, Donald E., and Rosemarie Skaine. 1982. Sexual harassment of blue-collar workers. *Journal of Sociology and Social Welfare* 9:682–695.

Messerschmidt, Jim. 1993. *Masculinity and crime.* Lanham, Md.: Rowman and Littlefield, 131–182.

Morgan, Phoebe. 2001. Sexual harassment: Violence against women at work. In *Sourcebook on violence against women*, ed. by Claire M. Renzetti, Jeffrey L. Edleson, and Raquel Kennedy Bergen. Thousand Oaks, Calif.: Sage.

Prieto, Maggie. 1983. Women coal miners fight sexual harassment. *Off Our Backs* (August/September): 16–17.

Schultz, Vicki. 1998. Reconceptualizing sexual harassment.*Yale Law Journal* 107:1683–1805.

Stoltenberg, John. 2002. Male-on-male sexual harassment. *Feminista* 1: n. 7.

U.S. Congress. 1979. House. Subcommittee on Investigations of the Committee on Post Office and Civil Service. *Sexual harassment in the federal government*, 96th Congress, 1st Session; October 23, November 1 and 13.

U.S. Congress. 1981. Senate. Committee on Labor and Human Resources. *Sex discrimination in the workplace*, 97th Congress, 1st Session; April 21. http://www.feminista.com/v1n7/stoltenberg.html (Accessed August 3, 2002).

Wehrli, Lynn. 1976. *Sexual harassment at the workplace: A feminist analysis and strategy for social change.* Master's thesis, Massachusetts Institute of Technology.

White, Connie, Barbara Angle, and Marat Moore. 1981. *Sexual harassment in the coal industry: A survey of women miners.* Oak Ridge, Tenn.: Coal Employment Project.

Women in construction. 1978. *Federal Register* 43:14891.

Women miners reassured. 1979, November 13. *Washington Post*, A-4.

Yount, Kirsten R. 1991, January. Ladies, flirts, and tomboys: Strategies for managing sexual harassment in an underground coal mine. *Journal of Contemporary Ethnography* 19:396–422.

12 THE ARCHITECTURE OF SEXUAL HARASSMENT

Carla Corroto

The quintessential example of men at work harassing women is the building construction work site: as women walk by, blue-collar men whistle, make catcalls, and generally call attention to women's bodies as sexual objects. Although not as renowned, sexual harassment at the architect's office where buildings are designed is just as deliberate. Here the translation of objectification and harassment is decidedly white collar, professional, and embedded in architects' formal education.[1] With this research, I investigate the version of sexual harassment that haunts the study and practice of architecture and helps maintain male domination in the profession. Unlike in the construction site, sexual harassment of women in architecture is unacknowledged. I will argue that sexual harassment is constitutive: part of the institutional practices and gendered organization that is considered architectural knowledge.

Architecture is historically, normatively, and numerically male dominated. However, the number of women enrolling in architecture school programs has steadily increased over the last twenty-five years. In many schools in North America and the United Kingdom, the first-year cohorts are upwards of 50 percent female. Yet, women are not graduating at the same rate as their male colleagues, since women make up less than 25 percent of most graduating classes. There is a significantly higher attrition rate for women in architecture at all levels when compared to men's persistence in the field. After earning a professional degree in architecture and then two to three years in professional office practice in the United States, an "interning architect" may take the registration or licensing exam. By some reports, the number of women who continue in the profession through licensure is actually decreasing. Today, approximately 11 percent of all licensed architects in the United States are women. Analyzing sexual harassment in architecture as a gendered organizational process and a professional culture that maintains male dominance will help us understand part of this chronic gender asymmetry.[2]

METHODS

This project was an in-depth long-term engagement in a comprehensive case study that took advantage of a three-year observational experience in architecture as a "complete participant" (Adler & Adler 1987, Marshall & Rossman 1999, Stake 1994). While holding an appointment as an assistant professor of architecture at a midwestern (U.S.) university from 1998 to 2000, I conducted "institutional ethnographic research" that connected the lived experiences of students and faculty to the institutional structure (Smith 1987). Employing traditional participant-observer fieldwork methods, I took detailed and extensive field notes, intending to use the data for ethnographic description and analysis (Lofland & Lofland 1995). My initial research questions centered on explaining why proportionally fewer women than men persisted in architecture school through graduation. At the university where I conducted my ethnographic research, the percentage of women in the program at all levels mirrored the national averages. The university architecture program was accredited and shared characteristics found in the majority of architecture programs in the United States.

This qualitative study uncovered institutional forms of harassment that another research method, such as a survey, would probably have missed (Arvey & Cavanaugh 1995). Researchers of sexual harassment across occupational types have been concerned that, for situations in which workers essentially "consent" to organizationally sanctioned harassing behaviors as part of their job, a generally worded questionnaire is inadequate (Williams 1997). As I will argue, harassment in architecture is embedded in everyday interaction as normative relations. Simply asking women to report unwanted sexual behavior or personal attention would miss the tacitly agreed-upon institutional interaction that constitutes the culture of architecture. Institutional ethnographic methods were effective empirical measurements and instrumental for uncovering male domination. As Dorothy E. Smith (1987) proposed, an institutional ethnography effectively illuminates the ideological procedures that are constituents of the social relations expressing work processes. When interpreting the context that produces architects and what counts as architectural knowledge, it is impossible to divorce the institutional value system from outcomes. Embedded in the social interaction between students, faculty, and practicing architects are answers to how sexual harassment is fostered in architecture and why some women do not continue in the field.

BACKGROUND

Architecture, in the university context, considers itself an exceptional avenue of study because of several heralded characteristics. Typically, it is an extended institutional commitment measured in years that involves unlimited hours of course work. Undergraduate professional degree programs entail a minimum of five years of enrollment, with some versions requiring a masters of architecture degree in six years. There are other avenues for graduates with nonarchitecture degrees, but the undergraduate path is the most prevalent. In those years directed toward a degree, architecture-the-institution requires an enormous time commitment for exertion in the design studio, which is central to the study of architecture. Architecture design studio is typically a five-, six-, or seven-credit-hour course (dependent upon institutional calendar), is taken each term a student is enrolled in a degree-granting program, and signifies all that is of value in architecture. Studio is considered the core of the program, where all knowledge garnered in *support* courses (such as architectural history, theory, engineering structures, and those outside the major in the humanities, natural sciences, and social sciences) is synthesized and integrated. Significantly, it is both a place where students are expected to work and a pedagogical type. The assignment for the studio is typically to design buildings by submitting extensive drawings and models that provide evidence of the student's *problem-solving abilities.*

It is also an exceptional course of study for several unheralded, yet equally defining, characteristics that reflect a masculinist ethos. First, requisite *all-nighters* spent toiling as a collective in a studio building on campus are institutional traditions. Second, the studio is an insular and time-consuming course of study in which only the toughest survive. Third, in this highly competitive environment, those students with no relationships or interests outside of architecture, who therefore spend the most time in studio, are often celebrated as the best and most committed designers. Fourth, technological and abstract theoretical sophistication is valued. Finally, students' studio design work is evaluated publicly in review sessions called juries with critics or jurors offering evaluation. This form of evaluation is infamous in architecture schools for its rather harsh and personally demeaning tone. Students are told "not to be defensive" and are expected to manage their emotions in what often devolves into a public haranguing. These evaluations amount to degradation ceremonies that students must "survive" as rites of passage to what is framed as an exclusive club (Anthony 1991).

This subtext can be explicated in the following promotional material for an architecture program that one university publishes:

The study of architecture is a group activity. It is a process of sharing, mentoring, and self-discovery surrounded by members of a community—students, faculty, and staff—equally passionate about learning, making, and experimenting. [Our university studio building] is a place alive around the clock with activity, inspiration and opportunity. The study of architecture is demanding, challenging, confusing, and expanding. No other discipline encompasses the breadth of knowledge—from the sciences to the humanities to the arts—as architecture. No other course of study expects as much of the student in creative thinking and synthesizing information. And no other learning environment is structured to foster self-discipline and individual accountability for his or her actions and conclusions. There are few "right" answers in design and rarely is the first "solution" even a good one. . . . Architects tend to welcome ambiguity—and look for opportunities to establish order to our experiences in the world. Architects, by their nature and training, enjoy the difficulty of reconciling and giving form to conflicting needs, desires, forces and dreams . . . architecture is hard work. It's a form of life.[3]

This passage speaks to many ideological components of architecture's self-definition, but especially to the all-consuming expectation that represents the institution; the study is, indeed, a "way of life." It is from this core of architecture's curriculum, pedagogy, and identity that I concentrate my research.

OBSERVATION

From the start of their formal education, architecture students are taught to "observe." Typically, opening assignments require intensive documentation via diagrams and freehand sketches of existing spaces, places, and buildings. At the university where I conducted my research, first-year students sit outside for hours in front of campus buildings and sketch how the sunlight casts shadows. Early-morning and late-afternoon light cast longer and less decisive shadows than noontime, brilliant, high-in-the-sky sun. They then appraise which of the buildings has the best play of light and shadows.

The student documentation is pinned up on the wall and evaluated based on observed design issues. What is the quality of their drawn lines? Do they vary in the conventional ways? Are the diagrams and sketches skillfully placed on the sheet of paper? Drawings and diagrams are labeled, and the lettering must be architectural, perfectly placed, and drafted using a straightedge so that vertical lines are, indeed, vertical and the titles reinforce compositional issues. The students are told that their "craft" matters. No messy drawings are permitted; only "museum quality" productions are acceptable. Perfection is the goal.

Making architects hyperaware of the way things look takes up much of their training. In a text advocating alternative design processes, an environmental psychologist wrote, "As a social scientist teaching in a school of architecture, I've been only too aware of how much architecture schools stress formal issues over human experience and activity" (Franck & Lepori 2000:5). Architects call their emphasis on the visual or aesthetic issues in design "formalism." Form is usually emphasized over content. To some critics, stressing form is a negatively abstract method of designing structures. Yet, even when individual instructors or architects value other design criteria, for example, how a building functions, they are still accustomed to appraising the merits of the architectural drawings and models, so that there is never ending attention paid to the aesthetics of some aspect of architects' designed objects.

Architects are also expected to evaluate design based on aesthetics. Regardless of the prevailing theory or style or paradigm, whether a building is evaluated in context or as an object, its appearance is debated in dualities and ultimately deemed "good or bad, exuberant or lackluster, successful or unsuccessful, elegant or awkward," based on its form. There is a language to design and composition, both visual and literal, and students as practitioners-in-training are taught to privilege the way things look as judges and evaluators.

This spotlight on design that we know from our sense of sight extends to almost all objects, from the personal—clothing, shoes, and lighters—to the domestic—tableware, furniture, and lamps. No object escapes the scrutiny of design-oriented architects. In informal conversation, I have heard them draw conclusions about the design merits of various eyeglass frames, automobiles, and fountain pens— exclaiming that beautiful objects are "fabulous." Indeed, it is peculiar to be in the company of architects who do not verbalize such pronouncements. One architecture studio professor created an assignment that found students shopping for a "well-designed object valued at fewer than five dollars." They bought and evaluated objects such as classic Pez dispensers, mouse pads, and soap holders from "design-oriented" stores. This sort of connoisseurship has many sociological implications, including social class initiation and consumerist culture validation. However, the impact I study here is how the institutional norm of appraising design based on aesthetics, in a society that objectifies women, extends to the review of women-as-objects, as well.

THE DATA

From my research site, I found two locations within the institution of architecture that promoted the objectification and sexualizing of women—at design juries and in the studio. Each place—with its attendant values, attitudes, beliefs, and artifacts—frames women as designed or sexual objects. The result is an environment in which women have attention paid to them personally rather than, or sometimes in addition to, because of their architecture design work.

The following descriptions of public design review juries illustrate how architects privilege form over content and attend to women in the same manner.

Architecture Design Juries

At the university where I conducted my ethnographic work, student projects were evaluated in juries at the end of the term in the traditional architecture school fashion. This rather theatrical event was the culmination of a semester of hard work. It was the focus, the goal, the climax that students seemed both to dread and relish, dependent upon their evaluation and place in the social and academic hierarchy. Here, individual stars were crowned and reputations created. Each student had approximately 20 to 30 minutes to present his or her architectural design and to receive an evaluation from a mix of architecture faculty and practicing architects invited to the university for this purpose.

In one studio class under review, each student had designed an interstate highway rest stop that spanned the boundary of two U.S. states. The four jurors were praising one student's "formal emphasis on horizontality that mimics the expansive plains of the Midwest." He had successfully designed a "beautifully balanced composition in (floor) plan and section that expressed the proper hierarchy of spatial relations." As a member of this review team, I pointed out that the student had included a bar in his rest stop and that Mothers Against Drunk Driving (MADD) would be less interested in his "horizontally configured elevation, than his facilitating drinking and driving." My comment was glossed over in lieu of more remarks regarding the aesthetics of the project.

At this same review, a woman presented her drawings for the rest stop that were a high contrast of black and white. The critique began with one architect who said that she "missed an important design opportunity," that the student should have worn an outfit that was black and white to match her drawings. The rest of the jury chimed in, trying to decide if her shirt should have been black and her skirt white or vice versa. After a rather lengthy discussion among the faculty and architect jurors about how this woman, as an architect, should dress to enhance her "design vocabulary," they briefly got around to critiquing her architecture. Meanwhile, as they discussed her wardrobe, the student stood in front of the room with her eyes averted, disengaged from what was posited as an educational process.

As women students stood up to make public presentations of their architectural designs, with audiences ranging from fifteen to seventy people, it became evident that more than schoolwork was under scrutiny. There were countless incidents of jurors making comments about women's clothing. A woman who wore a man's necktie was told, first, that the jury "liked her tie," then that its pattern was "anamorphic" like her project, and finally, that it was appropriate she wear a tie, as the assignment was to design a corporate office building. They were in fact suggesting that she was in costume. Other women were told that their outfits were too colorful, that they detracted from the drawings. Women students' haircuts, hair color, new eyeglasses, makeup (too much or too little,) tattoos, piercings, shoes, and jewelry all garnered attention and appraisal from architects, faculty, and some classmates. The terms used in critique were usually of an architectural character. For example, one architect told a student, "Your pin is so Baroque and I don't like it," associating the jewelry with a stylistic period. "Nice choice to go minimal" was sarcastically spoken to a woman who wore no makeup. Several women were told, in a paternalistic manner, that they were "getting too thin." It was cryptically noted that one woman had "a classic Roman nose" and she should "consider the historical reference." Another woman student with rather dark-toned skin was chided for her suntan, told that she should work as hard on her architecture as she had on getting a tan. A woman who wore eyeglass frames made popular by a famous deceased architect was sarcastically told not to "hide behind your Corb glasses. . . . they won't help your design, and you need help." A guest architect who wanted to refer to a previous project, but could not remember the name of the student, referred to her haircut and color instead by saying, "We should compare your project to that blonde girl's with the odd haircut." Conversely, I was witness to only one comment about a male student's appearance after he had dyed his hair electric blue.

As a faculty member, I was privy to the comments that professors made about students but that were seemingly not intended for the students to hear. While getting ready for jury, several professors whispered to each other about how they did not understand what a woman student, whom they characterized as particularly attractive, saw in her awkward-looking boyfriend. When I made a disapproving comment about their line of conversation, one faculty member said, "We all notice and talk about [the couple]." I was to believe that a consensus made their narrative valid. In another situation in which a student had become argumentative in reaction to a particularly negative critique, her professor suggested under his breath that because she is "so attractive" she is "used to getting her own way." When I again expressed displeasure with the line of commentary, he suggested that "we all think she had skated by on her looks." Some faculty would discuss the merits of women students' appearance amongst themselves and would allude to their having been easier on attractive women to keep them in the program.

Because these remarks directed to students were coded in terms used for design, or were in the context of the public formal review system, they were intrinsic to the institution. The attention paid to women or their appearance was made normative. These public rituals were considered part of their initiation into architecture, and they set the tone for the objectification of women in the design studio.

Architecture Design Studio Culture

Faculty at most architecture schools adamantly demand that their students complete architectural design work in the studio rather than at their homes. Where I conducted my research, the studio environments were highly competitive, with students regularly complaining that another had stolen a design idea or that their grade was unfair compared to their classmates'. Because of the emphasis on making designer stars and on individualism, the public nature of critiquing the work, the individual design awards, and the limited number of high grades, studio environments were often anything but supportive. The competition was not only for the best architectural design solutions, but also for who could work the longest, pull the most all-nighters, and literally be the toughest. Often, when students were not succeeding in the traditional manner in design studio, a professor would suggest that the poor performance was because he or she "does not work in studio." Their attendance was informally monitored, and it was not unusual for faculty to walk through the studio at night to see which students were at their desks. After several students changed majors out of architecture, I heard them described, by both faculty and students, as "not tough enough to cut it, weak, uncommitted, and lazy." It was clear that working in the studio was not optional and that it was a proving ground for architects.

Studios are generally large open rooms in campus buildings where students get a drafting table and a stool and use that furniture to stake out a space to call their own. This university was no different. There was typically no privacy. The only respite from attending to a room full of people was to wear earphones and listen to music. Frequently, students reported that studios became very loud at night, with radios blaring and raised voices in conversations. Certainly more than assigned work occurs in studio. At night, I saw male students appropriate space by moving desks aside and playing a type of broomball or floor hockey. Others would toss a football. Because time immersion is one way that architecture measures commitment to its discipline, many students thought of their studio as home base. Some brought in mattresses, placed them under their desks, and tried to catch a few hours of sleep before returning to their drawings or going to a class. Late nights and long hours were normative, and students spent a large amount of time together, isolated from the rest of campus and from family.

In such a studio environment, physical segregation from the rest of campus and society contributes to gender segregation. Here, testing and proving masculinity take on a parochial character, such that what otherwise may be a gender-neutral campus environment becomes rooted in masculine behavior, symbols, and objects. Some aspects of individual gender identity—particularly masculinity—are products of organizational processes and pressures (Acker 1990). At this studio, the valuable men proved their worth by sleeping the least, producing the most beautiful drawings via digital technology, and constructing intricate models, and they took on the design vocabulary heard at juries. Because architecture student work is publicly evaluated, all the students were aware of the class rankings. Design awards were given every year to the best of the best design students, although that distinction was rarely patently obvious.

At the university where I conducted my research, the studio environment was problematic for some women students, who formally and informally reported that they did not feel comfortable working there. The three women in the graduate degree program told of very deliberate harassment by men in the studio at night. The male students would turn their radios to channels that broadcast a sex-talk call-in show. The topics were explicit, and the men in attendance would laugh loudly, add to the radio topics, and intimidate the women with personal remarks about their sex lives. The department had a standing mandate that radios be used only with earphones, but there was no one of authority there at night and that rule was not enforced.

Male students would also leave pornographic images on their computer screen savers in view of whoever walked by or worked in their areas. Although I asked them to remove the images, they would disappear only so long as I was in their studio. Many first- and second-year women students felt targeted, and they acknowledged that their presence garnered much negative attention from faculty and male students. Older architecture students frequently asked this cohort of women out on dates. One woman told me that she and her peers were loath to socialize with these men because they felt as though they "actually lived with them in studio." In addition, they feared that, by going on dates, the women would be labeled "slackers" because they spent time away from studio work. Many said that they wished the requests for dates would stop and described serious relational pressures. Worse for some of the women were requests for sexual behavior and sexual commentary from the older, more prestigious male students. One woman student told me that although she knew "they were just kidding around," she found the sex talking "shocking." Faculty often joked about the first-year women students as magnets for the older men; when they were absent from their assigned studios, the male students could often be found "hitting on the freshmen" (sic). I taught a second-year studio and often heard male students evaluate the appearance of women in the school. There was one particularly industrious woman student who regularly overachieved, producing more and better drawings than most anyone in the class. It was not difficult to listen in to the group of men, who would crassly joke and conjure up what her standards might be for a man with whom she would have sex. Other women in the studio heard these conversations as well. A woman student told me the men had a ranking system that was known to all. The categories were for best body parts—the women students with the best legs, breasts, and so on—and they kept a running spreadsheet regularly going through the studios to take notes.

There were several male students who were so threatening that women would maneuver to never be alone with them in the studio. The women took to working in groups and planning their time around each other's schedules because these men would leer at them, ask them for sexual acts, and speak loudly about sexual situations. The other men in the studio did not sanction them but were said to find their behavior humorous. Several departmental administrators and the university affirmative action office were alerted to this situation by one of the women graduate students, but seemingly no action was taken.

In another situation, a lecture was given about the perils of using inauthentic drawing techniques to hide architectural design miscues. After the lecture, several high-prestige male students took advertisements from magazines featuring a lingerie line that cast women as angels with wings. They drew nipples and pubic hair on the models and scripted, in perfect architectural lettering, "real men don't airbrush" and on others, "this is a misuse of Photoshop." The images were tacked up on the studio walls. Their messages conveyed that women-objects, like architecture, could be depicted inauthentically via photo-altering techniques. Several faculty members saw the depictions, and no one made a move to remove the pictures.

Frequently, men would wallpaper their studio area with images of scantily clad or naked women. However, these pictures were not your ordinary calendar model pinups. They could be considered art photos, since compositionally the framing, position, lighting, and so forth were deliberately designed using concepts from visual composition, like architectural design. At this university setting, no one in authority resisted the pinups, nor did they articulate regulations against such sexualized depictions of women. I instructed individual men to remove the images, telling them that the pictures were inappropriate for a public work setting. In response, I would hear the myriad of design reasons that the pictures were pinned up— symmetry, balance, rhythm, repetition, harmony. They wanted me to believe that the content of the pictures was tangential to the formal relationships that they found attractive, interesting, or inspiring.

As a woman faculty member who taught a course titled "Gender Constructions in Architecture," I was often a sounding board for students' concerns. On three occasions I brought studio situations to the attention of department administrators and encouraged students to use the formal university system, such as it was, to wage complaints. Although this university had a sexual harassment policy, it was not common knowledge, and the enforcement of an appropriate code of conduct was never evident. On one occasion, a department administrator spoke with an individual student who exhibited threatening behavior toward women, although to my knowledge he was not sanctioned nor his behavior further monitored. Behaviors such as sexual harassment were viewed as deviations of gendered actors, not, as MacKinnon (1987) might argue, as components of organizational structure. Rather than seeing this locker-room atmosphere as an institutional problem, it was viewed as the individual problem of a select few. The conversation between administrator and student did not alleviate the behavior.

DISCUSSION

Sexual harassment plays a role in the maintenance of male dominance in architecture via the cultural reproduction of asymmetrical images of gender and the creation of a hostile environment for women. Architecture school is organized around making masculinity and men the subject while constructing women as the lesser "other" and the object. The two locales of harassment have varying dynamics, but in tandem they reproduce a climate that objectifies and sexualizes women while constructing a narrow definition of acceptable masculine behavior. Although it shares features found in other occupations and professions and manifests the same outcomes, the way that architects sexually harass, or the architecture of sexual harassment, is distinctively woven into their knowledge base and gendered organization.

Constructing Objects

Women in architecture experience objectification much like women do in occupations where sexualized treatment is institutionalized, like restaurants where women servers are required to wear short skirts or low-cut shirts (Loe 1996). The difference in architecture is that objectification in the design jury is intellectualized via the language of architecture; though not explicit, it is institutionalized as normal practice. Architects privilege and elevate the role of form and aesthetics in design; therefore, attention is directed to observation and then critique of objects. In a society where women are routinely positioned as objects, and in a culture where observing is rewarded, women in architecture become the observed, the assessed, and the objects of the gaze.

It is over a decade since theorists reintroduced the study of the social and cultural meanings attached to *the body* (Bordo 1993, Schilling 1993, Witz 2000), although feminists have all along documented the harm connected with the preoccupation with the female body as the object of male gaze (e.g., Brownmiller 1975). The common thread running through all forms of objectification is the experience of being treated as a body (or collection of body parts) valued predominantly for its use to (or consumption by) others and appraised on the basis of appearance (Fredrickson & Roberts 1997). Evaluation is enacted through a visual inspection of the form of a woman's body or her choices in clothing, accessories, and so on. In architecture it is enacted in the continual attention to all aspects of women's appearance through direct observation, evaluation, and institutionally sanctioned commentary. Objectification occurs in the design jury whenever aspects of a woman's appearance are separated out from her person and regarded as if those aspects were capable of representing her or her schoolwork. An example was referring to an architectural design as "that blonde girl's with the odd haircut" rather than by the name of the architecture student by whom it was created. When objectified, women are treated as bodies, and in particular as bodies that exist for the inspection and delectation of others. Objectification is only one type of gender oppression, but it influences other forms of harassment.

Visual evaluation of the female body, which can lead to sexual objectification, is integral to male domination. Connell (2000) argues that the cultural custom of objectifying female bodies stems from the creation, maintenance, and expression of patriarchy. Sexual harassment is believed to arise from and reinforce the subordinate position of women in society and is a consequence of gendered institutions that promote male dominance and the sexual objectification of women (Fitzgerald 1993, Pagelow 1992, cited in Cleveland & McNamara 1996).

Instrumentally, commenting on a woman's appearance in architecture has the effect of unreasonably interfering with her learning opportunity. Some women students simply did not get proper attention paid to their architectural design solutions and were therefore deprived of an important part of their education. Most women would make certain that they allowed time to attend to their personal grooming before the public presentations because they knew there was a chance that as much attention would be paid to their appearance as their design achievements. Although some women resisted, more women enacted traditional gendered behavior and would dress up for their reviews, putting on nicer clothing, doing their hair, and wearing makeup, than would not. Few of the male students gave this kind of attention to their appearance, attending their juries in conventional casual student garb.

Among other issues, distracting women from the task at hand with unwanted personal comments put them in a less competitive position relative to their male peers. It also had the effect of replicating architecture's message that their form was more important than the content of their schoolwork. Psychologists have outlined the harm that befalls individual women when they are subject to such scrutiny. Objectification positions women to take an observer's view of themselves (Bartky 1990). As external pressure encourages women's preoccupation with their own physical appearance, the potential exists for their thoughts and actions to be interrupted and distracted by images of how their bodies appear and for them to lose concentration on their work or activities (Fredrickson & Roberts 1997). Architecture is a time-consuming pursuit that requires great attention to detail, so being distracted again places women at a disadvantage. Other psychological problems stemming from objectification include eating disorders and depression.[4]

Even if an individual woman was not herself a target of this sort of commentary in the jury, it affected all present generally by creating a climate that was inhospitable to taking women's architecture work seriously. Women had to accommodate themselves as best they could to looking the part of a competent architect. This bystander stress found women listening in as their colleagues were objectified, with no sanctions for the commentators, wondering if or when such attention would be paid to them. This experience may be nearly as stressful as being a direct target of personal attention (Schneider

1996). Objectification from architecture's authorities set a tone that had an effect on the men as well. It influenced the general organizational environment in that paying unwanted personal attention to the women students, as modeled by faculty and visiting architects, was replicated throughout the institution. Essentially, institutional reality was communicated to students through repeated examples in the design juries.

Constructing Masculinity

The design studio was a site of gender harassment that created a hostile learning environment because it played a prime role in the construction and maintenance of one kind of masculinity. Gruber (1998) asserts that for contexts that are numerically and normatively male dominated, the learning or work culture is essentially an extension of male culture. To understand male dominance, then, it is important to recognize the influence that the institution has on the hegemonic state of relations between different males and masculinities and women (Connell 2001). Hegemonic masculinity is circumscribed against various subordinated masculinities as well as in opposition to women and femininity (Connell 1987). The dominant architecture student contributes to a heterosexist locker-room atmosphere that sexualizes women and establishes intimacy among men (Curry 1991). This socially constructed masculinity is *done* as part of the gendered processes of the organization of architectural education via heterosexuality and power, and it facilitates harassment (West & Zimmerman 1987, Lorber 1994). Quinn (2002:399) cautions that sexual objectification of women as a form of sexual harassment is a mechanism "through which gendered boundaries are patrolled and evoked and by which deeply held identities are established." In the architecture studio, the behavior directed toward women students may be described most often as gender harassment (Fitzgerald, Gelfand, & Drasgow 1994). Indiscriminate sexist comments that expressed insulting, degrading, and sexist attitudes, soliciting women for dates, and objectifying and evaluating their appearance was as much about male social bonding as it was about distinguishing the men from the women students and ensuring male dominance.

In this male-dominated institution, where women are competing with men for rewards such as grades, design prizes, and prestige, men attempt to emphasize women classmates' status as women over their status as architects (Reskin 1988). Femaleness is salient and visible when there are fewer women (Stockdale 1996.) In architecture schools, the ratio of men to women becomes increasingly skewed as the students, then professionals, progress through the system. Creating a hostile environment allows men to put women in their proper or subordinate places in architecture.

RESPONSES

Cleveland and McNamara (1996) posit that sexual harassment is more likely to occur when women have low social power and are socially isolated. As students, the relatively few women in architecture are not positioned to easily challenge the existing order. As an assistant professor with no social support, when I suggested augmenting the jury format, attending to behavior in the studio, or preventing students from working as many consecutive hours together in the studio, the response was to caution that those changes would limit architecture's "rigor." Creating a draconian institution is the most identifiable aspect of architecture, and it is the most oft-cited reason for maintaining the status quo.

Social isolation has an influence on sexual harassment (Gutek 1985). It is a requisite characteristic of the architecture discipline that students absent themselves from most aspects of campus and community life to toil for extended hours on their drawings and models. This demand effectively diminishes an architect's social networks, so that the harassment is rarely revealed outside of the studio. Research has shown that women with extended support systems are more likely to take action and report their negative experiences with harassment (Stockdale 1996). Architecture students are essentially rewarded for having no social relations outside of their studios. Further, because students often begin their studies in architecture studio right out of high school, the younger women are more vulnerable and have less life experience on which to draw. In my study, only the graduate student women made formal complaints.

In architecture, the studio and jury culture is constitutive. Many women who remain in the discipline may choose passive responding or making light of the situation because they accept that to challenge the situation is futile. If architecture school is indeed experienced as a way of life, then objectification and maneuvering in a hostile climate are a consequence and part of that life course for women. When women change majors or drop out of architecture, the picture painted explaining their attrition is usually that architecture is just too difficult. Considering the hostile environment and objectification, their assessment, while incomplete, is not incorrect.

NOTES

1. Because architecture is categorized as a profession and because the harassment that I uncover is encouraged by the professional values, attitudes, and beliefs in the normative operation of studying and practicing architecture, I have labeled it a "white-collar" version for contrast. However, as Gruber, Smith, and Kauppinen-Toropainen (1996) find, there is "not a variety of sexual harassment experiences that are unique to different categories of working women. . . . In terms of range and prevalence of experiences, and the emotional impact of each type of experience, there is simply sexual harassment" (p. 152).
2. http://www.aia.org/diversity/statistics are gathered by the American Institute of Architects. The Royal Institute of British Architects (RIBA) is currently sponsoring research to ascertain why women in the United Kingdom are exiting the profession in such great numbers.
3. http://www.tulane.edu/%7Etsahome/lifetsa.html.
4. This population of women in architecture is consistent with the profile most often affected by eating disorders—white, middle to upper-middle class, in a context that encourages perfection.

REFERENCES

Acker, J. 1990. Hierarchies, jobs, bodies: A theory of gendered organizations. *Gender and Society* 4 (2): 139–158.

Adler, P. A., and P. Adler. 1987. *Membership roles in field research.* Newbury Park, Calif.: Sage.

Anthony, K. H. 1991. *Design juries on trial: The renaissance of the design studio.* New York: Van Nostrand Reinhold.

Arvey, R. D., and M. A. Cavanaugh. 1995. Using surveys to assess the prevalence of sexual harassment: Some methodological problems. *Journal of Social Issues* 51 (1): 39–52.

Bartky, S. L. 1990. *Femininity and domination: Studies in the phenomenology of oppression.* New York: Routledge.

Bordo, S. R. 1993. *Unbearable weight: Feminism, Western culture, and the body.* Berkeley: University of California Press.

Brownmiller, S. 1975. *Against our will: Men, women, and rape.* New York: Simon and Schuster.

Cleveland, J. N., and K. McNamara. 1996. Understanding sexual harassment: Contributions from research on domestic violence and organizational change. In *Sexual harassment in the workplace: Perspectives, frontiers and response strategies,* ed. M. Stockdale, 217–240. Thousand Oaks, Calif.: Sage.

Connell, R. W. 1987. *Gender and power.* Stanford, Calif.: Stanford University Press.

———. 2000. *The men and the boys.* Berkeley: University of California Press.

———. 2001. Understanding men: Gender sociology and the new international research on masculinities. *Social Thought and Research* 24:13–31.

Curry, T. J. 1991. Fraternal bonding in the locker room: A pro-feminist analysis of talk about competition and women. *Sociology of Sport Journal* 8 (2): 119–135.

Fitzgerald, L. F. 1993. Sexual harassment: Violence against women in the workplace. *American Psychology* 48:1070–1076.

Fitzgerald, L., C. Hulin, and F. Drasgow. 1994. The antecedents and consequences of sexual harassment in organizations: An integrated model. In *Job stress in the changing workforce: Investigating gender, diversity, and family issues,* ed. G. Keita and J. Hurrell, 55–73. Washington, D.C.: American Psychological Association.

Franck, K. A., and R. B. Lepori. 2000. *Architecture inside out.* Chichester, West Sussex: Wiley-Academy.

Fredrickson, B. L., and T. Roberts. 1997. Objectification theory: Toward understanding women's lived experiences and mental health risks. *Psychology of Women Quarterly* 21:173–206.

Gruber, J. E. 1998. The impact of male work environments and organizational policies on women's experiences of sexual harassment. *Gender and Society* 12 (3): 301–320.

Gruber, J. E., M. Smith, and K. Kauppinen-Toropainen. 1996. Sexual harassment types and severity: Linking research and policy. In *Sexual harassment in the workplace: Perspectives, frontiers and response strategies,* ed. M. Stockdale, 151–173. Thousand Oaks, Calif.: Sage.

Gutek, B. A. 1985. *Sex and the workplace: The impact of sexual behavior and harassment on women, men, and organizations.* San Francisco: Jossey-Bass.

Loe, M. 1996. Working for men: The intersection of power, gender and sexuality. *Social Inquiry* 66 (4): 399–421.

Lofland, J., and L. Lofland. 1995. *Analyzing social settings.* Belmont, Calif.: Wadsworth.

Lorber, J. 1994. *Paradoxes of gender.* New Haven: Yale University Press.

MacKinnon, C. 1987. *Feminism unmodified: Discourses on life and law.* Cambridge, Mass.: Harvard University Press.

Marshall, C., and G. V. Rossman. 1999. *Designing qualitative research.* Thousand Oaks, Calif.: Sage.

Pagelow, M. 1992. Adult victims of domestic violence. *Journal of Interpersonal Violence* 7:87–120.

Quinn, B. A. 2002. Sexual harassment and masculinity: The power and meaning of "girl watching." *Gender and Society* 16 (3): 386–402.

Reskin, B. 1988. Bringing the men back in. *Gender and Society* 2:58–81.

Schneider, K. T. 1996. *Bystander stress: Effects of sexual harassment of coworkers.* Paper presented at a symposium on responses to sexual harassment, APA annual conference, Toronto, Ontario, Canada.

Shilling, L. 1993. *The body and social theory.* London: Sage.

Smith, D. E. 1987. *The everyday world as problematic: A feminist sociology.* Boston: Northeastern University Press.

Stake, R. E. 1994. Case studies. In *Handbook of qualitative research*, ed. N. K. Denzin and Y. S. Lincoln, 236–247. Thousand Oaks, Calif.: Sage.

Stockdale, M. S. 1996. What we know and what we need to learn about sexual harassment. In *Sexual harassment in the workplace: Perspectives, frontiers and response strategies*, ed. M. Stockdale, 3–28. Thousand Oaks, Calif.: Sage.

West, C., and D. H. Zimmerman. 1987. Doing gender. *Gender and Society* 1 (2): 125–151.

Williams, C. (1997). Sexual harassment in organizations: A critique of current research and policy. *Sexuality Culture* 1:19–43.

Witz, A. 2000. Whose body matters? Feminist sociology and the corporeal turn in sociology and feminism. *Body and Society* 6:1–4.

13

THE NEXUS OF RACE AND GENDER DOMINATION

Racialized Sexual Harassment of African American Women

NiCole T. Buchanan

Despite their growing presence in organizations and educational settings, women still face significant inequities in salary, promotional opportunities, and experiences of harassment (Budwig 2002, U.S. Bureau of the Census 1993). More specifically, half of all working women are harassed over the course of their working lives (Fitzgerald & Shullman 1993). This makes sexual harassment the single most common occupational hazard facing American women today.

In an attempt to understand why sexual harassment is so pervasive, feminists have examined patriarchy and the role of male dominance (Koss et al. 1994, McKinnon 1979, Morgan 2001). They have done so because sexual harassment occurs most frequently when men have positions of social and/or structural power over women, when women enter occupations traditionally dominated by men, or when women challenge definitions of masculinity and femininity (Brogan et al. 1999, DeCoster, Estes, & Mueller 1999, Gruber 1998, Gutek 1985, Vartia & Hyyti 2002).

While mainstream feminist research treats all women as the same, multiculturalists warn that not all women experience oppression in similar ways (Collins 1998, 2000, hooks 1989, 1990, Hurtado 2003).

Specifically, as a result of the combined effect of both male and racial domination, black women may be targeted in unique ways (Buchanan & Ormerod 2002, DeFour 1990, Martin 1994, Murrell 1996, Texeira 2002). Although previous research has increased our general knowledge about the harassment of women, little is understood of the nuances of race regarding it.

Men's studies and masculinity research have theorized a connection between racial and sexual dominance. Conceptualizing masculinity as a socially constructed hierarchy, they note a rank ordering in which some masculinities are more privileged than others (Carrigan, Connell, & Lee 1987, Connell 2000, Hearn 1996, Messerschmidt 1993, 1998). At the top are white men, who reap the greatest benefits of both masculine and racial privilege. Located further down are subgroup hierarchies defined by race. While white women and black women may have their own hierarchies, theirs are excluded from the masculine hierarchy altogether. Privileged status within these hierarchies is often maintained through the harassment of those lower in the hierarchy as well as those located outside it altogether. Therefore, harassment of black women also reflects the specific location of the perpetrator within both the masculinity and racial subgroup hierarchies. These factors further demonstrate the additional complications resulting from intersecting systems of domination (Collins 2000).

The work of research—even critical research—is racialized and gendered. It is dominated by both whites and men. While the thoughts and experiences of white women have dominated sexual harassment studies, those of white men have dominated the study of masculinity and male dominance. In the following pages I offer a challenge to the status quo of research on sexual harassment and male dominance. Drawing upon culturally sensitive methodologies, I use the words of black women to analyze their unique experience of sexual harassment, recorded in a series of semistructured focus groups.

RACIALIZED SEXUAL HARASSMENT

Racial and sexual harassment have traditionally been studied as separate experiences and by separate sets of researchers. Research on sexual harassment rarely includes racial harassment and vice versa. Moreover, despite their commonalities as forms of workplace harassment, these two bodies of research rarely inform one another. As a result, the nexus of race and gender, embodied by black women, has fallen through the cracks and as a consequence been inadequately studied.

Nevertheless, the recognition of sexual harassment as a serious social problem was based upon the complaints of black women. In fact, one of the first cases to establish sexual harassment as a form of discrimination, and therefore as illegal, was filed by a black woman, and her complaints included both sexual and racial forms of harassment (see *Meritor Savings Bank, FSB v. Vinson* 1986; *Vinson v. Taylor* 1986). Furthermore, in 1991, Professor Anita Hill's testimony of harassment by then Supreme Court justice nominee Clarence Thomas awakened the American public to the unique experience of black-on-black sexual harassment (Hill 1997). Nevertheless, analysis of their experiences have been generalized to apply to all women, and their unique experience of racialized sexism has been ignored.

When women of color are the targets of harassment, multiple systems of oppression and dominance are involved (Collins 1998, Crenshaw 1995, White 1999). Specifically, black women experience male dominance from both white and black men and racial dominance from white women and white men. In addition, because formal organizational power does not mitigate their status as members of two oppressed groups, black women in positions of authority are at a greater risk of contrapower harassment than either black men or white women (Rospenda, Richman, & Nawyn 1998).

The legacy of race and sexual relations from the time of institutionalized slavery continues to shape how black women experience sexual harassment, as well as how it is perpetrated (Adams 1997).

During slavery, black women's bodies were a bartered commodity, and their reproduction was an economic necessity for white slave owners. As a result, the rape of black women served dual purposes: as a method of creating wealth, and as a form of social control (Davis 1998).

During slavery, stereotypes of the mammy, Sapphire, and Jezebel were institutionalized, and their images continue to permeate American culture (Collins 2000, Simms 2001, West 1995, 2000). Such portrayals have successfully woven themselves into individuals' beliefs, with many describing black women with negative traits associated with these images (Donovan 2002, Hudson 1998, Weitz & Gordon 1993). Access to legal and social services is limited as a result of these stereotypes, and their endorsement by black men is associated with the use of violence toward black women (Gillum 2001, Campbell et al. 2001).

Despite the relative absence of research on the combination of racial and sexual harassment, an emerging literature supports the proposition that racialized sexual harassment exists and produces perceptions and outcomes uniquely experienced by African American women (Buchanan 1999, Collins 1998, 2000, DeFour 1990, Wyatt & Riederle 1995, Murrell 1996, C. West 2000, T. West 1999).

Buchanan and Ormerod (2002) propose that the harassment of African American women is likely to be unique both in its perception as well as its form. Specifically, the nature of sexual harassment is likely to draw upon aspects of race, whether subtle or overt, when directed toward women of color. For example, although white women may be referred to as sluts or whores, an African American woman is more likely to be called a *black* whore, creating an experience that combines aspects of both gender and race. Therefore, the experience of events as both racist and sexist is not solely an issue of the target's perception—it is an accurate interpretation of a racialized sexist event.

Additional studies support the relationship between racial and sexual harassment. For example, Mansfield and colleagues (1991) found that African American tradeswomen had extensive gender-based *and* race-based harassment, suggesting that to some extent the two experiences co-occur among women of color. In their studies of African American women firefighters, Yoder and Aniakudo (1995, 1996, 1997) found that respondents refused to define their experiences as solely racial or sexual, asserting instead that their experiences fused both forms of harassment simultaneously. In their study of black college students, Mecca and Rubin found that "for many African American women, the issue of sexual harassment seems inextricably intertwined with racism" (1999:817), and a unique category of harassment emerged in which sexual attention was based on racial stereotypes of African American women's sexuality or on physical features thought to vary by race (e.g., that black women have large behinds). These studies demonstrate that sexual harassment, when directed toward women of color, often fuses racial and gender domination and may be better defined as racialized sexual harassment (Buchanan & Ormerod 2002, Martin 1994, Texeira 2002). Furthermore, experiencing this combination of harassment is likely to have a deleterious effect on targets.

METHOD

Giving consideration to the many concerns listed, this chapter's analysis focuses on black women's experiences of racialized sexual harassment. Particular attention is paid to the systems of structural oppression that create and maintain domination over women of color by prefacing the needs and desires of men and Caucasians. Thirty-seven African American women participated in one of six focus group interviews. They came from both a large and a midsized city in the Midwest. Participants ranged in age from 23 to 56 years (M = 39.3). Most participants were highly educated, with 40 percent having graduate degrees; 23.3 percent were either part- or full-time graduate students, an additional 10 percent had completed college, 30 percent had some college education and/or an associate's degree, and only one person ended her formal education with a high school diploma or GED. The women also represented a wide range of professions: they were nurses, mental health and social service caseworkers, elementary and high school teachers, accountants, librarians, secretaries, engineers, college administrators, university academic advisors, executive directors/managers, city housing coordinators, delivery personnel, therapists, and research assistants. Their positions included those in government, private industry, and self-owned businesses. Thus, despite their commonality as black women, demographically speaking, there was considerable variation among them.

The focus group approach was chosen for two primary reasons. First, focus groups facilitate honest dialogue about sensitive topics of conversation (Madriz 2000, Wilkinson 1998, 1999). Perhaps more important to this study, focus groups are more culturally congruent for African American women than are many other forms of data acquisition. In particular, focus groups capitalize upon a group narrative, similar to the folk narratives and communal sharing common to collectivist communities. Therefore, focus groups are a truly innovative approach to examining harassment and may uniquely allow aspects of male and racial dominance to be further explored among women of color.

Each focus group began with an overview of the general topics to be discussed, a review of the rights of participants and the role of the moderators, a reminder that participation was voluntary and confidential, a request that each participant honor the privacy of other group members, and a discussion of how the data and audiotapes of the sessions would be handled in the future. Moderators followed a general protocol to guide the discussion, which asked about unwanted race-based and sex-based behaviors experienced personally or described to them by other African American women. The terms *racial harassment* and *sexual harassment* were not used unless mentioned by participants; instead, moderators used those terms generated by participants (e.g., *inappropriate behavior*). Further, to ensure adequate coverage of each topic across focus groups, one-half of the focus groups began with racial harassment and the other half with sexual harassment (counterbalancing).

Working within the grounded theory tradition, focus groups were organized until theoretical saturation had been achieved (Charmaz 2000, Glaser & Strauss 1967, Krueger 1994). In other words, at the conclusion of each group discussion, the moderators examined the topics and themes and then used this information to modify the discussion protocol for the next focus group. After six focus groups it was determined that little or no new information was being gleaned and theoretical saturation had been reached, and the data collection phase of the project ended.

Data analysis progressed in two stages: (1) line-by line microanalysis and (2) conceptual ordering analysis. This process identified the more salient conceptual categories for theory development and defined their properties as well as their relationships to one another (Strauss & Corbin 1998).

RESULTS

The harassment experiences reported by participants centered around two core theoretical propositions. First, the nature of their harassment was best defined as racialized sexual harassment, with examples reflecting intersecting systems of domination in which both racial and gender oppression were present. Although the nature of many of the examples explicitly combined both, the perceptual experience of participants also reflected their knowledge of this intersection, even under ambiguous circumstances. The second core finding was the impact of slavery and the ways in which its legacy continues to influence contemporary manifestations of harassment and dominance. Examples reflected various negative stereotypes specific to black women. In particular, many drew upon the historic image of the Jezebel, which originated during slavery, as the sexually insatiable black woman. Also, women noted that role expectations of black women as servants had remained stable and that harassment often occurred when they violated these presumptions. It should be noted that although these core theoretical propositions are addressed in turn, this is not to give the appearance of independence. For example, harassment often exploited stereotypes of black women, which emerged during slavery, while harassing them in ways that combined race and gender simultaneously. Therefore, these propositions are better represented as a venn diagram, reflecting their interdependence and relationship to one another.

The first core theoretical proposition demonstrated the ways in which racial and sexual harassment intersect to form a distinct type of harassment called racialized sexual harassment. When given the opportunity to discuss harassment, black women in this study shared several common experiences, ranging from the sexualization of their clothing to presumptions about their competence and hygiene. These experiences demonstrate the unique ways in which racial and gendered dominance intersect when the targets are both black and female. Several examples follow.

Several women reported comments that sexualized their dress and appearance in a racially charged manner. These comments ranged from relatively innocuous statements about their appearance, such as hinting that an outfit would be worn by a prostitute, to direct comments about the color and style of clothing as exotic or offensive. For example, one participant reported the following interaction with a white female supervisor:

> My husband and I were getting ready to go out after work and I changed at work and put on a red dress. A head nurse said, "You looking like you're getting ready to go stand on the corner." Don't assume just because I put on a red dress that I'm a whore, because there are a lot of white ones out there too.

Though she was wearing plain tan slacks and a loose-fitting white button-down shirt, another woman was chastised by her white male supervisor because he considered her clothing to be too sexy. "I had on a white blouse and tan slacks and a week later he told me that I was not dressed appropriately. . . . I knew what he was getting at."

In another surprising finding, women reported negative comments regarding their shoes and accessories. These included comments about their color or the print on the material. The following example is an interaction between a participant and a white coworker: "I had on a scarf that was a kind of a safari print, and she asked me, 'Why do black women always wear leopard skin print?' and another day I had a particular pair of shoes that had a lot of color and she told me that my shoes were too exotic, they offended her." In another example regarding footwear, a participant reported that she was not hired, ostensibly because of her shoes.

> I applied for a job and this guy says, "I'm sorry, you got on the wrong shoes, and you just wouldn't fit this job. You wouldn't fit this job, come back when you get better shoes." I looked around at the white girl that was working there and she had on sandals, flip flops, and I knew what he meant.

In sum, a theme emerged surrounding the style, color, and type of clothing and shoes worn by African American women. Often this manifested as a double standard, where at best, the appearance of African American women was held to a higher standard than that of Caucasian women. At its worst, clothing worn by African American women was often sexualized in a way that directly or indirectly focused on race. Specifically, the term *exotic* appeared as a way of simultaneously sexualizing clothing and denigrating it. At other times, certain styles, such as colorful accessories or animal prints, were specifically associated with African American women and then, presumably as a result of this association, were deemed offensive or inappropriate for the workplace.

In addition to examples about their clothing, several women discussed questions and comments about their personal cleanliness, particularly regarding hair care. These examples demonstrated a perception that black women were dirty, unkempt, and unusual. As one woman describes, "These women would just come and touch my hair—they touch what they think is odd." Another woman ex-

plained her anger with repeated questions by white female coworkers regarding her hair and their assumptions that black women are
unclean.

> White women continually ask me, "how often do black women wash
> their hair?" and so I said, "you know this is like the third time you
> asked me how many times black women wash their hair, you already
> know the answer." And then it becomes an issue of personal hygiene
> or whatever, like black women are dirty.

Regardless of their feelings about having to answer such questions, the women continued to struggle with such comments. They
found repeated questions regarding black women's hair care to be
condescending and insulting, but struggled with a sense of obligation to educate whites on such issues. This placed them in the precarious position of wanting to answer their questions in the hopes
of lessening the barriers between them, while resenting being placed
in such a position and fearing that their answers would be used to
further denigrate black women. Furthermore, despite hoping that
white coworkers were well meaning, they could not ignore the feelings of objectification that accompanied such comments. They did
not feel respected as individuals, but rather as objects of curiosity to
be touched and probed at will. Their personal and physical space
was violated and their discomfort ignored. In particular, they were
disturbed by the interpretation that racial differences in skin and
hair care reflected poor hygiene on the part of black women.

In addition to negative assumptions regarding their hygiene, another theme emerged: black women were presumed to be incapable
of managing work-related tasks or holding positions of leadership.
As the following quotes illustrate, presumptions of incompetence
were sometimes present prior to hiring and reappeared in various
settings.

> I went on the interview and he said, "Well, the only reason I had you
> come in for an interview was to see if you really were all that you
> looked like on paper, because your resume was impressive. And I just

wanted to see because I've never hired a black woman, and I don't really want to lower my standards to hire a black woman.

In the following example, a computer engineer describes repeated competence tests as a normal part of her work.

> I teach computer-based classes to faculty, too. In one class of older white men—on a technical level they don't want to be taught by an African American woman. They don't think that I know what I'm talking about. During the first 5 or 10 minutes someone would ask me some question that had nothing to do with what I was teaching, but it was a really complex technical question and I answered it correctly and they were shocked.

As a result of living in an environment where their competence is continually challenged, participants reported feeling compelled to demonstrate additional knowledge and recognized that they were being subjected to repeated "competence tests" before being valued in their positions. Often these tests and assumptions of incompetence persisted over extended periods of time, if they ended at all. The assumption that black women are incompetent and incapable of leadership roles again demonstrates that their particular location in the matrix of privilege results in their continued harassment based on both race and gender.

Deconstructing these interactions demonstrates various aspects of dominance and privilege. It is evident that the white coworkers described here believed they had a right to impose their ideas, beliefs, and curiosities on black women at work. Participants were surprised by the freedom others felt to comment on their clothing, even when the others were not in a position of authority. Their comments also cause one to question who has the power to define their clothing as exotic or inappropriate as a result of its color. It is important to examine the privilege that accompanies the freedom to demand personal information about hygiene from others. Much like they felt free to make comments on black women's clothing, white coworkers were unrestrained in their curiosity regarding black women's hygiene. Participants described their astonishment with being physically touched by coworkers and felt that this reflected the privilege that whites, regardless of gender, have relative to African American women. Moreover, these women were subjected to both forms of dominance specific to their status as African American women. The questions and comments described here specifically isolated them as black women rather than as women in general or as blacks as a group. The freedom to touch and probe black women and the belief that satisfying one's curiosity trumps respect for the other's personal boundaries are but one manifestation of dominance over black women.

The second core theoretical proposition asserts that the legacy of slavery continues to affect how sexualized behavior and acts of dominance are experienced and perceived by both targets and perpetrators. Regardless of their position or rank within an organization, black women report treatment by white bosses, coworkers, and employees that reflect images born of this time period. Beyond the stereotypes of the Jezebel and Sapphire, which originated during slavery, the women also believed that former norms governing the work roles of black women relative to white women and men persisted in the present. More specifically, the women in this study noted that they were expected to fulfill the roles of servant and seductress, regardless of their organizational rank.

Perceptions of black women as seductive and hypersexed manifested in many ways. Often the nature of the sexual comments directed toward black women exploited the legacy of slavery and the sexualization of black female slaves. For example, one woman described an interaction with a white male coworker who, in attempting to flirt with her, commented, "I bet you're a *slave* to sex." Not only was this offensive because he believed that being sexual with her was an appropriate way of flirting, but he also conjured the painful legacy of slavery while doing so. As a white man, he may not have fully comprehended the gravity of such a statement. More importantly, because of his relative social status in relation to black women, he did not need to fully consider the ramifications of such a comment.

In addition, the women in this sample believed that their treatment was different from that of Caucasian women, specifically because they continued to be seen as the Jezebel, a sexually insatiable black woman, which leads to negative presumptions regarding their sexuality. For example, participants reported that white coworkers and supervisors often felt free to be sexually explicit or to request information about their sex lives (e.g., seeking sexual advice, asking about sexual positions participants have tried, or telling participants of their own sexual exploits). These discussions occurred without sufficient opportunity to build the rapport or relationship that would normally precede such intimate conversation. Consequently, participants asserted that this behavior reflected an underlying assumption that African American women's sexual boundaries, both the behaviors they will engage in and their comfort in discussing sex, are looser than those of Caucasians. For example:

> People will say things to a black woman, I don't care how much education she has, or what her position is, they'll say things to black women that they would never say to a white woman—no matter what position the white woman is in. They [white men] are more likely to not only say direct things, but to come out and do things to a black woman.

One woman said, "Not only are you supposed to accept it because you're black, but even like it, more than they would expect from white women." Several nodded and indicated agreement. One replied, "Yeah, you're there for their amusement."

It is important to note that negative stereotyping not only defined the manifestation of their harassment and the role of dominance for African American women, but also the way in which such events were perceived and responded to by targets. In addition to being targeted in ways that reflected sexualized stereotypes, participants believed that knowledge of these images and the sexually abusive relationships between white men and black female slaves affected their reactions to those behaviors. The following quotes illustrate these feelings.

> It is more offensive from white men. I don't know if it's from *Roots* and slavery, but in the back of my mind I'm thinking, "Don't come at me that way."

> As African American women coming out of traditional slavery work, we were owned body and soul by white men. . . . We already have stereotypes working against us, we don't want to promote them. Sometimes you are an individual; sometimes you're the race.

Thus, these women were continuously conscious of the stereotypes of black women as both hypersexual and aggressive, as well as the history of sexually abusive interactions between white men and black women. For some, this knowledge made the acts more offensive when the perpetrator was a Caucasian man, but these stereotypes also presented a conflict in responding. Namely, women felt torn between protecting themselves from harassment at the risk of reinforcing racial stereotypes of black women as Sapphires (i.e., aggressive, domineering, amoral) and protecting their ethnic community, perhaps at great personal sacrifice.

In addition to the stereotypes of the Jezebel and the Sapphire, the structure of black women's work during slavery and beyond impacted their current experience of racial and gendered domination. During slavery, African American women were relegated to roles as servants to white men and women, and these continue to define work roles and expectations for many black women today. As a result, white men and women are unaccustomed to being in a subordinate role to black women. This was most obvious in their examples of white women subordinates' hostility and outright refusal to engage in behaviors that may be construed as "serving" a black woman—despite performing the same duties without incident for their former white male supervisors. The following were reported by an assistant dean and an accountant regarding their interactions with white female secretaries:

> The first thing my secretary did was say that she wasn't going to make the coffee. She said, "Oh there's no coffee today, you should make it." ME? I'm not making the coffee! Literally the dean had to stand there and say, "you make the coffee" to my secretary. Well, one day she was there and she had to get some stuff that I needed, some files. She was throwing them at me and they were hitting the floor. And she was looking at me like, "you black B——, how dare you."

Historically, black women were servants in the homes of whites and worked under the close supervision of white women. After slavery, the occupational opportunities of black women continued to be restricted to subservient roles as cooks, maids, and caretakers. To date, despite their economic and educational gains, women of color continue to be disproportionately represented in such occupations. As a result of these role expectations, white people are unfamiliar with images of powerful black women, let alone those whose commands are to be respected and obeyed. The historical demarcation of power, privilege, and dominance that defines the roles and status of black women in relation to white men and women led participants to perceive these experiences as a refusal by whites to engage in behaviors that may be constructed as "serving" a black woman. In an attempt to remedy this reversal of dominant roles, white coworkers and subordinates made overt and covert attempts to return the structure of power to their favor. As a result of both racial and gender dominance that disfavors black women, their attempts were often successful in reminding black women of "their place" according to white America. As one woman concluded: "They think we shouldn't be making that type of money, regardless of whether I have a master's degree or not. I could have a Ph.D. and they would still think I should be serving them."

DISCUSSION

Since the term *sexual harassment* was first coined, feminists have argued that a focus on the role of patriarchy and male domination is critical to understanding sexual harassment. The resulting research is almost exclusively dominated by white feminists using white women as participants. As a result, theories about the relationship between sexual harassment and male domination have not incorporated the role of race or the experiences of black women and other women of color. Without an examination of intersecting systems of domination, specifically gendered and racial dominance, the harassment experiences of African American women are unlikely to be fully understood.

To address these limitations, the current study is unique in that it examines black women's racial and sexual harassment as intersecting experiences. In addition, it draws upon new methodology and underutilized bodies of thought to examine the phenomenon. First, the study is rooted in a black feminist epistemology, which focuses on systems of oppression and their dominance over women of color. Second, focus groups composed exclusively of African American women were used because they are both effective when exploring sensitive topics with women of color and empowering for participants. Third, the strategies of analysis were rooted in grounded theory as an inductive method of theory generation. This is in stark contrast to most research on sexual harassment, which utilizes feminist theory without a multicultural perspective, does not include representative numbers of women of color, and enlists deductive methods of analysis in order to confirm established theory rather than generate new theoretical propositions. Specifically, these results demonstrate that examinations of the nexus of race and gender yield results that are often overlooked in traditional research.

When given the opportunity to discuss their experiences, the black women in this study claimed they commonly experienced racialized sexual harassment, that is, harassment with racial and sexual overtones. Not all their experiences were the same. The types of racialized sexual harassment described ranged from racial sexualization and denigration of clothing worn by black women to assumptions regarding their competence and personal hygiene. Their stories demonstrate how the history of slavery shapes contemporary experi-

ences of harassment, particularly regarding the persistence of stereotypes and assumptions regarding their sexuality.

Their experiences also illustrate how multiple systems of dominance impact everyday life. Within the interlocking hierarchies of
gender and race, privilege is relational. For example, the women in
this study experienced class privilege relative to poor women of
color, but if compared to white men, even poor white men, the
balance of privilege and dominance shifts against them. Their stories
show with great specificity how racialized sexual harassment is used
by white women, as well as black and white men, to protect and
steal power (Johnson 2001).

The women in this study defined as harassment experiences that
did not clearly fit commonly accepted definitions of either sexual or
racial harassment. This may reflect the racial differences in perceptions of an environment, which develop as a result of their differing
history of oppression. For example, in one study of professional
black and white women, it was found that black women were much
more likely to perceive gender and racial inequality in the workplace
(Higginbotham & Weber 1999). This implies that, at least in the
workplace, black and white women are experiencing different
worlds, and racialized sexual harassment is one experience that divides them.

The finding that black women feel sexually harassed by white
women was surprising. Because of their common experience of gender oppression, it would be natural for African American and Caucasian women to unite around workplace harassment. Unfortunately, this was not the case. Instead, white women often
perpetuated and/or responded to myths and stereotypes of black
women as incompetent, dirty, and sexually immoral. Moreover, because of their racial privilege, white women appeared additionally
offended by having to "serve" black women (e.g., by making coffee,
getting files).

Although white women also experience gender oppression, they
have a stake in maintaining aspects of the matrix of domination

because they experience white privilege (Collins 1998, 2000, Hurtado 1996, 2003, Johnson 2001) and identification with the aggressor, white men. This can manifest in acts of actual harassment perpetrated by white women, or in their silence when they witness the harassment of another. Women in this study voiced frustration with those who observed harassment and said nothing, or later apologized for a witnessed event. The reluctance of others to publicly state their discomfort with inappropriate comments or behaviors acts as collusion with perpetrators, whether they agreed with the events or not. As Allan G. Johnson states, "oppression and dominance name social realities that we can participate in without being oppressive or dominating people" (2001:13). By virtue of their silence, white women hid behind their own matrix of privilege and benefited from that privilege as a result.

These findings also suggest that African American women are particularly vulnerable to contrapower harassment, defined as harassment directed toward an employer or supervisor by subordinates (Rospenda et al. 1998). As members of two socially marginalized demographic groups (women and ethnic minorities), black women experience multiple forms of dominance and limited social privilege. As a result, both male and Caucasian employees may feel that their lower social status as women of color overrides their formal organizational power, thereby increasing their vulnerability to contrapower harassment.

Interestingly, some of these experiences also required a re-creation of the race and gender hierarchy to reach resolution. Specifically, in the earlier example in which the secretary refused to make coffee, the situation was not resolved until the dean of the college, a white male, issued a direct order to the secretary to make coffee. To legitimate her own status, she had to appeal to someone of greater social and organization power, the college dean (a white man). This "power by proxy" keeps black women, even professional women, in a precarious position. Because others do not afford them the benefits of their status, they may be forced to align themselves with white men, who may also exert varying levels of racial and gendered dominance over them. As a result, African American women are continually vulnerable at work, even when acquiring positions of organizational power.

Expectations of racialized sexual harassment and vulnerability to contrapower harassment may explain the reluctance of African American women to establish mentoring relationships and/or friendships with Caucasian coworkers and employers. Specifically, the black women who participated in these focus groups were fearful of interactions with white men being interpreted as an invitation for a sexual relationship, which may lead to harassment (Richie et al. 1997). The choices these women made to protect themselves from possible harassment not only had personal costs, but likely limited their access to the benefits such relationships can provide, such as promotional opportunities and career enhancement.

Future examinations of interlocking dominance must consider how social class influences the experience of racialized sexual harassment. Although none of our participants identified as lower or working class, it is important to consider how class privilege may have impacted their experiences as well as those of other African American working women (Hurtado 1996). Classism has been used as justification for differential pay for women, and because of its interaction with other forms of subordination and dominance, it has a differential impact on African American women (Johnson 2001). Historically, black women have been among the lowest paid in the workforce, falling far below men of all races and white women in salaries, even for similar positions (Corcoran 1999, England, Christopher, & Reid 1999). Although not addressed in this study, it is also possible that these women experienced more severe harassment because their education and organizational status were a greater challenge to the social hierarchy than black women in more traditional occupations. Nevertheless, their elevated class status is likely to provide privileges not afforded to working-class African American women, particularly those in blue-collar jobs. For example, Gruber and Bjorn (1982) found that black women in blue-collar employment experienced more severe forms of sexual harassment. Therefore, it is likely that women in this study were spared the more overt and/or severe forms of racialized sexual harassment that may be directed toward blue-collar black women. So, although their position within the matrix of domination placed them lower than both men and white women, the women in this study still enjoyed some privilege based on class.

Current mainstream research on coping with sexual harassment does not adequately incorporate black women's responses to racialized sexual harassment (Buchanan, Langhout, and Fitzgerald 2000). Black women's coping strategies vary depending upon the gender and race of the perpetrator. For example, the strategies chosen take into account the belief that official action against a black male perpetrator may result in harsher consequences than similar accusations against a white man. Participants in the current study recognized that black men can exert gender dominance over them, but their power was different from that of white men because of their location in the racial hierarchy.

In another study of black women's ways of coping, Jenkins (2002) found that participants experiencing community violence utilized strategies rarely addressed in the coping literature (e.g., prayer and political activism). Moreover, demographic factors, such as education and income, influenced participants' coping styles, such that more highly educated women with higher incomes responded to violence by isolating themselves from potential harm and becoming politically active in their communities. Based on these research findings and the intersections of racial, gendered, and sometimes also economic oppression, it is likely that they will utilize or reject certain coping strategies based on their utility in addressing their intersecting oppressions.

CONCLUSION

Although the goal of this project was to examine the experiences of African American women's workplace harassment, the applicability of this data to the general population, indeed, to the population of African American women, is limited. Participants who elected to participate may have been more likely to have negative work experiences, more likely to conceptualize these experiences as hostile, or more willing to discuss such events than people who did not participate. Also, because advertisements for participation in the study specifically requested African American women, those who responded may have a stronger racial, gender, or combined identification than those who did not. This may have made them more likely than other African American women to label experiences along dimensions of race and gender or their intersection.

The findings point to the need for interventions and training that integrate issues of both racial and gendered dominance. As the women in this study asserted, race and gender are inextricable in their lives because participants embody the nexus of the two. Therefore, workplace training must address these intersections and understand the nuances of racialized gender oppression. In addition, when these interconnections are understood, it becomes clear that perpetrators, as was the case here, can be of many forms, including Caucasian women and African American men. To be truly effective, trainings will need to broaden their conceptualization of harassment. However, change requires more than new trainings or simply giving people of color and women positions of power while the current gender and racial hierarchies still exist (Guinier & Torres 2002). Instead, change requires that we deconstruct the matrices of domination and privilege that create conditions where racialized sexual harassment flourishes. Such efforts require all stakeholders to recognize and take action against the harm resulting from workplace harassment and the subordination of women and people of color.

Overall, this study makes a strong argument for the importance of not overlooking either racial or gendered components when examining the harassment experiences of ethnic minority women. Participants described events they considered both racist *and* sexist, and unique to them because they were both black *and* female. Indeed, many examples were specific to them as black women, and few of these experiences would happen to either white women or black men. This places African American women at a crossroads, where their particular location in the matrix of domination and privilege puts them at risk for multiple, intersecting forms of oppression. As a result, they are continually sexualized for their race and for their gender.

REFERENCES

Adams, Jann H. 1997. Sexual harassment and black women: A historical perspective. In *Sexual harassment: Theory, research, and treatment,* ed. by William O'Donohue. Boston: Allyn and Bacon.

Brogan, Donna J., et al. 1999. Harassment of lesbians as medical students and physicians. *JAMA: Journal of the American Medical Association* 282:1290–1292.

Buchanan, NiCole T. 1999. *Sexual harassment and the African American woman: A historical analysis of a contemporary phenomena.* Paper presented at the annual meeting of the Association for Women in Psychology at Providence, Rhode Island.

Buchanan, NiCole T., Regina D. Langhout, and Louise F. Fitzgerald. 2000. *Predictors of African American women's responses to sexual harassment.* Paper presented at the annual meeting of the Society for Industrial and Organizational Psychology. New Orleans, La.

Buchanan, NiCole T., and Alayne J. Ormerod. 2002. Racialized sexual harassment in the lives of African American women. *Women and Therapy* 25:107–124. Copublished simultaneously in *Violence in the lives of Black women: Battered, Black, and Blue,* ed. Carolyn M. West. New York: Haworth Press.

Budwig, Michelle J. 2002. Male advantage and the gender composition of jobs: Who rides the glass escalator? *Social Problems* 49:258–277.

Campbell, Rebecca, Sharon M. Wasco, Courtney E. Ahrens, Tracy Sefl, and Holly E. Barnes. 2001. Preventing the "second rape": Rape survivors' experiences with community service providers. *Journal of Interpersonal Violence* 16:1239–1259.

Carrigan, T., Robert W. Connell, and J. Lee. 1987. Hard and heavy: Toward a sociology of masculinity. In *Beyond patriarchy: Essays by men on plea-*

sure, power and change, ed. Michael Kaufman. Toronto: Oxford University Press.

Charmaz, Kathy. 2000. Grounded theory: Objectivist and constructivist methods. In *Handbook of qualitative research*, ed. Norman K. Denzin and Yvonna S. Lincoln. Thousand Oaks, Calif.: Sage.

Collins, Patricia H. 1998. *Fighting words: Black women and the search for justice.* Minneapolis: University of Minnesota Press.

———. 2000. *Black feminist thought: Knowledge, consciousness, and the politics of empowerment*, 2d ed. New York: Routledge.

Connell, Robert W. 2000. *The men and the boys.* Berkeley: University of California Press.

Corcoran, Mary. 1999. The economic progress of African American women. In *Latinas and African American women at work: Race, gender, and economic inequality*, ed. Irene Brown. New York: Russell Sage Foundation.

Crenshaw, K. 1995. Mapping the margins: Intersectionality, identity politics, and violence against women of color. In *Critical race theory: The key writings that formed the movement*, ed. K. Crenshaw, N. Gotanda, G. Peller, and K. Thomas. New York: New Press.

Davis, Angela Y. 1998. Reflections on the Black woman's role in the community of slaves. In *The Angela Y. Davis reader*, ed. Joy James. Malden, Mass.: Blackwell.

DeCoster, Stacy, Sarah B. Estes, and Charles W. Mueller. 1999. Routine activities and sexual harassment in the workplace. *Work and Occupations* 26:21–49.

DeFour, Darlene C. 1990. The interface of racism and sexism on college campuses. In *Ivory power: Sexual harassment on campus*, ed. Michele A. Paludi. Albany: State University of New York Press.

Donovan, Roxanne A. 2002. *Tough or tender: White college students' beliefs about Black and White women.* Master's thesis, University of Connecticut, Storrs.

England, Paula, Karen Christopher, and Lori L. Reid. 1999. Gender, race, ethnicity, and wages. In *Latinas and African American women at work: Race, gender, and economic inequality*, ed. Irene Brown. New York: Russell Sage Foundation.

Fitzgerald, Louise F., and Sandra L. Shullman. 1993. Sexual harassment: A research analysis and agenda for the 1990's. *Journal of Vocational Behavior* 42:5–27.

Gillum, Tameka L. 2001. Exploring the link between stereotypic images and intimate partner violence in the African American community. *Violence Against Women* 8:64–86.

Glaser, Barney F., and Anselm L. Strauss. 1967. *The discovery of grounded theory: Strategies for qualitative research.* Chicago: Aldine.

Gruber, James E. 1998. The impact of male work environments and organizational policies on women's experiences of sexual harassment. *Gender and Society* 12:301–320.

Gruber, James E., and Lars Bjorn. 1982. Blue-collar blues: The sexual harassment of women autoworkers. *Work and Occupations* 9:271–298.

Guinier, Lani, and Gerald Torres. 2002. *The miner's canary: Enlisting race, resisting power, transforming democracy.* Cambridge, Mass.: Harvard University Press.

Gutek, Barbara A. 1985. *Sex and the workplace: Impact of sexual behavior and harassment on women, men, and organizations.* San Francisco: Jossey-Bass.

Hearn, Jeff. 1996. Is masculinity dead? A critique of the concept of masculinity/masculinities. In *Understanding masculinities: Social relations and cultural arenas,* ed. Máirtín Mac an Ghaill. Buckingham, Penn.: Open University Press.

Higginbotham, Elizabeth, and Lynn Weber. 1999. Perceptions of workplace discrimination among Black and White professional-managerial women. In *Latinas and African American women at work: Race, gender, and economic inequality,* ed. Irene Brown. New York: Russell Sage Foundation.

Hill, Anita. 1997. *Speaking truth to power.* New York: Doubleday.

hooks, bell. 1989. *Talking back: Thinking feminist, thinking black.* Boston, Mass.: South End Press.

———. 1990. *Yearning: Race, gender, and cultural politics.* Boston, Mass.: South End Press.

Hudson, Shawna V. 1998. Re-creational television: The paradox of change and continuity within stereotypical iconography. *Sociological Inquiry* 68:242–257.

Hurtado, Aida. 1996. *The color of privilege: Three blasphemies on race and feminism.* Ann Arbor, Mich.: University of Michigan Press.

———. 2003. *Voicing Chicana feminisms: Young women speak out on sexuality and identity.* New York: New York University Press.

Jenkins, E. J. 2002. Black women and community violence: Trauma, grief, and coping. *Women and Therapy* 25:29–44.

Johnson, Allan G. 2001. *Privilege, power, and difference.* Boston: McGraw-Hill.

Koss, Mary P., Lisa A. Goodman, Angela Browne, Louise F. Fitzgerald, Gwendolyn P. Keita, and Nancy F. Russo. 1994. *Male violence against women at home, at work, and in the community.* Washington, D.C.: American Psychological Association.

Krueger, Richard A. 1994. *Focus groups: A practical guide to applied research.* Thousand Oaks, Calif.: Sage.

MacKinnon, Catharine A. 1979. *Sexual harassment of working women.* New Haven, Conn.: Yale University Press.

Madriz, Esther. 2000. Focus groups in feminist research. In *Handbook of qualitative research,* ed. Norman K. Denzin and Yvonna S. Lincoln, 2d ed. Thousand Oaks, Calif.: Sage.

Mansfield, Phyllis K., Patricia B. Koch, Julie Henderson, and Judith R.Vicary. 1991. The job climate for women in traditionally male blue-collar occupations. *Sex Roles* 25:63–79.

Martin, Susan E. 1994. "Outsider within" the station house: The impact of race and gender on Black women police. *Social Problems* 41:383–400.

Mecca, Susan J., and Linda J. Rubin. 1999. Definitional research on African American students and sexual harassment. *Psychology of Women Quarterly* 23:813–817.

Meritor Savings Bank FSB v. Vinson. 477 U.S. 57 (1986).

Messerschmidt, James W. 1993. *Masculinities and crime: Critique and reconceptualization of theory.* Lanham, Md.: Rowman and Littlefield.

———. 1998. Men victimizing men: The case of lynching, 1965–1900. In *Masculinities and violence,* ed. Lee H. Bowker. Thousand Oaks, Calif.: Sage.

Morgan, Phoebe. 2001. Sexual harassment: Violence against women at work. In *Sourcebook on violence against women,* ed. Claire M. Renzetti, Jeffrey L. Edleson, and Raquel K. Bergen. Thousand Oaks, Calif.: Sage.

Murrell, Audrey J. 1996. Sexual harassment and women of color: Issues, challenges, and future directions. In *Sexual harassment in the workplace: Perspectives, frontiers, and response strategies,* ed. Margaret S. Stockdale. London: Sage.

Richie, Beth S., Ruth E. Fassinger, Sonja G. Linn, Judith Johnson, Joanne Prosser, and Sandra Robinson. 1997. Persistence, connection, and passion: A qualitative study of the career development of highly achieving African American-Black and White women. *Journal of Counseling Psychology* 44:133–148.

Rospenda, Kathleen M., Judith A. Richman, and Stephanie J. Nawyn. 1998. Doing power: The confluence of gender, race, and class in contrapower sexual harassment. *Gender and Society* 15:879–897.

Simms, R. 2001. Controlling images and the gender construction of enslaved African women. *Gender and Society* 15:879–897.

Strauss, Anselm L., and Juliet M. Corbin. 1998. *Basics of qualitative research: Techniques and procedures for developing grounded theory*, 2d ed. Thousand Oaks, Calif.: Sage.

Texeira, Mary T. 2002. "Who protects and serves me?" A case study of sexual harassment of African American women in one U.S. law enforcement agency. *Gender and Society* 16:524–545.

U.S. Bureau of the Census. 1993. *1990 Census of the population supplementary reports: Detailed occupation and other characteristics from the EEO file for the United States.* Washington, D.C.: U.S. Government Printing Office.

Vartia, Maarit, and Jari Hyyti. 2002. Gender differences in workplace bullying among prison officers. *European Journal of Work and Organizational Psychology* 11:113–126.

Vinson v. Taylor. D.C. Cir. 753 F.2d 141, 36 FEP Cases (1986).

Weitz, Rose, and Leonard Gordon. 1993. Images of Black women among Anglo college students. *Sex Roles* 28:19–34.

West, Carolyn. 1995. Mammy, Sapphire, and Jezebel: Historical images of Black women and their implications for psychotherapy. *Psychotherapy: Theory, Research, Practice, Training* 32:458–466.

———. 2000. Developing an "oppositional gaze" toward the images of Black women. In *Lectures on the psychology of women*, ed. Joan C. Chrisler, Carla Golden, and Patricia D. Rozee, 2d ed. Boston: McGraw-Hill.

West, Traci C. 1999. *Wounds of the spirit: Black women, violence, and resistance ethics.* New York: New York University Press.

White, Aaronette M. 1999. Talking feminist, talking Black: Micromobilization processes in a collective protest against rape. *Gender and Society* 13:77–100.

Wilkinson, Sue. 1998. Focus groups in feminist research: Power, interaction, and the co-construction of meaning. *Women's Studies International Forum* 21:111–125.

———. 1999. Focus groups: A feminist method. *Psychology of Women Quarterly* 23:221–245.

Yoder, Janice D., and and Patricia Aniakudo. 1995. The responses of African American women firefighters to gender harassment at work. *Sex Roles* 32:125–137.

———. 1996. When pranks become harassment: The case of African American women firefighters. *Sex Roles* 35:253–270.

———. 1997, June. "Outsiders within" the firehouse: Exclusion and difference in the social interactions of African American women firefighters. *Gender and Society* 11:324–341.

INDEX

Boseley, S., 99
Brannon, Robert, 151
British Crime Survey, 102
Brittan-Powell, C., 125
Brodsky, C. M., 109
Brown, Jennifer, 196–97
Brown, Phyllis, 258
Buchanan, NiCole T., xvii, 168–69, 297
Bularzik, Mary, 247
bullying, 92–94, 97–100, 103–7. *See also* sexual harassment; violence
Bundy, Sandra, 258, 260–63
Bundy v. Jackson, 261–62
Burawoy, Michael, 73
Burger, Justice Warren, 155–56
Burt, Martha R., 70

California Psychological Inventory, 10
capitalism, and sexual harassment, 245–46, 247–48, 249
Cardy, C., 106, 107
CEP (Coal Employment Project), 253–56, 257, 258
Chiapuzio v. BLT Operating Corp., 120
Chicana Rights Project, 251
Chicana Service Action Center, 251, 252
children, gender socialization of, 87
Chodorow, Nancy, 78
Chrysler Corporation, 256
Clarke, Elissa, 257
class privilege, 310–13
Cleveland, J. N., 289
Coal Employment Project (CEP), 253–56, 257, 258
coal mining: feminist collective action and, 253–56; and group relationship strategies, 71–75; and harassment of women, 80–85; harazzment and, 67–71; male

dominance in, 65–66, 88n1; sexualized interactions and homophobia, 76–80
Coal Mining Women's Support Team, 255
Coalition of Labor Union Women, 257, 258, 262
collective action, feminists and, 251–52, 253–56, 263–67
Collinson, D. L., 31, 37
Collinson, M., 31, 37
Connell, R. W., 33–34, 286
Consolidation Coal Company (CONSOL), 253–55
construction industry, 251–53
Continental Can Company, 259–60
contrapower harassment, 311–12
Cooper, Cary, 99
Corroto, Carla, xvii–xviii, 168
criminal action: gender skew and, 3, 4–5; perpetrator motivations and, 4–7, 8, 20; sexual harassment as, 4–5, 6–7, 8, 20–21, 29
criminology theory, and sexual harassment, 3–4, 5–9, 20–21
critical criminological theory, 3, 6, 8, 20, 21
Crull, Peggy, 248, 262
cultural differences in reporting sexual harassment, 180–82
culture of management, 108–10

David, Deborah, 151
de Certeau, Michel, 33, 40
Defense Department, U.S., 219, 236
Department of Defense Sexual Experience Questionnaire (SEQ-DoD), 122, 127, 130–31*t*
DePauw, Linda Grant, 236
design vocabulary, 278, 280, 285
District of Columbia Department of Corrections, 260
Doe v. City of Belleville, 157

Kanter, Rosabeth Moss, 31, 198
Katz, Jack, 27, 28, 33, 39, 40, 41
Kauppinen, Kaisa, xix, 167–68, 209
Kauppinen-Toropainen, Kaisa, 210
Kentucky Commission on Human
    Rights, 255, 256
Kimmel, Michael S., xix
Kinnunen, A., 107
Klein, Freada, 247

la perruque masculine, 33–39
Labor Department, U.S., 251–53
Labor Education and Research Proj-
    ect, 257
Lady Miners of Utah, 257
language: and architecture, 278, 280,
    285; male control and, 105; sexist,
    55–56, 60; sexual banter, 83
Largen, Mary Ann, 264
Larwood, Laurie, 197
*Last Man Down: The Fireman's
    Story* (Picciotto), 60
Law Commission, 103
Lee, Deborah, 160
legality of sexual harassment, 118–21,
    129, 132
lesbians: experienced sexual harass-
    ment and, 228–30, 231–33, 234;
    military ban on, 215, 220, 237–38;
    perceived sexual harassment and,
    226, 227–30
Leymann, Heinz, 206
Likelihood to Sexually Harass Scale
    (LSHS), 9–10, 11, 13, 15, 21
Longshore, D., 10
Lyman, Peter, 78

McDonald, Nancy, 246
MacKinnon, Catharine A., 40, 97,
    156, 243, 248, 284
McNamara, K., 289
*McWilliams v. Fairfax County Board
    of Supervisors,* 124
mainstream (traditional) crimino-

logical theory, 7, 8, 9, 10, 20–21,
    27–28
male dominance: collective action
    and, 251–52, 253–56, 263–67; cul-
    ture of management and, 108–10;
    degrees of, 183–85, 187–90; femi-
    nist theory of, 245–49, 263–67;
    gender self-image and, 185–86;
    gender socialization and, 67,
    70–71; organizations and, 105,
    107–10; sexual harassment and,
    5–6, 20, 246–48, 263–65
male dominated workplaces, sexual
    harassment and, 183–85, 188–91
male emotion management strate-
    gies, 70–75
male gender deviance, 124, 125, 133,
    151–52, 156–63
management, culture of, 108–10
Mansfield, Phyllis K., 297
Martin, S. E., 6
Marx, Karl, 86
masculine identity construction: in
    architecture, 288–89; criminal ac-
    tion and, 5–6, 20; embedded so-
    cial structure and, 27–29, 31–32,
    38, 40–41; and male dominance,
    32–34, 39, 40–41; occupational
    characteristics and, 70–71; self-
    image and, 40–41, 47, 56, 59, 61,
    125; sexual harassment and,
    40–41; traditional elements of, 47,
    56, 59, 61, 151
masculine legal gender model, 144–
    45, 148–49, 150–52, 156–61
masculine women, 150, 230, 231*t*
matrix of domination, 309–13
Measure of Self-Control (MSC), 10–
    11, 13, 15, 21
Mecca, Susan J., 298
media: masculine identity construc-
    tion and, 37; portrayal of fire-
    fighters by, 60, 61; as violent cul-
    tural force, 247

Men and Women of the Corporation (Kanter), 31

Men's Sexual Harassment Experiences (MSHE) scale, 127–29, 130–31*t*, 132, 133

Merit System Protection Board, U.S. (USMSPB), 121, 130–31*t*

Meritor Savings Bank v. Vinson, 256, 257–58

Messerschmidt, James W., 3, 17, 20, 28

Mexican American Legal Defense and Education Fund, 251

Milburn, M. A., 31

military, U.S.: experience of sexual harassment in, 231–33; handling of sexual harassment by, 219, 227–30; history of women in, 216–17, 239–40n5; homophobia in, 220–21, 226–27; perceptions of sexual harassment in, 226, 227–31

Miller, Arnold, 256

Miller, Joyce, 262

Miller, L., 136

Minerva's Bulletin Board: The News Magazine on Women and the Military, 218, 221

Minnesota Human Rights Act, 259–60

Minnesota Multiphasic Personality Inventory, 10

Morasch, Bruce, 5, 197

Morgan, Phoebe, xx, 3, 4, 6, 19, 267, 294

Mothershed, K. F., 163n1

Motoike, Janice, 127, 132

MSC (Measure of Self-Control), 10–11, 13, 15, 21

multiple masculinities, 151, 162

Murphy, R., 137

Myers, Frieda, 255

National Conference of Women Coal Miners, 253, 254

National Organization for Women (NOW), 260

New Responses, Inc., 264

New Way Community Center, 259

New York City Fire Department, 262

New York Times Magazine, 143

Non-Traditional Employment for Women, 258

nonverbal sexual harassment, 199

normalization of male sexual harassment behavior, 30

Norton, Eleanor Holmes, 257

NOW (National Organization for Women), 260

Oncale v. Sundowner Offshore Services, Inc., 117–18, 124, 161–62

organizational model of sexual harassment, 70

organizations: bullying and, 97–100; changing face of, 111–12; changing power model and, 185–90; male dominance in, 105, 107–10, 197–98; male resistance in, 34, 37, 40–41; physical violence and, 100–103; sexual harassment in, 95–97; violations within, 103–7, 110, 111–12

Ormerod, Alayne J., 297

ostracism of outsiders, 76, 85

other-sex sexual harassment (OSSH), 122–26, 152–56

Ott, E. Marlies, 197–98

outsider status of women, 187–90, 198

overperformance pressure in women, 135, 197

Parker, Sharon K., 135, 197

Parkin, Wendy, xx–xxi, 2

Patoluoto, Saara, xx, 167–68

patriarchal hierarchies, 48–51, 55

Peabody Coal Company, 255

Peirce, E. R., 147
perceptions of environment, 310
perpetrators of sexual harassment:
    demographic research on, 17–19;
    embedded social structure and,
    27–29, 31–32, 38, 40–41; motives
    of, 5–6, 7, 8, 9–10, 13–16, 20–22
Perry, William J., 219
Phoenix Institute, 257
physical violence. See bullying; sex-
    ual harassment; violence
Picciotto, Rob, 60
Plantinga, J., 181
policewomen: overperformance
    pressure and, 135, 197; research
    studies on, 196–98; sexual harass-
    ment of, 199–200, 204–6; super-
    visor and coworker attitudes
    toward, 202–4; work environ-
    ment of, 200–202, 207–8; work-
    related violence and, 198–99,
    206–8
*Polly v. Houston Lighting and Power
    Company*, 124, 152, 158–61
power balance shifting process, 185–
    90, 192–93
Poyner, B., 101
preferential treatment of women, 85
"Propensity to Harass" measure
    (Pryor), 30–31
Pryor, J. B., 9, 11, 20, 30–31
psychological violence, 199, 206
public reprimands of women, 84

quid pro quo sexual harassment:
    early legal focus on, 145, 244, 249,
    258; likelihood to harass studies
    and, 11, 21
Quine, L., 98
Quinn, Beth A., xxi, 1–2, 125, 288

racialized sexual harassment: analy-
    sis methods of, 298–300; assump-
    tions of incompetence and,

303–4; clothing sexualization
    and, 301–2; and contrapower ha-
    rassment, 311–12; overview of,
    296–98; personal hygiene as-
    sumptions, 302–3; sexualized ste-
    reotypes and, 305–7; work role
    subordination and, 307–8. *See
    also* African American women
Radcliffe-Brown, A. R., 69
rape, in military, 225
razzing, among coal miners, 68–69,
    71–75
"reasonable person" legal standard,
    146, 147
Register, The, 221
rejection-based sexual harassment,
    120–21
"Repeat After Me: We Are Different.
    We Are the Same" (Gomez), 148
research of sexual harassment. *See*
    sexual harassment research
*Review of Workplace-Related Vio-
    lence*, 101
rites of passage, 55, 57, 61
rogue masculinity, 37, 40
roughhousing among men, 78–79,
    81
Rubin, Linda J., 298
Rudman, L. A., 10

Salin, D., 109
same-sex sexual harassment
    (SSSH): approach-rejection the-
    ory and, 121–26; landmark legal
    cases and, 156–63
Sauvigné, Karen, 262
Schulhofer, Steven, 26
Schultz, Vicki, 264
Scott, James, 33
Sedley, A., 97
Self-Control Schedule, 10
self-control, sexual harassment and,
    6–8, 10–11, 20–21, 22n3

social power theory of gender inequality, 197–98
social testing, coal miners and, 74–75
sociocultural model of gender socialization, 70–71
SSSH (same-sex sexual harassment): approach-rejection theory and, 121–26; landmark legal cases and, 156–63
stereotyping: of African American women, 305–8; of legal sex-role norms, 150–52, 156–61
Stockdale, Margaret S., xxi, 2
Stoller, L. M., 9
Suzy Lamplugh Trust, 100
Syme, M., 109

Tailhook convention, 218
Talbot, Margaret, 143–44
Tangri, Sandra S., 70
"technology of sexism," 120
theories of wrongness of sexual harassment, 118–21
Thomas, Clarence, 296
Thomas, Marie D., 236
Thomas, Patricia J., 236
Till, F. J., 126
Timmerman, Greetje, xxi–xxii, 167
Title VII (Civil Rights Act): and hostile environment sexual harassment, 244, 258, 266; same-sex sexual harassment rulings on, 119, 157, 159–60, 161–62
Titunik, Regina, 218
tolerance threshold, 81, 83–84
"tomboys," 83
Trades Union Congress (TUC), 108
traditional (mainstream) criminology, 7, 8, 9, 10, 20–21, 27–28
transition, in power balance change process, 187, 189–90
Tucson Women's Commission, 251

union organizing, 256–58
United Auto Workers (UAW), 256, 257, 262
United Kingdom, 135
United Mine Workers of America, 254, 256
United Trade Workers Association, 251
Urban League, 259
U.S. Merit System Protection Board (USMSPB), 121, 130–31*t*

Vaught, Charles, 78
verbal sexual harassment, 69, 81–82, 199
victimological sexual harassment research, 27, 29–32
violations of the person, 103–7, 110, 111–12
violence: and bullying, 103–7; male dominance and, 5–6, 20, 246–47; organizations and, 100–103, 198–99, 206–8; perpetrator likelihood of, 5–7, 8, 9–10, 11–16, 17–19, 20, 21–22; and sexual harassment, 4–5, 103–7. *See also* bullying; sexual harassment
Violent Times: Preventing Violence at Work (TUC), 108
visual evaluation of women, 286

Wade, J. C., 125
Walby, S., 95
Waldo, C. R., 123, 127
Wall of Honor, 60
Warling, Cliff, 259
Warne, C., 101
Wehrli, Lynn, 245–46
Western Kentucky Coalmining Women's Support Team, 257, 262
"When Men Taunt Men, Is It Sexual Harassment?" (Talbot), 143
"white knight" male image, 47, 61